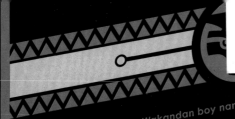

There once was a Wakandan boy named N'Jadaka who was taken from his homeland during an invasion.

Eventually, he would find his way back to Wakanda, now going by the name Erik Killmonger. After many attempted coups, including one that saw him defeat the Black Panther in ritual combat, Killmonger died in battle.

This is the story of what happened between when N'Jadaka was taken from Wakanda and when Erik Killmonger returned to take it.

BY ANY MEANS

BRYAN HILL WRITER
JUAN FERREYRA ARTIST

EDUARDO FERRERYA COLOR ASSISTS
VC'S JOE SABINO LETTERER
JUAN FERREYRA COVER ART

SARAH BRUNSTAD ASSOCIATE EDITOR
WIL MOSS EDITOR
TOM BREVOORT EXECUTIVE EDITOR

JENNIFER GRÜNWALD COLLECTION EDITOR
CAITLIN O'CONNELL ASSISTANT EDITOR
KATERI WOODY ASSOCIATE MANAGING EDITOR
MARK D. BEAZLEY EDITOR, SPECIAL PROJECTS
JEFF YOUNGQUIST VP PRODUCTION & SPECIAL PROJECTS
DAVID GABRIEL SVP PRINT, SALES & M
JAY BOWEN BOOK DESIGNER

C.B. CEBULSKI EDITOR IN CHIEF
JOE QUESADA CHIEF CREATIVE OFFICER
DAN BUCKLEY PRESIDENT
ALAN FINE EXECUTIVE PRODUCER

BLACK PANTHER: KILLMONGER — BY ANY MEANS. Contains material originally published in magazine form as KILLMONGER #1-5. First printing 2019. ISBN 978-1-302-91586-5. Published by MARVEL WORLDWIDE, INC., a subsidiary of MARVEL ENTERTAINMENT, LLC. OFFICE OF PUBLICATION: 135 West 50th Street, New York, NY 10020. © 2019 MARVEL No similarity between any of the names, characters, persons, and/or institutions in this magazine with those of any living or dead person or institution is intended, and any such similarity which may exist is purely coincidental. Printed in Canada. DAN BUCKLEY, President, Marvel Entertainment; JOHN NEE, Publisher; JOE QUESADA, Chief Creative Officer; TOM BREVOORT, SVP of Publishing; DAVID BOGART, Associate Publisher & SVP of Talent Affairs; DAVID GABRIEL, SVP of Sales & Marketing, Publishing; JEFF YOUNGQUIST, VP of Production & Special Projects; DAN CARR, Executive Director of Publishing Technology; ALEX MORALES, Director of Publishing Operations; DAN EDINGTON, Managing Editor; SUSAN CRESPI, Production Manager; STAN LEE, Chairman Emeritus. For information regarding advertising in Marvel Comics or on Marvel.com, please contact Vit DeBellis, Custom Solutions & Integrated Advertising Manager, at vdebellis@marvel.com. For Marvel subscription inquiries, please call 888-511-5480. Manufactured between 3/8/2019 and 4/9/2019 by SOLISCO PRINTERS, SCOTT, QC, CANADA.

1

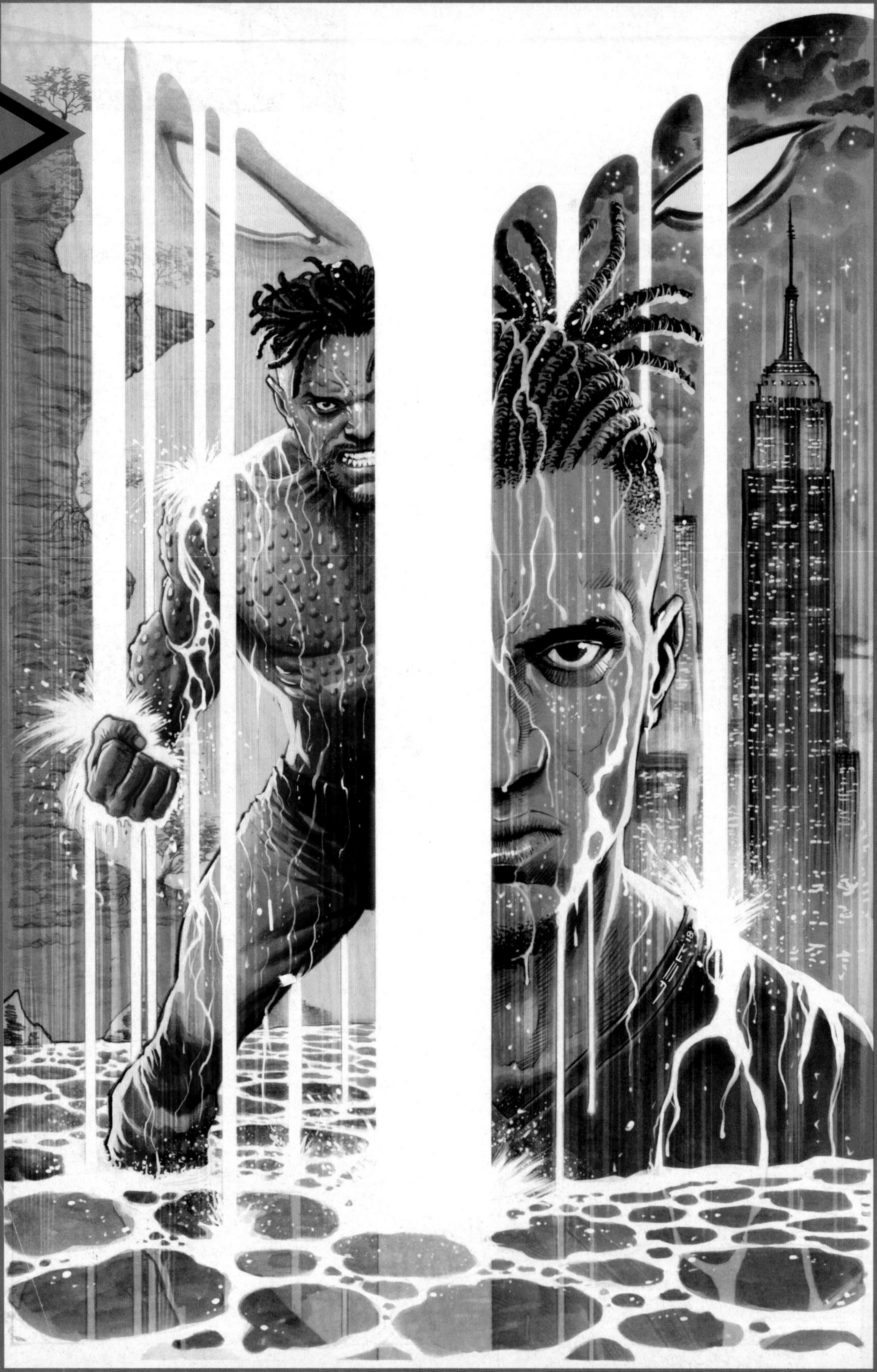

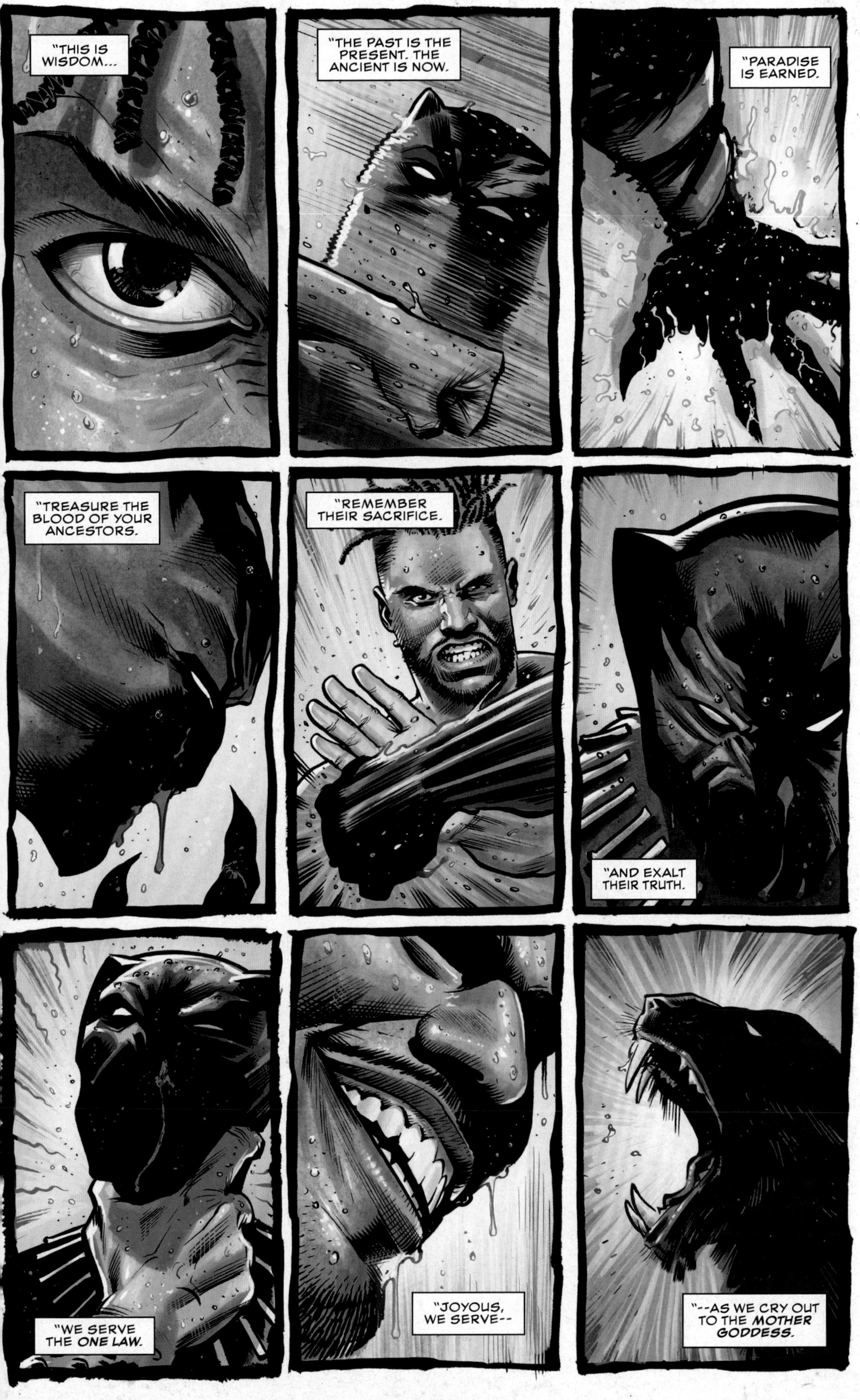
"THIS IS WISDOM...
"THE PAST IS THE PRESENT. THE ANCIENT IS NOW.
"PARADISE IS EARNED.
"TREASURE THE BLOOD OF YOUR ANCESTORS.
"REMEMBER THEIR SACRIFICE.
"AND EXALT THEIR TRUTH.
"WE SERVE THE *ONE LAW.*
"JOYOUS, WE SERVE--
"--AS WE CRY OUT TO THE *MOTHER GODDESS.*

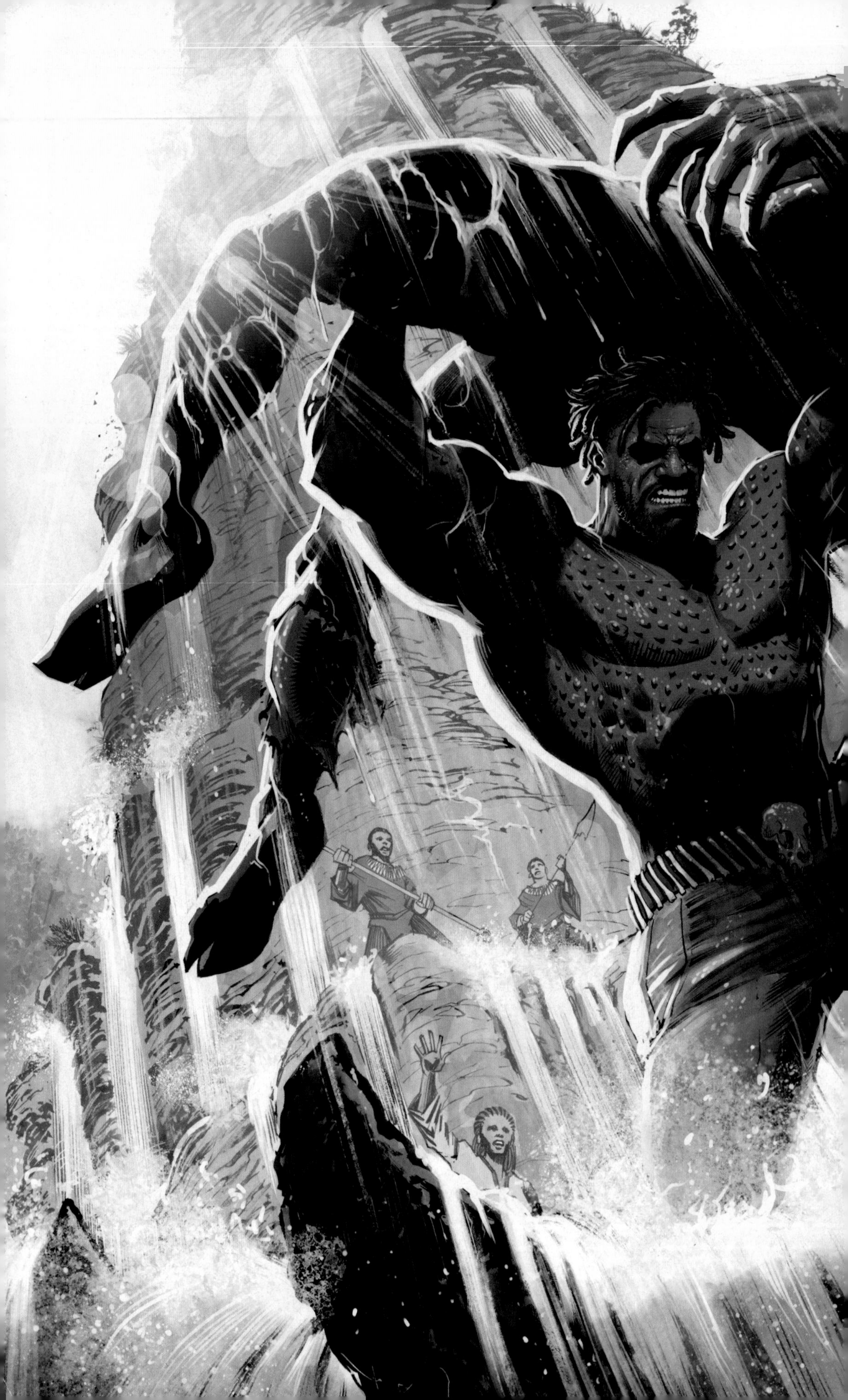

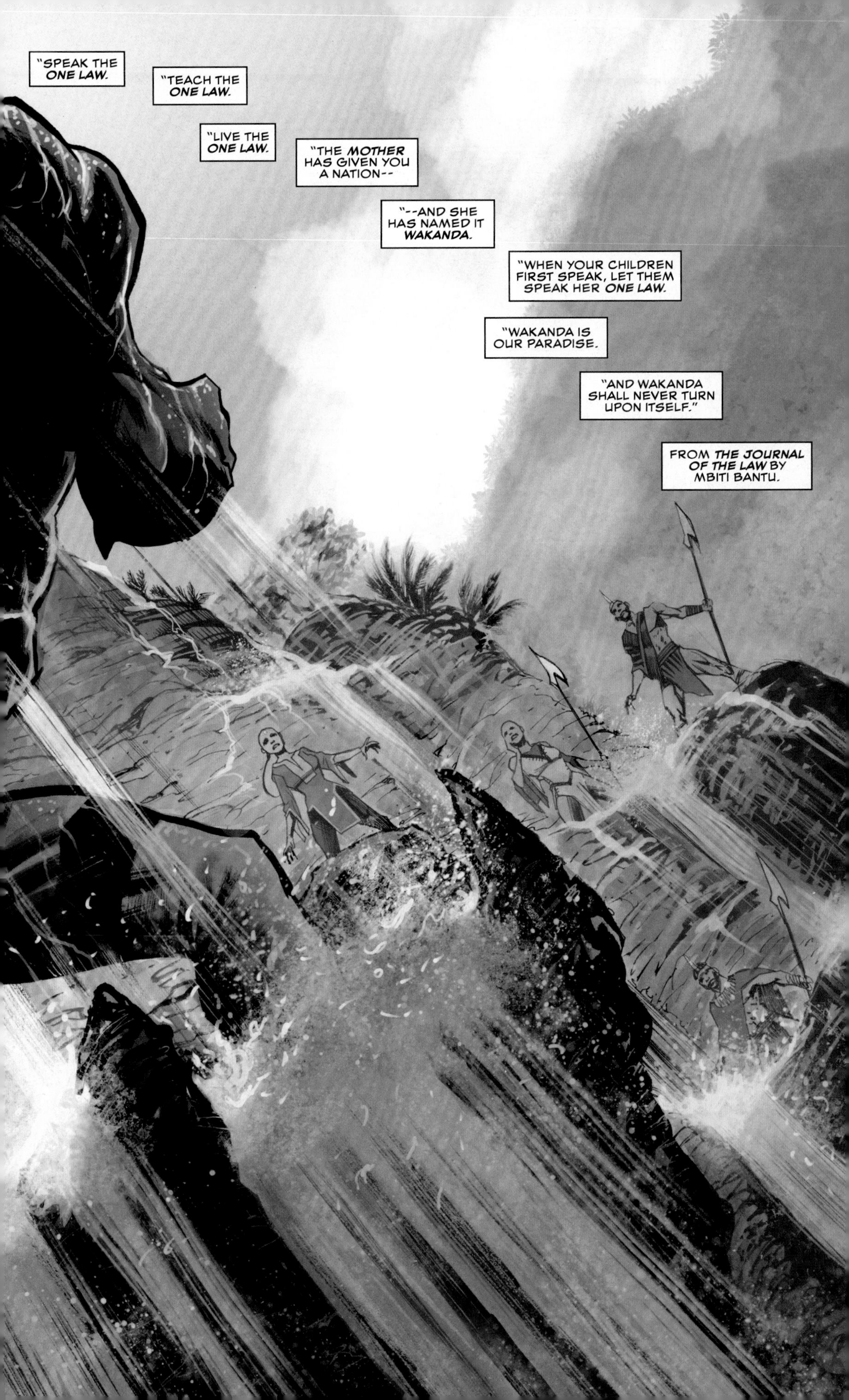
"SPEAK THE *ONE LAW.*
"TEACH THE *ONE LAW.*
"LIVE THE *ONE LAW.*
"THE *MOTHER* HAS GIVEN YOU A NATION--
"--AND SHE HAS NAMED IT *WAKANDA.*
"WHEN YOUR CHILDREN FIRST SPEAK, LET THEM SPEAK HER *ONE LAW.*
"WAKANDA IS OUR PARADISE.
"AND WAKANDA SHALL NEVER TURN UPON ITSELF."
FROM *THE JOURNAL OF THE LAW* BY MBITI BANTU.

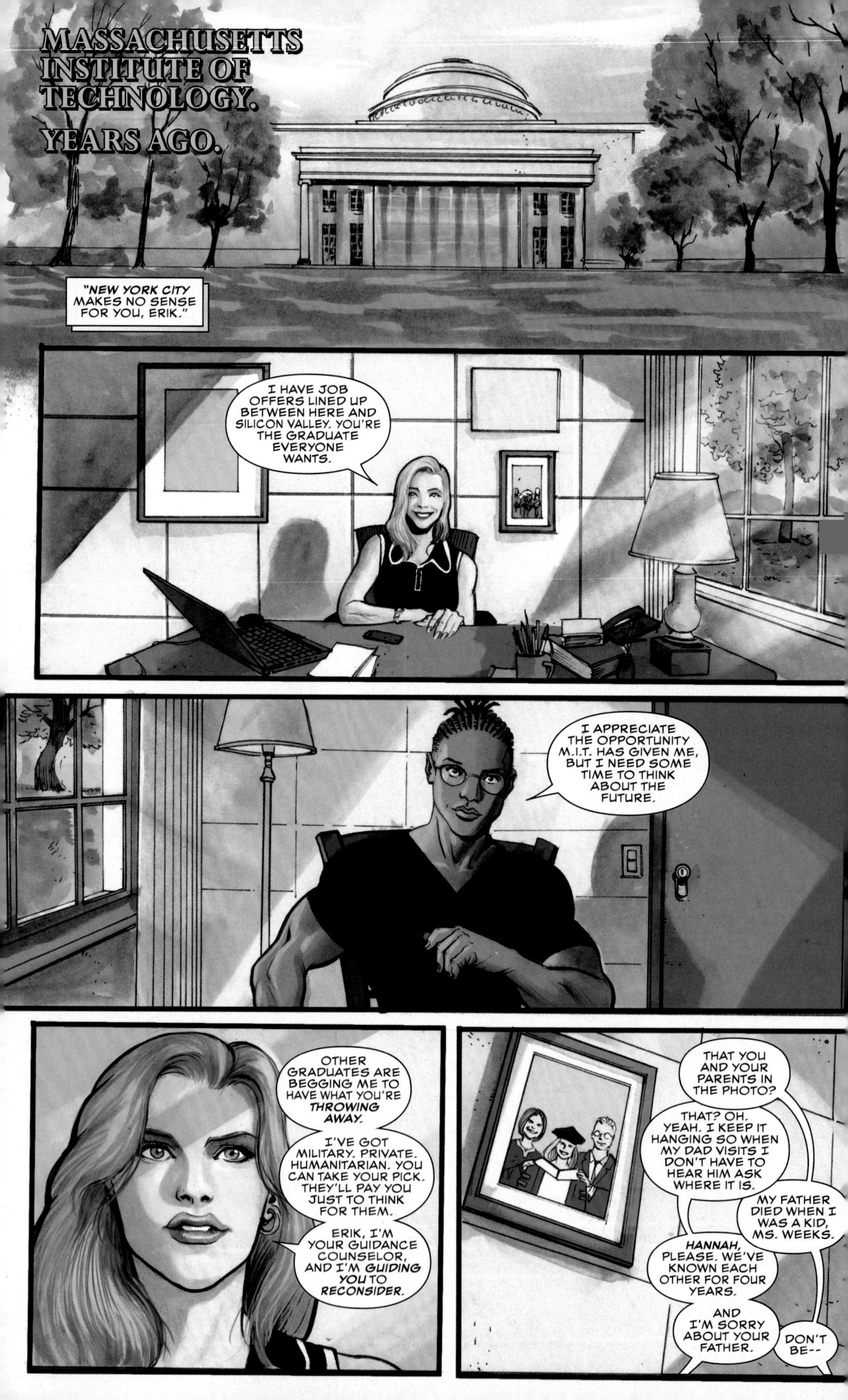
MASSACHUSETTS INSTITUTE OF TECHNOLOGY.
YEARS AGO.
"NEW YORK CITY MAKES NO SENSE FOR YOU, ERIK."
I HAVE JOB OFFERS LINED UP BETWEEN HERE AND SILICON VALLEY. YOU'RE THE GRADUATE EVERYONE WANTS.
I APPRECIATE THE OPPORTUNITY M.I.T. HAS GIVEN ME, BUT I NEED SOME TIME TO THINK ABOUT THE FUTURE.
OTHER GRADUATES ARE BEGGING ME TO HAVE WHAT YOU'RE THROWING AWAY.
I'VE GOT MILITARY. PRIVATE. HUMANITARIAN. YOU CAN TAKE YOUR PICK. THEY'LL PAY YOU JUST TO THINK FOR THEM.
ERIK, I'M YOUR GUIDANCE COUNSELOR, AND I'M GUIDING YOU TO RECONSIDER.
THAT YOU AND YOUR PARENTS IN THE PHOTO?
THAT? OH. YEAH. I KEEP IT HANGING SO WHEN MY DAD VISITS I DON'T HAVE TO HEAR HIM ASK WHERE IT IS.
MY FATHER DIED WHEN I WAS A KID, MS. WEEKS.
HANNAH, PLEASE. WE'VE KNOWN EACH OTHER FOR FOUR YEARS.
AND I'M SORRY ABOUT YOUR FATHER.
DON'T BE--

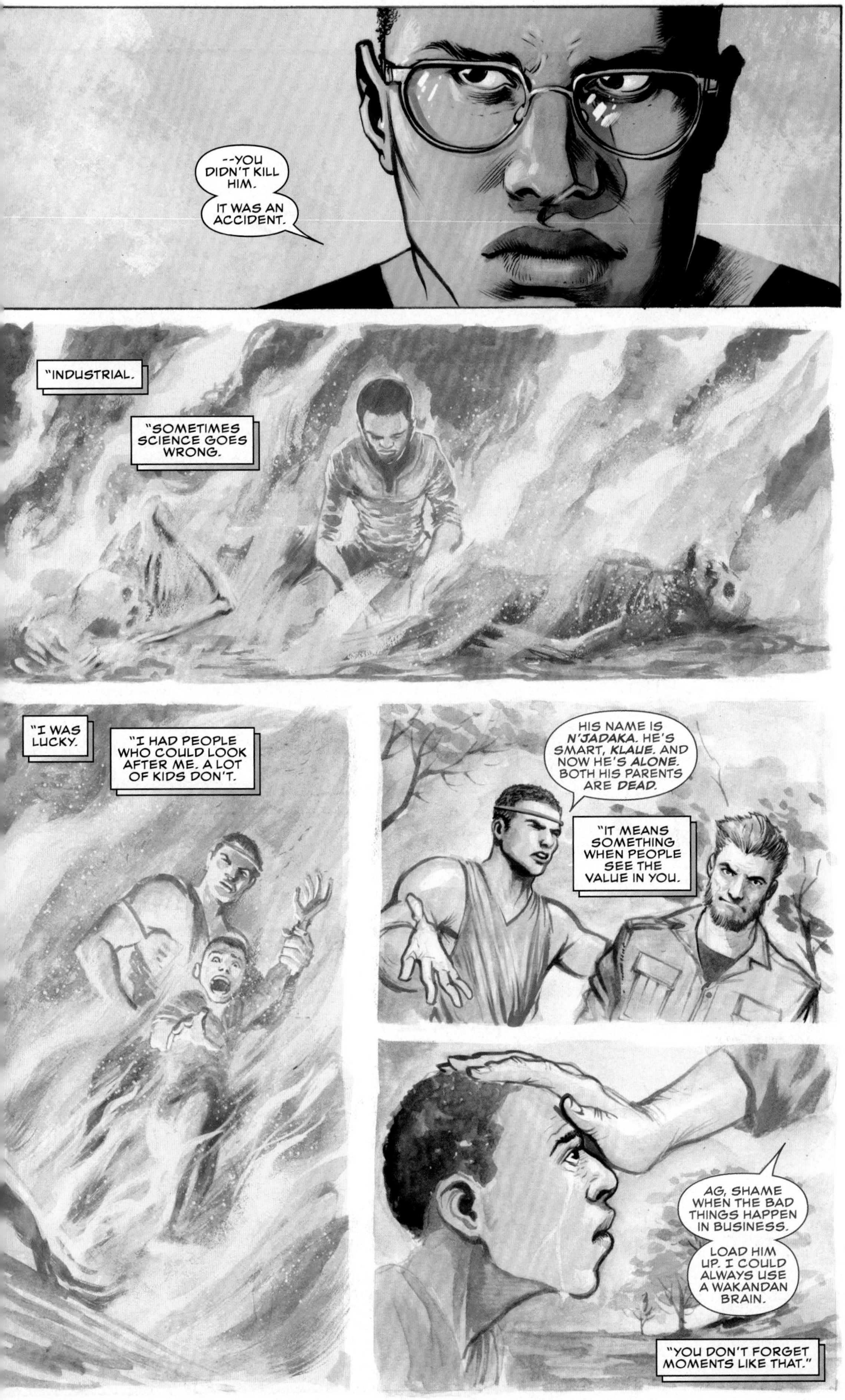
--YOU DIDN'T KILL HIM.
IT WAS AN ACCIDENT.
"INDUSTRIAL.
"SOMETIMES SCIENCE GOES WRONG.
"I WAS LUCKY.
"I HAD PEOPLE WHO COULD LOOK AFTER ME. A LOT OF KIDS DON'T.
HIS NAME IS N'JADAKA. HE'S SMART, KLAUE. AND NOW HE'S ALONE. BOTH HIS PARENTS ARE DEAD.
"IT MEANS SOMETHING WHEN PEOPLE SEE THE VALUE IN YOU.
AG, SHAME WHEN THE BAD THINGS HAPPEN IN BUSINESS.
LOAD HIM UP. I COULD ALWAYS USE A WAKANDAN BRAIN.
"YOU DON'T FORGET MOMENTS LIKE THAT."

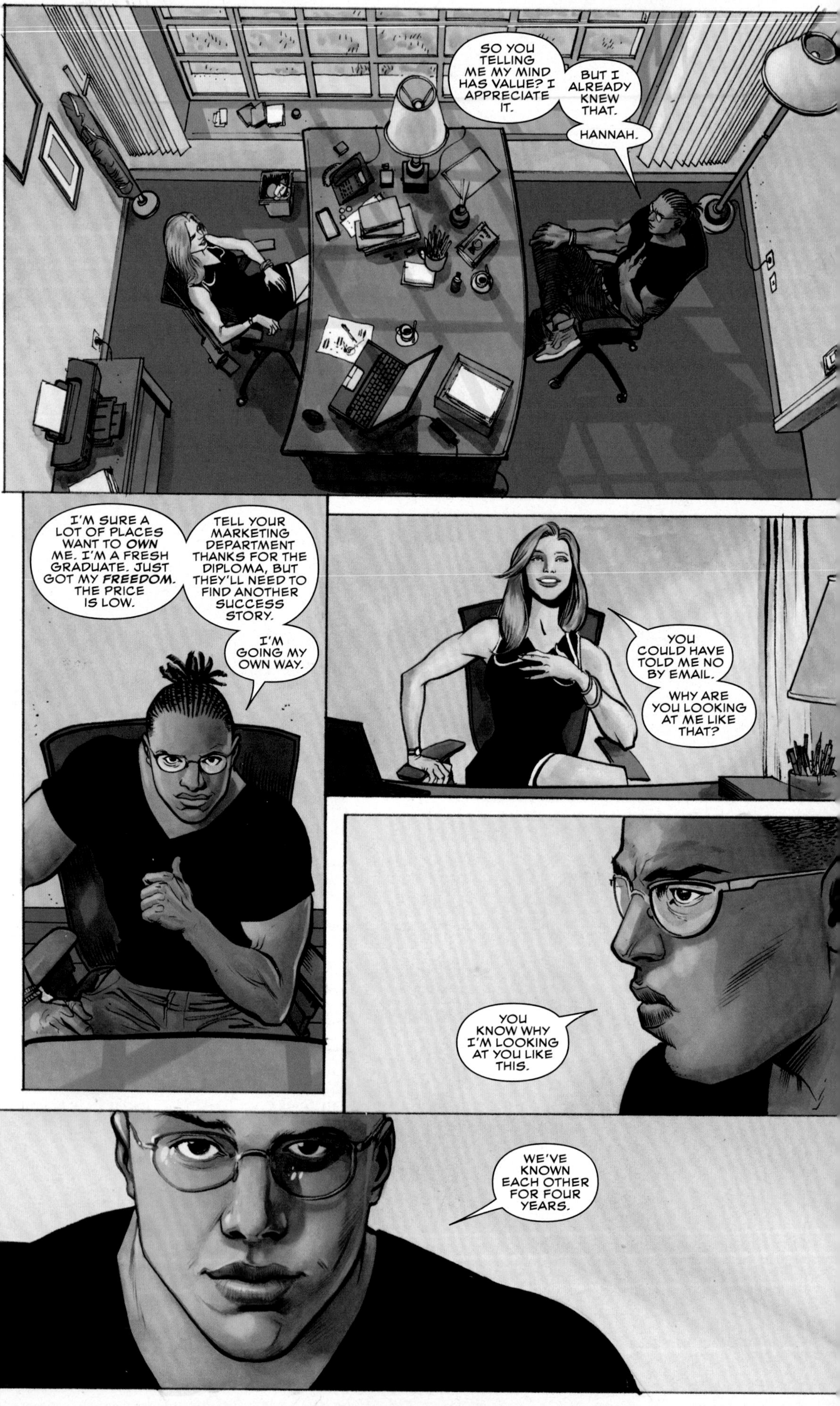
SO YOU TELLING ME MY MIND HAS VALUE? I APPRECIATE IT.
BUT I ALREADY KNEW THAT.
HANNAH.
I'M SURE A LOT OF PLACES WANT TO OWN ME. I'M A FRESH GRADUATE. JUST GOT MY FREEDOM. THE PRICE IS LOW.
TELL YOUR MARKETING DEPARTMENT THANKS FOR THE DIPLOMA, BUT THEY'LL NEED TO FIND ANOTHER SUCCESS STORY.
I'M GOING MY OWN WAY.
YOU COULD HAVE TOLD ME NO BY EMAIL.
WHY ARE YOU LOOKING AT ME LIKE THAT?
YOU KNOW WHY I'M LOOKING AT YOU LIKE THIS.
WE'VE KNOWN EACH OTHER FOR FOUR YEARS.

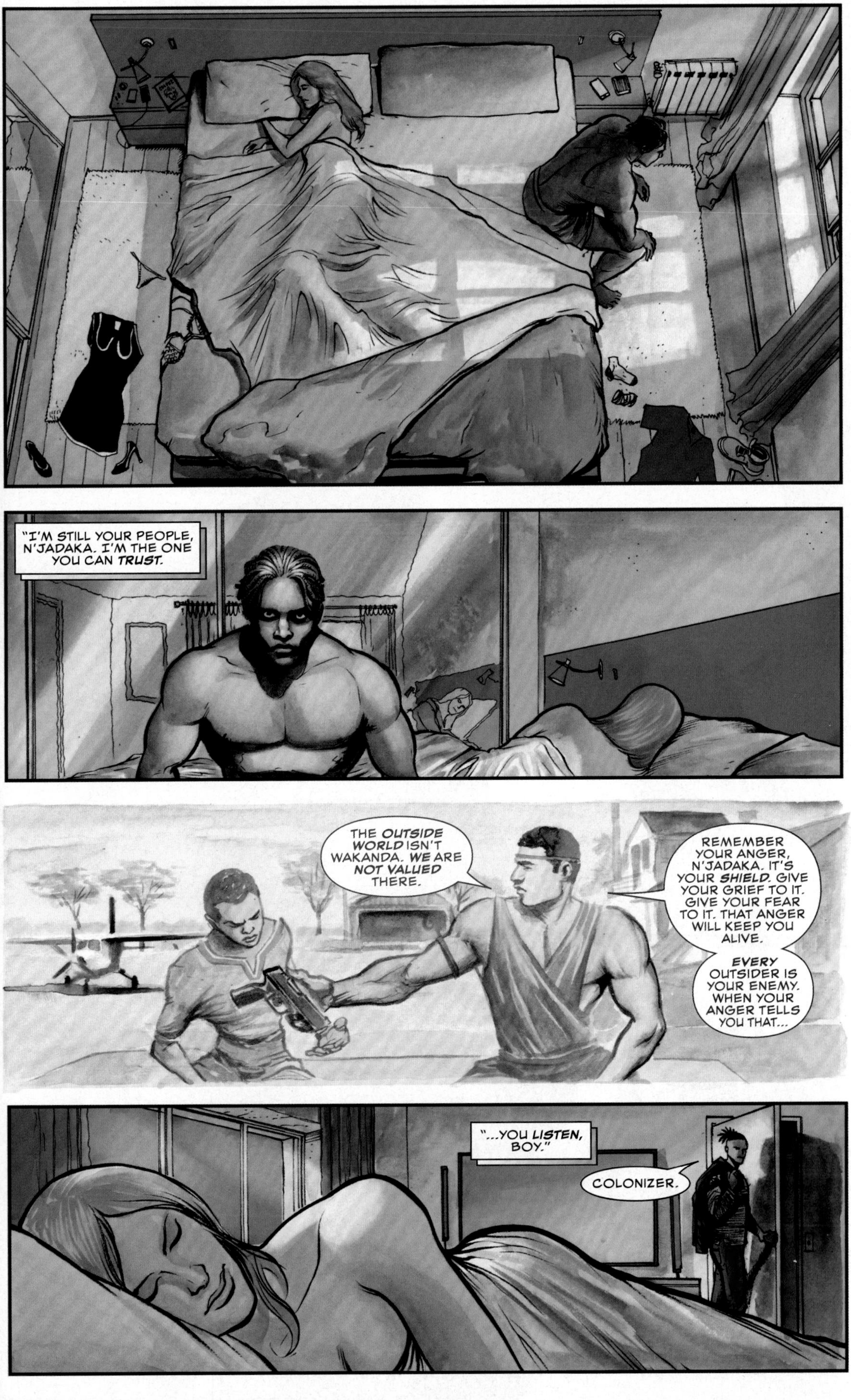
"I'M STILL YOUR PEOPLE, N'JADAKA. I'M THE ONE YOU CAN TRUST.
THE OUTSIDE WORLD ISN'T WAKANDA. WE ARE NOT VALUED THERE.
REMEMBER YOUR ANGER, N'JADAKA. IT'S YOUR SHIELD. GIVE YOUR GRIEF TO IT. GIVE YOUR FEAR TO IT. THAT ANGER WILL KEEP YOU ALIVE.
EVERY OUTSIDER IS YOUR ENEMY. WHEN YOUR ANGER TELLS YOU THAT...
"...YOU LISTEN, BOY."
COLONIZER.

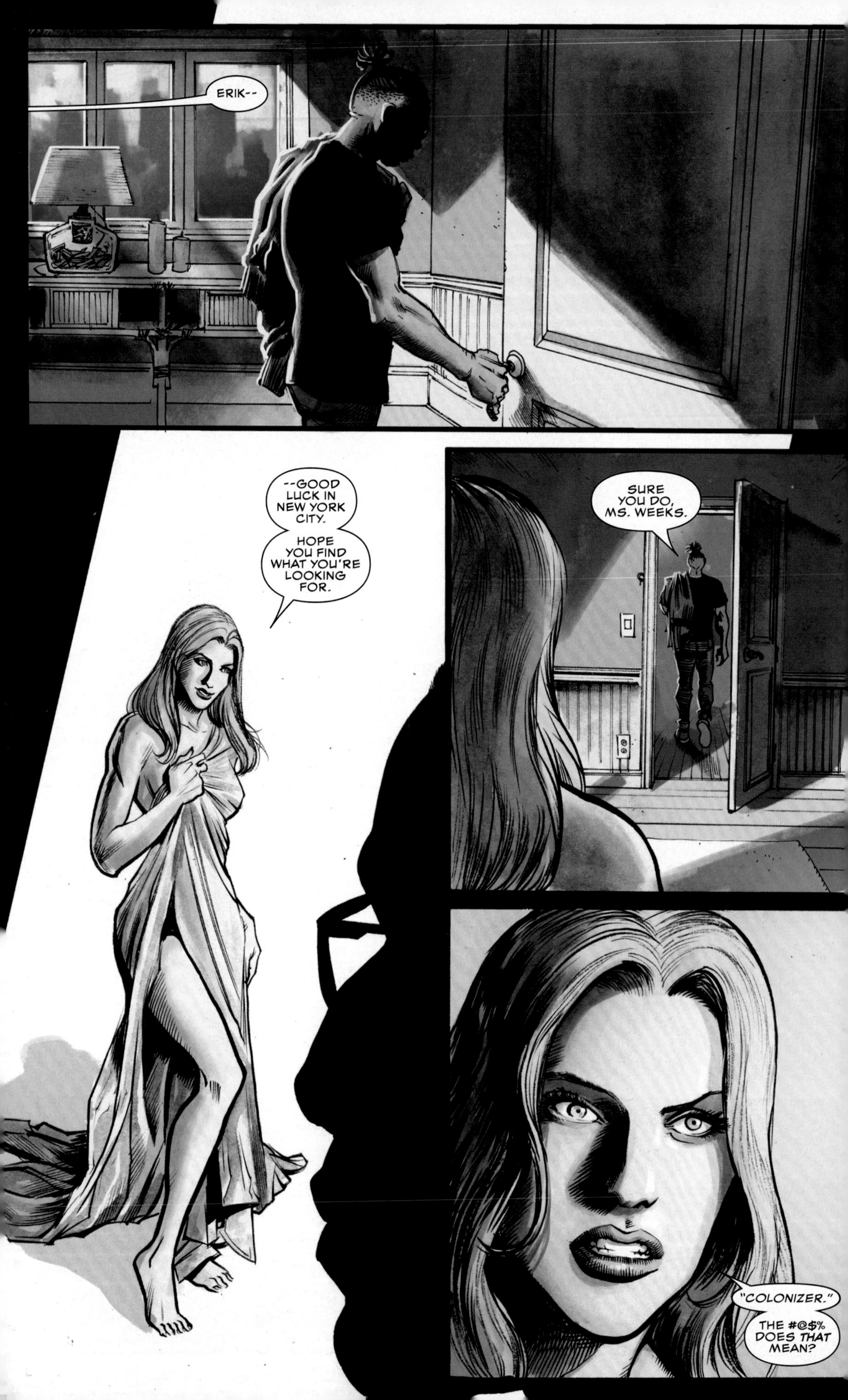
ERIK--
--GOOD LUCK IN NEW YORK CITY.
HOPE YOU FIND WHAT YOU'RE LOOKING FOR.
SURE YOU DO, MS. WEEKS.
"COLONIZER."
THE #@$% DOES THAT MEAN?

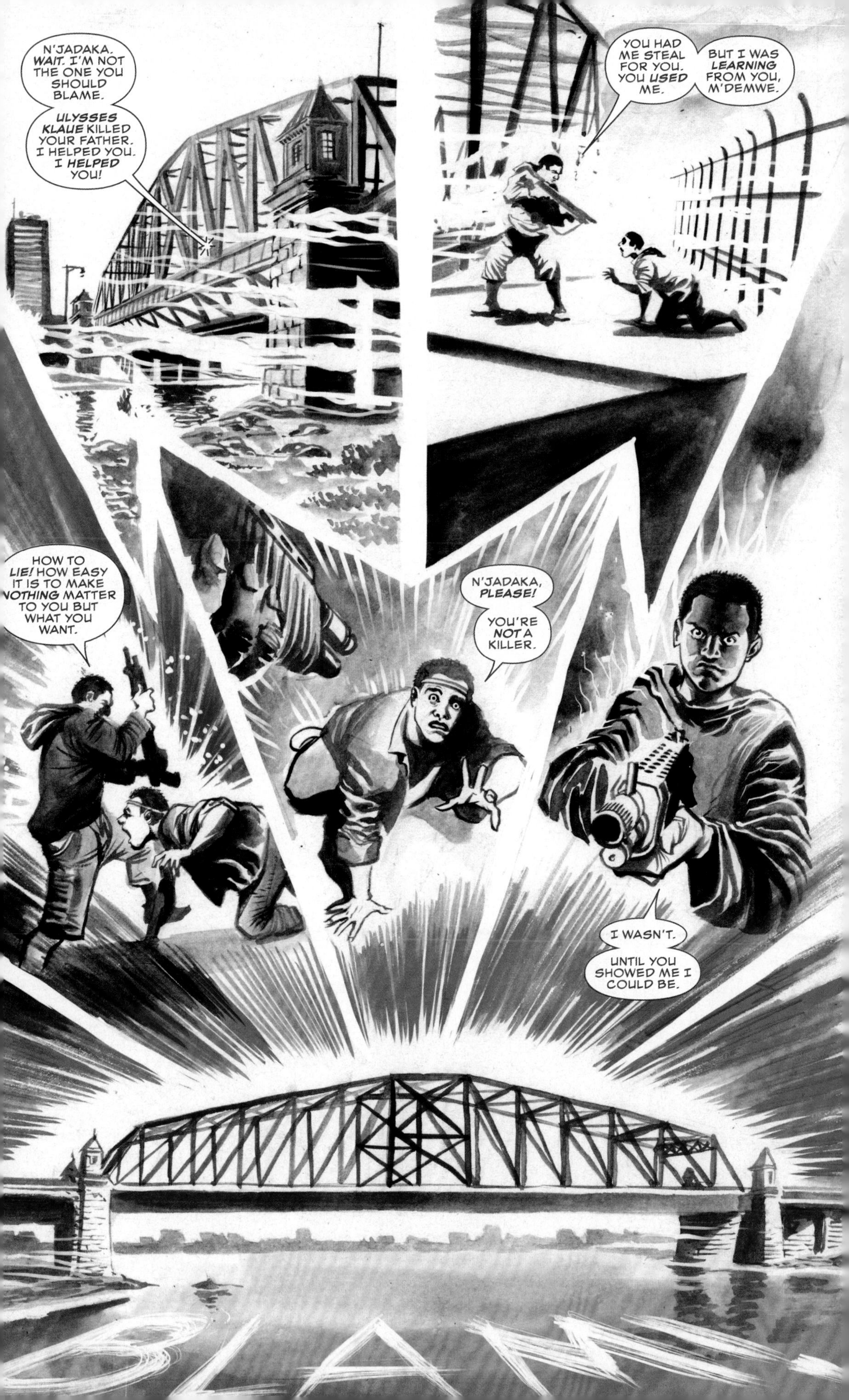
N'JADAKA. WAIT. I'M NOT THE ONE YOU SHOULD BLAME.
ULYSSES KLAUE KILLED YOUR FATHER. I HELPED YOU. I HELPED YOU!
YOU HAD ME STEAL FOR YOU. YOU USED ME.
BUT I WAS LEARNING FROM YOU, M'DEMWE.
HOW TO LIE! HOW EASY IT IS TO MAKE NOTHING MATTER TO YOU BUT WHAT YOU WANT.
N'JADAKA, PLEASE!
YOU'RE NOT A KILLER.
I WASN'T.
UNTIL YOU SHOWED ME I COULD BE.
BLAM

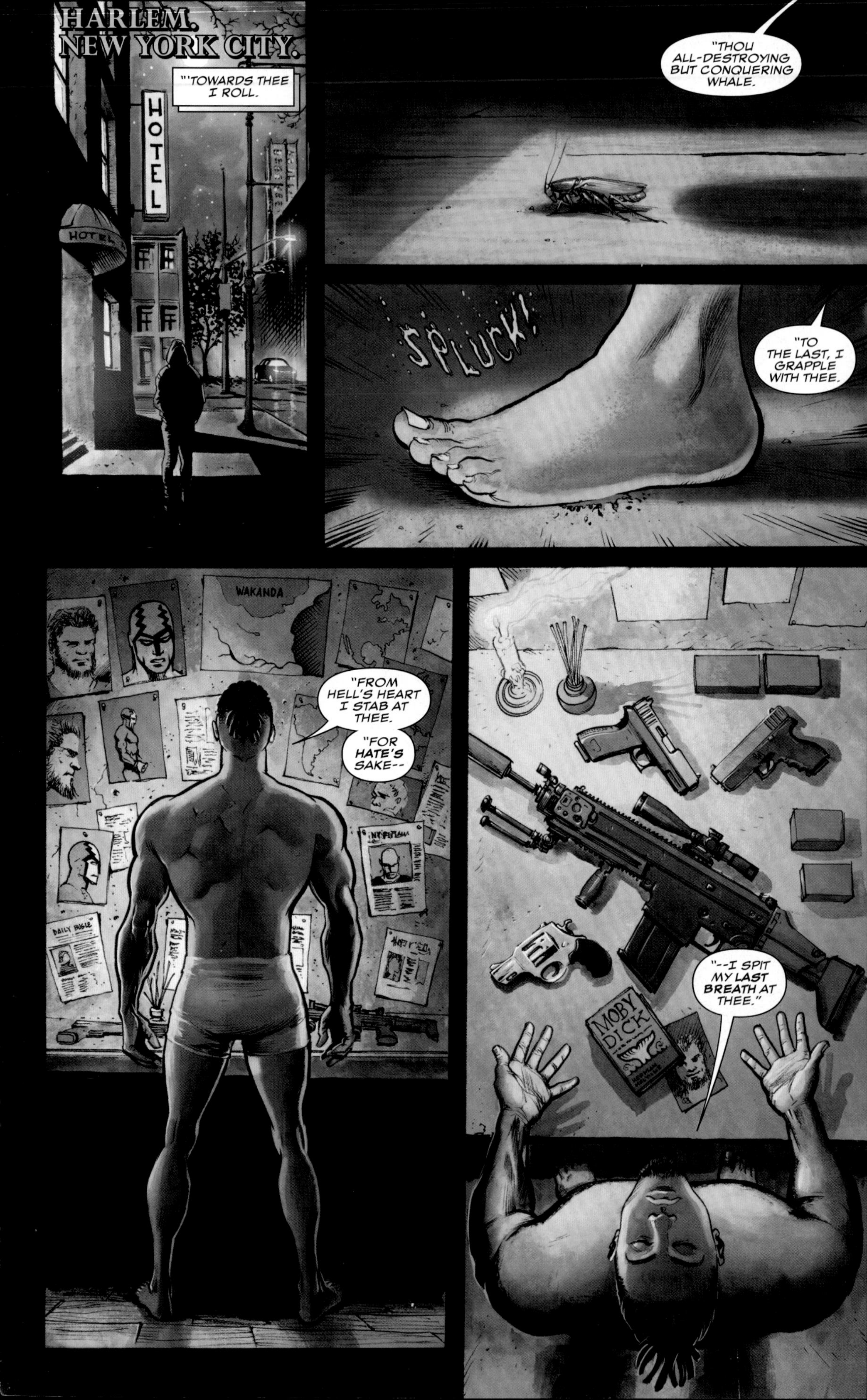
HARLEM, NEW YORK CITY.
"'TOWARDS THEE I ROLL.
HOTEL
HOTEL
"THOU ALL-DESTROYING BUT CONQUERING WHALE.
SPLUCK!
"TO THE LAST, I GRAPPLE WITH THEE.
WAKANDA
"FROM HELL'S HEART I STAB AT THEE.
"FOR HATE'S SAKE--
DAILY BUGLE
"--I SPIT MY LAST BREATH AT THEE."
MOBY DICK

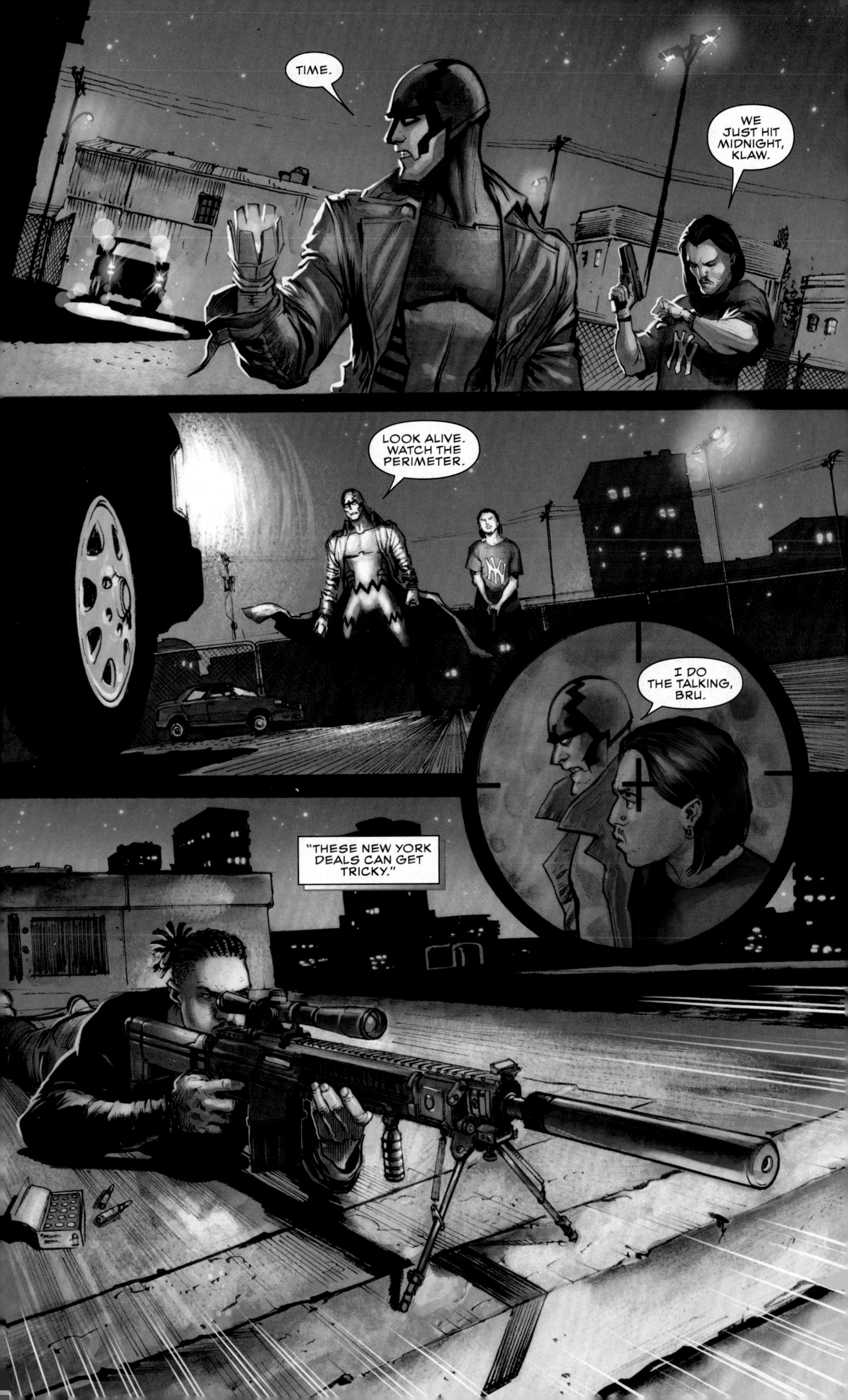
TIME.
WE JUST HIT MIDNIGHT, KLAW.
LOOK ALIVE. WATCH THE PERIMETER.
I DO THE TALKING, BRU.
"THESE NEW YORK DEALS CAN GET TRICKY."

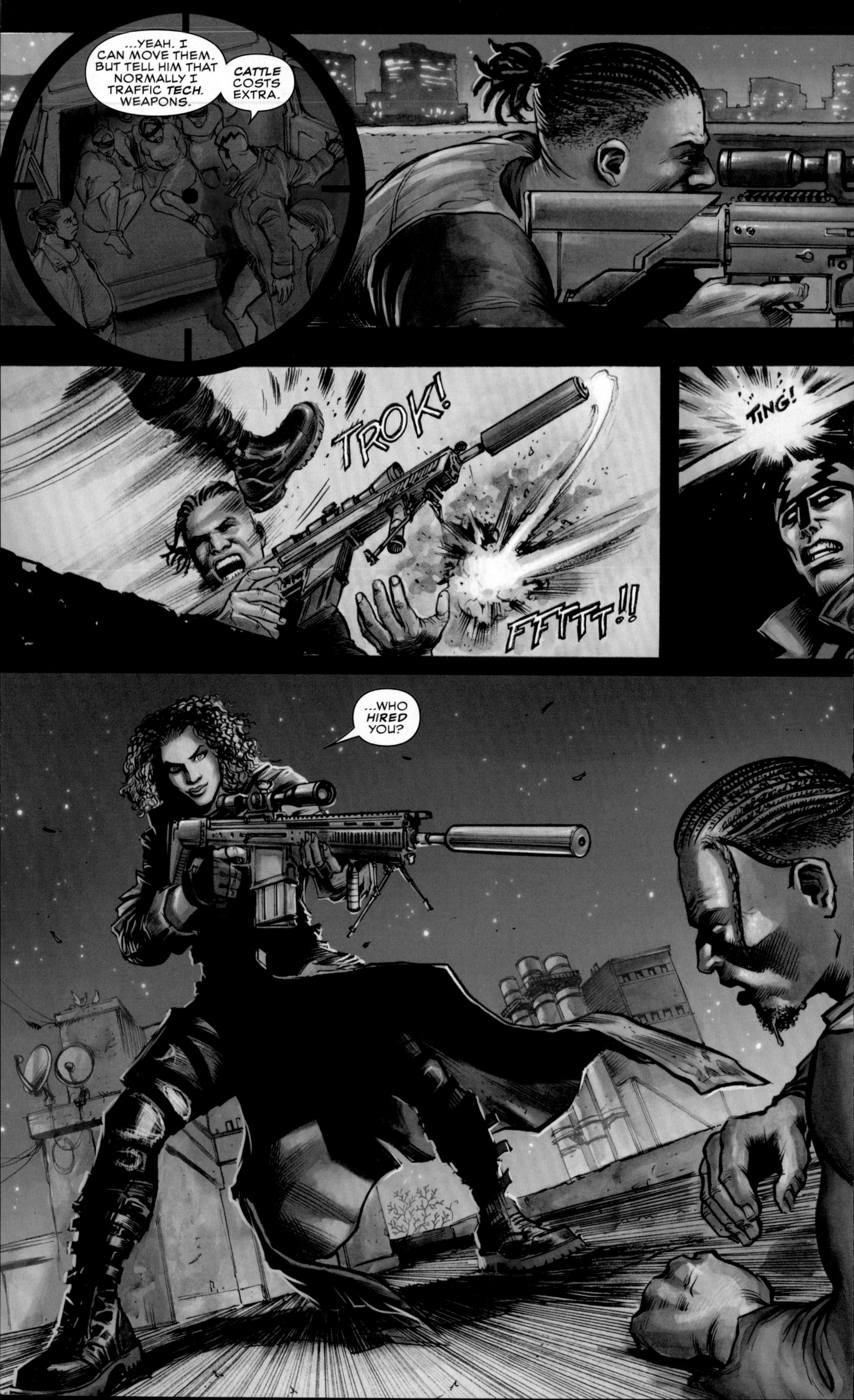
...YEAH. I CAN MOVE THEM. BUT TELL HIM THAT NORMALLY I TRAFFIC TECH. WEAPONS.
CATTLE COSTS EXTRA.
TROK!
FFTTT!!
TING!
...WHO HIRED YOU?

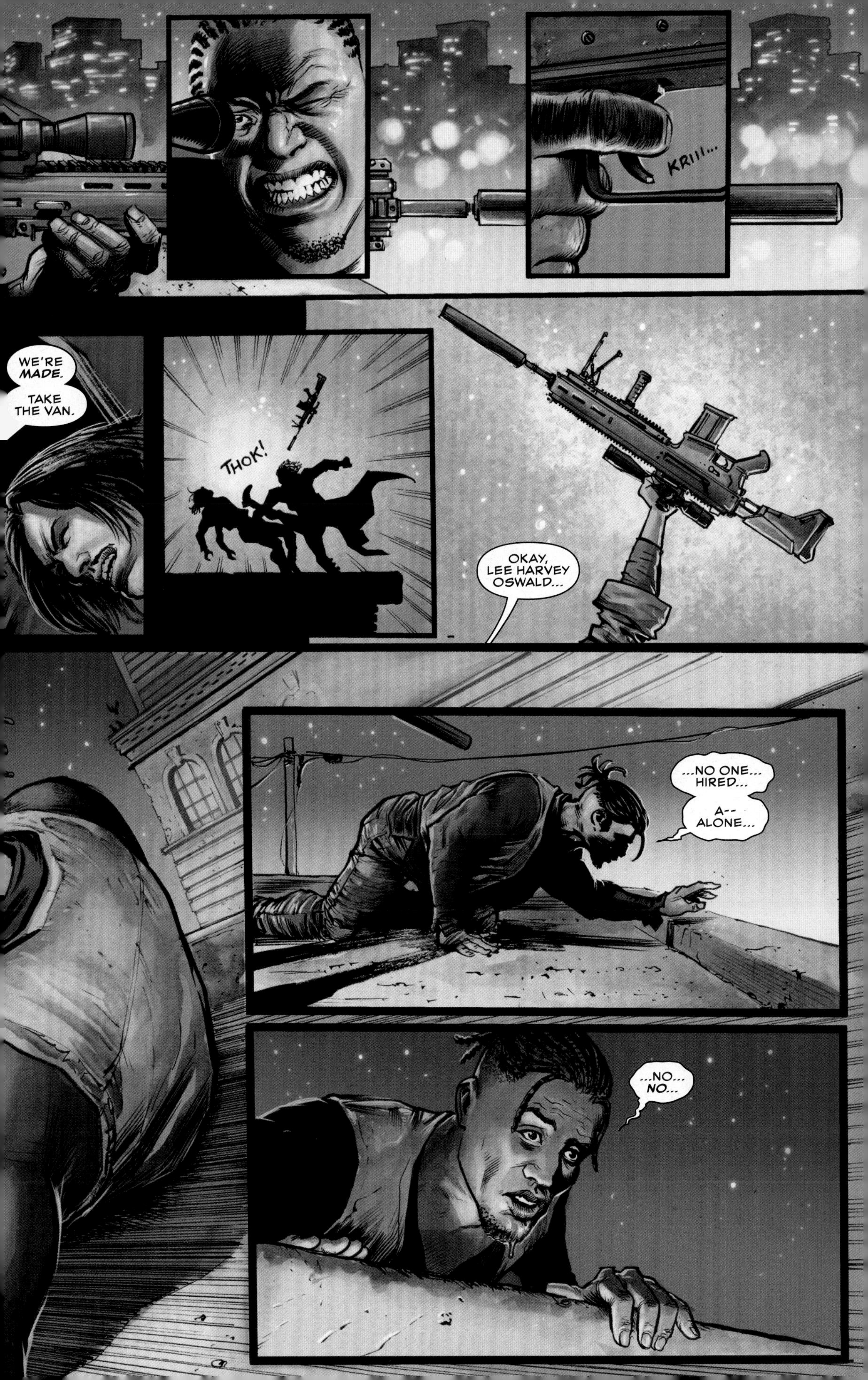
KRIII...
WE'RE MADE.
TAKE THE VAN.
THOK!
OKAY, LEE HARVEY OSWALD...
...NO ONE... HIRED...
A-- ALONE...
...NO... NO...

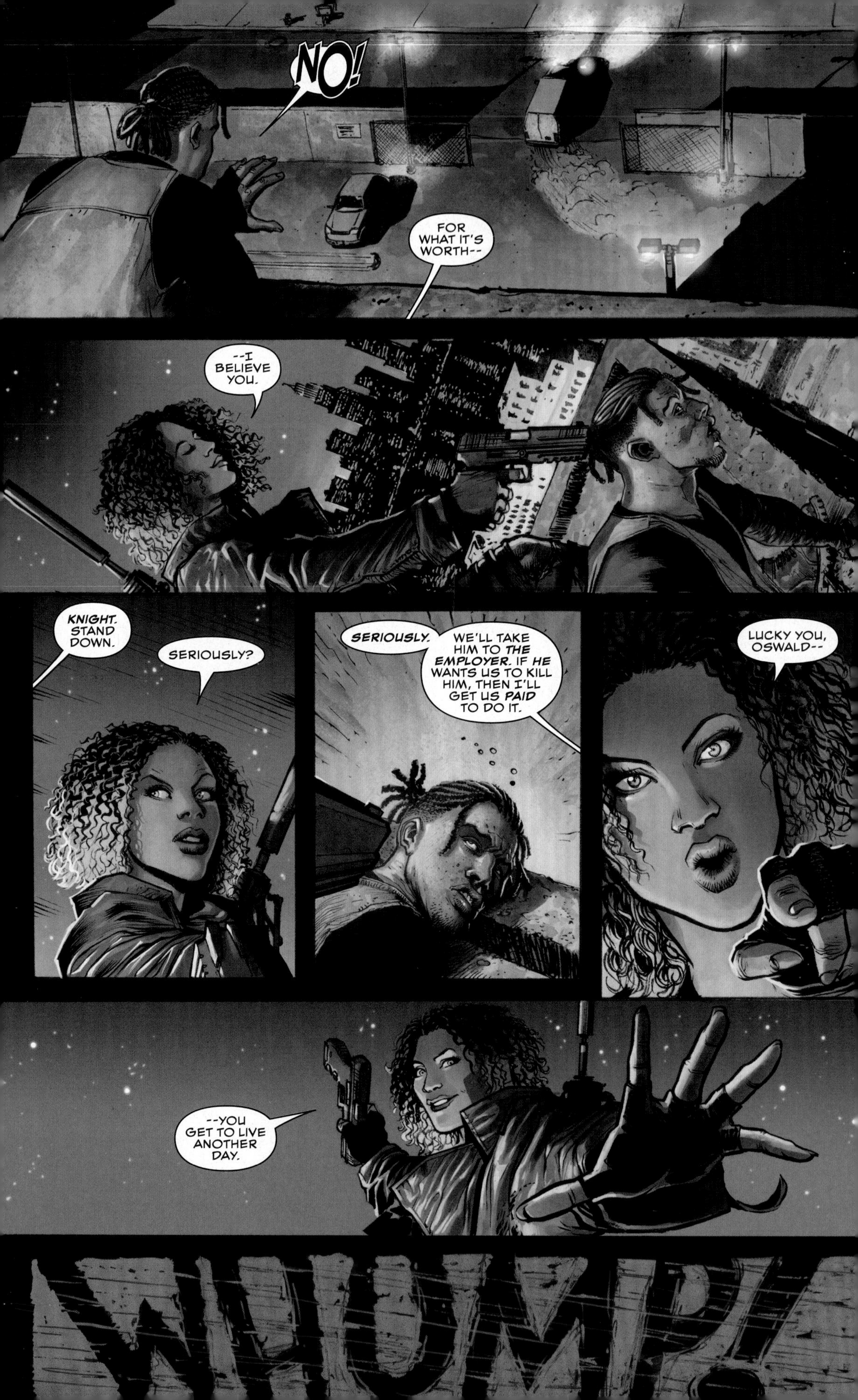
NO!
FOR WHAT IT'S WORTH--
--I BELIEVE YOU.
KNIGHT. STAND DOWN.
SERIOUSLY?
SERIOUSLY.
WE'LL TAKE HIM TO THE EMPLOYER. IF HE WANTS US TO KILL HIM, THEN I'LL GET US PAID TO DO IT.
LUCKY YOU, OSWALD--
--YOU GET TO LIVE ANOTHER DAY.
WHUMP!

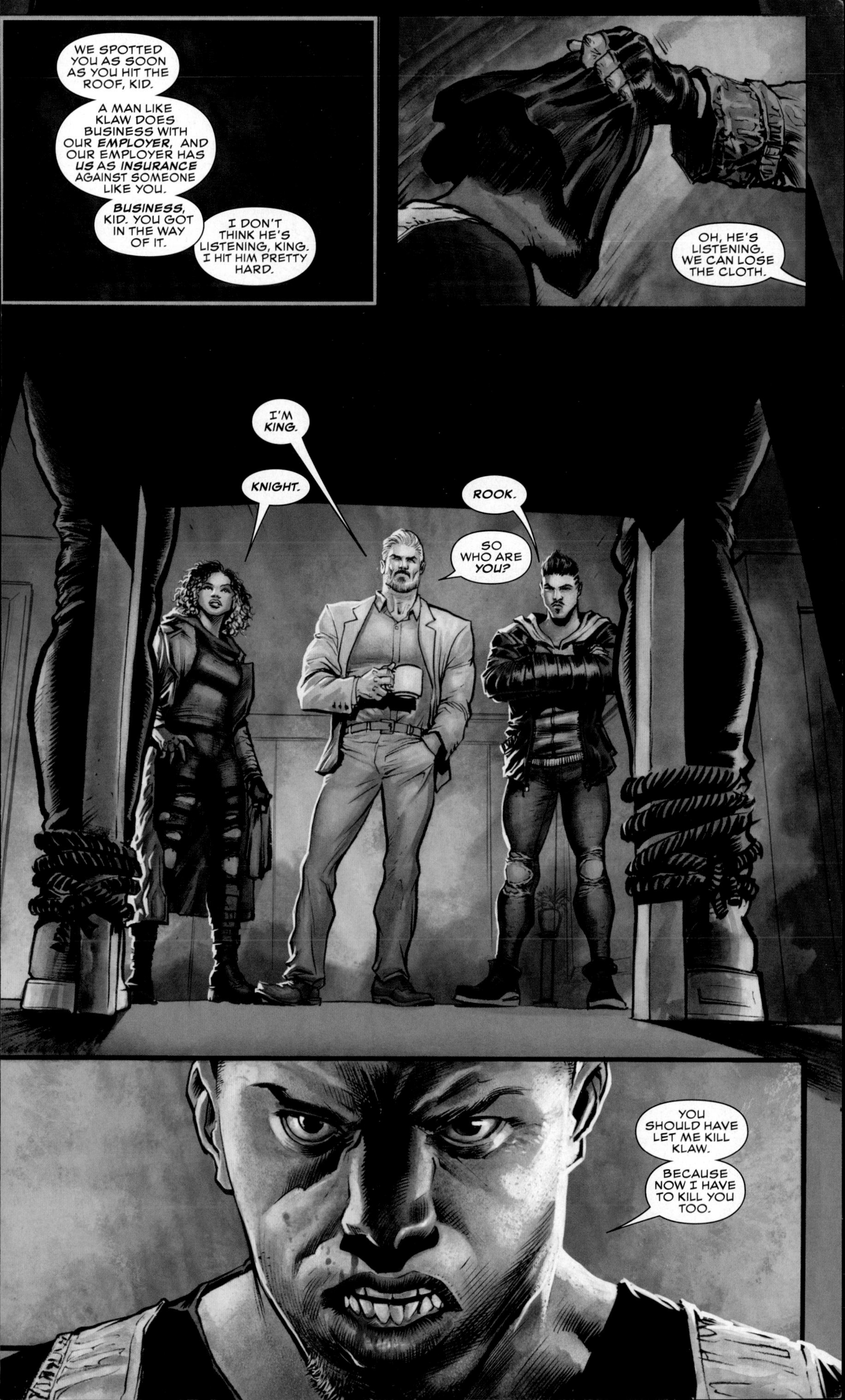
WE SPOTTED YOU AS SOON AS YOU HIT THE ROOF, KID.
A MAN LIKE KLAW DOES BUSINESS WITH OUR EMPLOYER, AND OUR EMPLOYER HAS US AS INSURANCE AGAINST SOMEONE LIKE YOU.
BUSINESS, KID. YOU GOT IN THE WAY OF IT.
I DON'T THINK HE'S LISTENING, KING. I HIT HIM PRETTY HARD.
OH, HE'S LISTENING. WE CAN LOSE THE CLOTH.
I'M KING.
KNIGHT.
ROOK.
SO WHO ARE YOU?
YOU SHOULD HAVE LET ME KILL KLAW.
BECAUSE NOW I HAVE TO KILL YOU TOO.

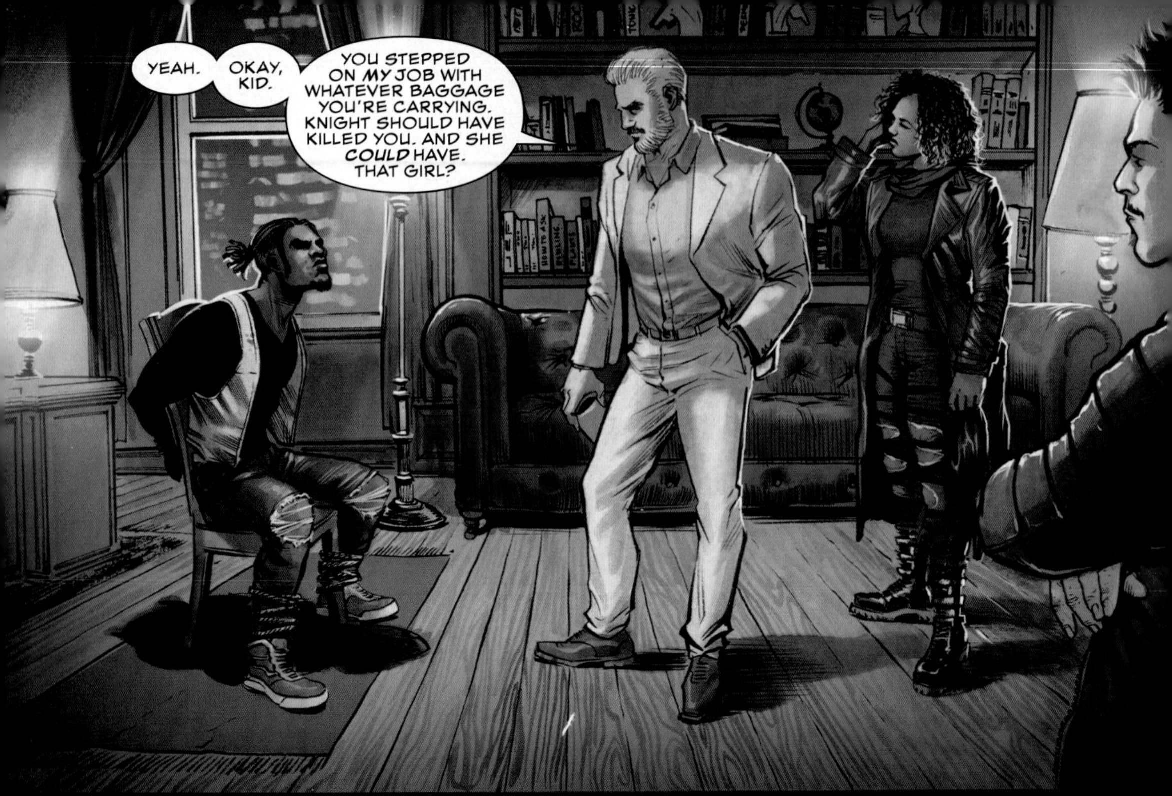
YEAH.
OKAY, KID.
YOU STEPPED ON MY JOB WITH WHATEVER BAGGAGE YOU'RE CARRYING. KNIGHT SHOULD HAVE KILLED YOU. AND SHE COULD HAVE. THAT GIRL?

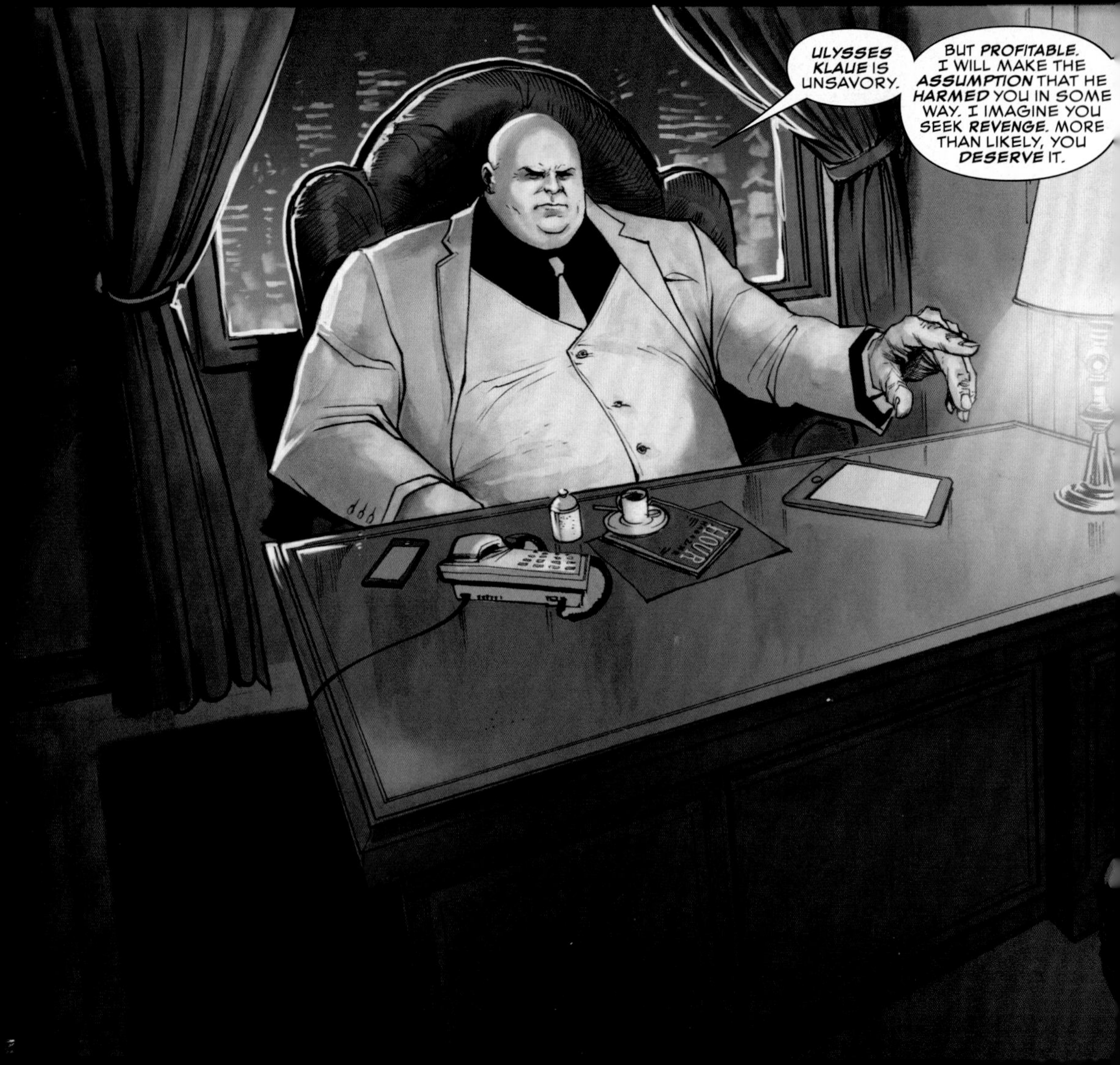
ULYSSES KLAUE IS UNSAVORY.
BUT PROFITABLE. I WILL MAKE THE ASSUMPTION THAT HE HARMED YOU IN SOME WAY. I IMAGINE YOU SEEK REVENGE. MORE THAN LIKELY, YOU DESERVE IT.

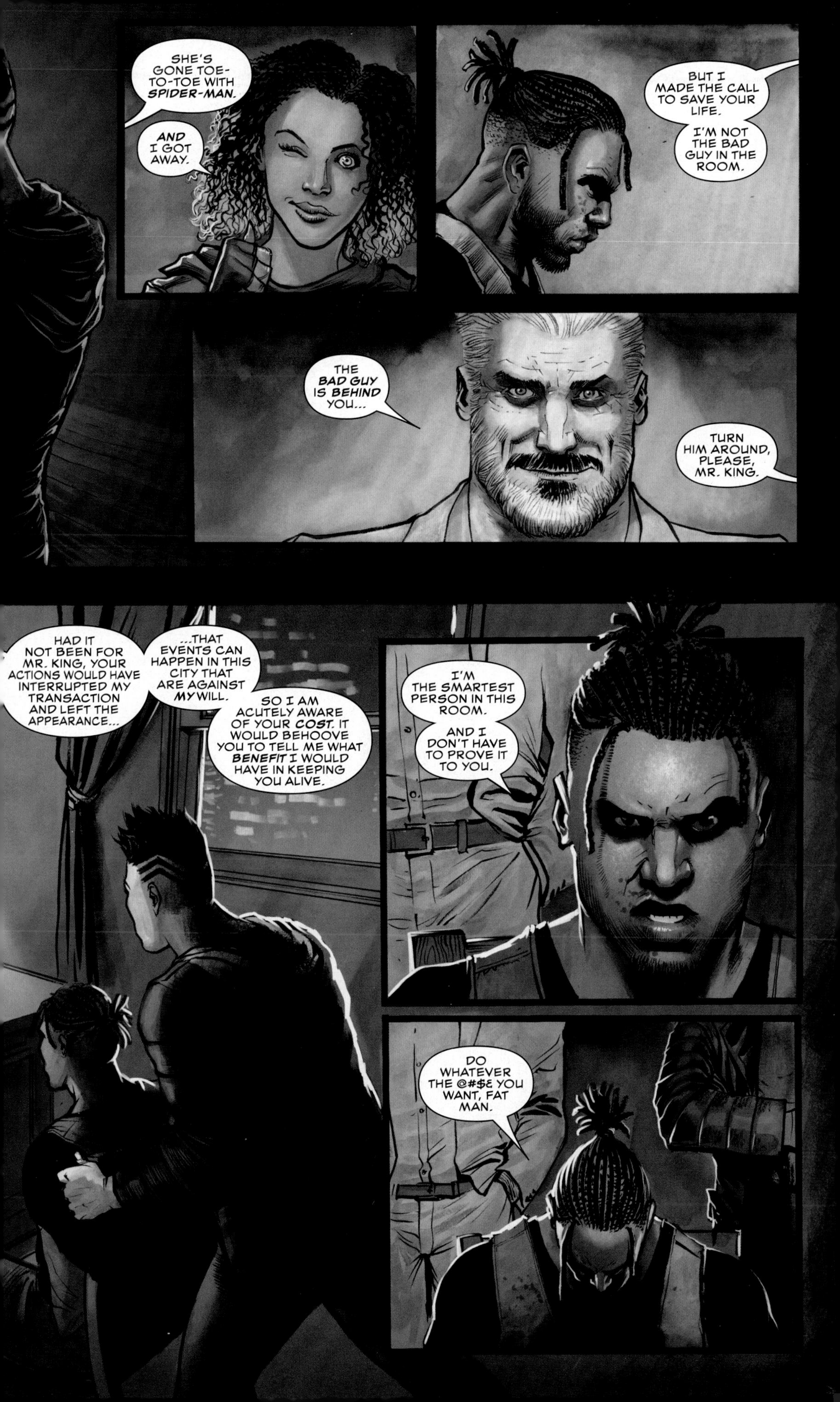
SHE'S GONE TOE-TO-TOE WITH SPIDER-MAN.
AND I GOT AWAY.
BUT I MADE THE CALL TO SAVE YOUR LIFE.
I'M NOT THE BAD GUY IN THE ROOM.
THE BAD GUY IS BEHIND YOU...
TURN HIM AROUND, PLEASE, MR. KING.
HAD IT NOT BEEN FOR MR. KING, YOUR ACTIONS WOULD HAVE INTERRUPTED MY TRANSACTION AND LEFT THE APPEARANCE...
...THAT EVENTS CAN HAPPEN IN THIS CITY THAT ARE AGAINST MY WILL.
SO I AM ACUTELY AWARE OF YOUR COST. IT WOULD BEHOOVE YOU TO TELL ME WHAT BENEFIT I WOULD HAVE IN KEEPING YOU ALIVE.
I'M THE SMARTEST PERSON IN THIS ROOM.
AND I DON'T HAVE TO PROVE IT TO YOU.
DO WHATEVER THE @#$& YOU WANT, FAT MAN.

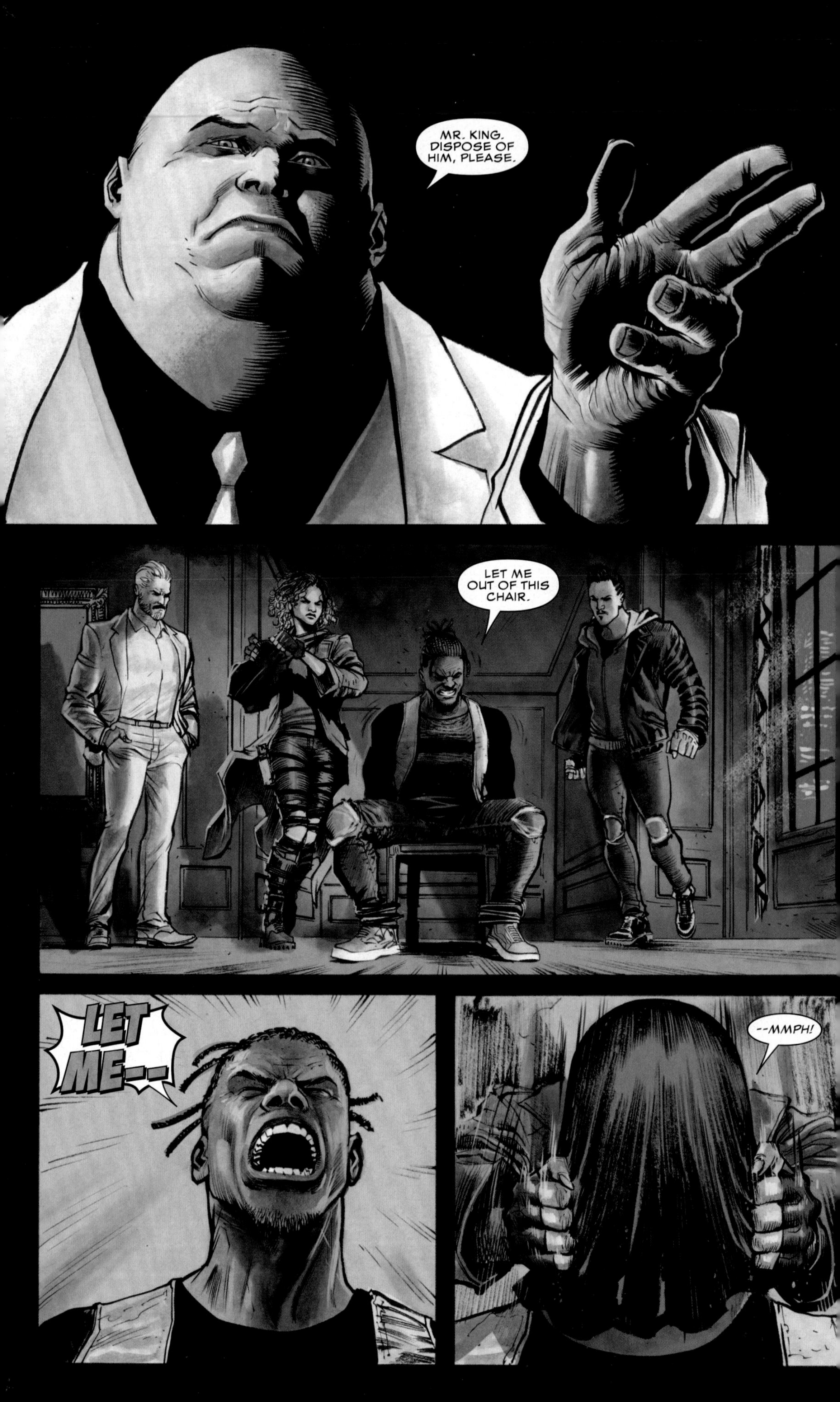
MR. KING. DISPOSE OF HIM, PLEASE.
LET ME OUT OF THIS CHAIR.
LET ME--
--MMPH!

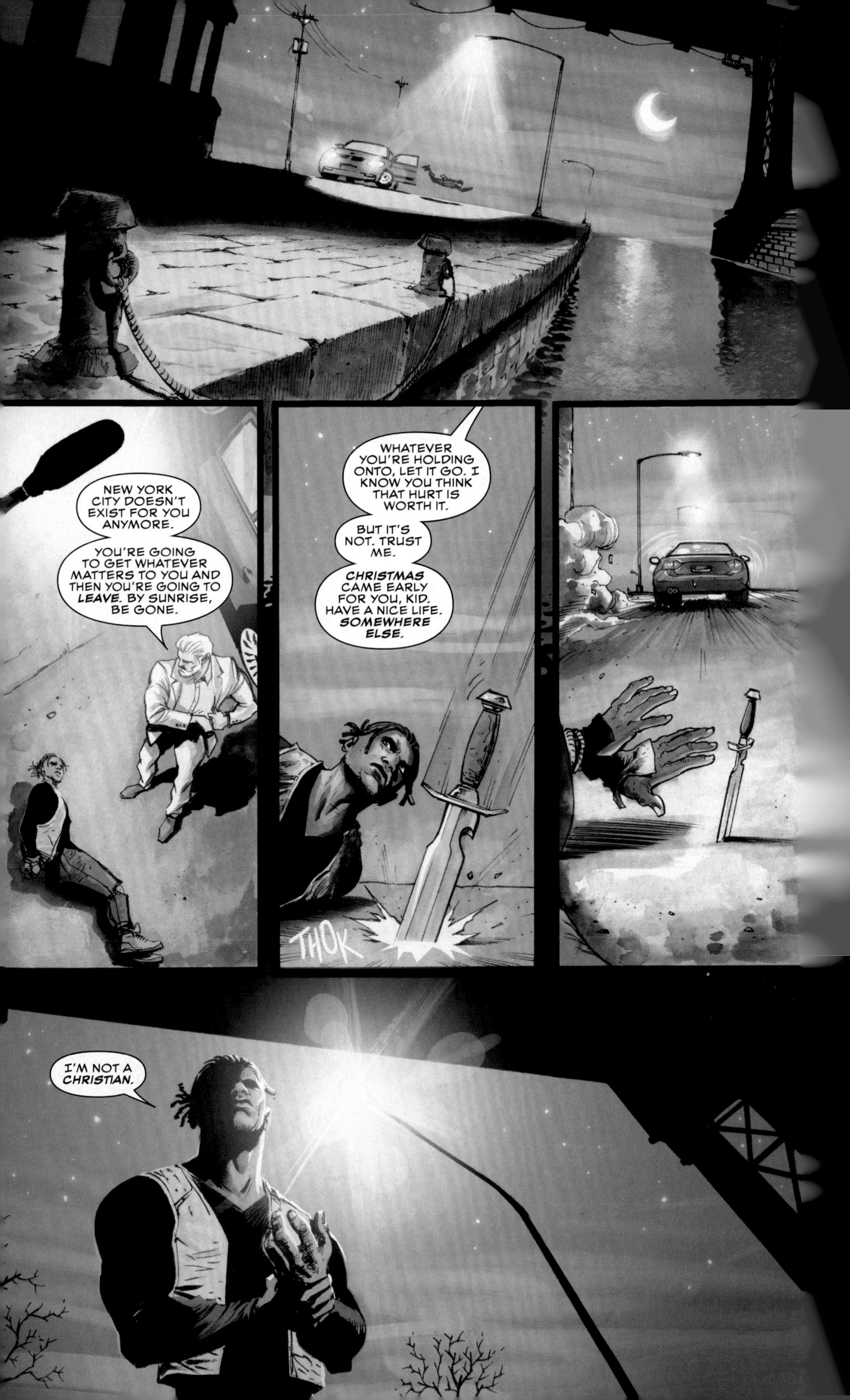
NEW YORK CITY DOESN'T EXIST FOR YOU ANYMORE.
YOU'RE GOING TO GET WHATEVER MATTERS TO YOU AND THEN YOU'RE GOING TO LEAVE. BY SUNRISE, BE GONE.
WHATEVER YOU'RE HOLDING ONTO, LET IT GO. I KNOW YOU THINK THAT HURT IS WORTH IT.
BUT IT'S NOT. TRUST ME.
CHRISTMAS CAME EARLY FOR YOU, KID. HAVE A NICE LIFE. SOMEWHERE ELSE.
THOK
I'M NOT A CHRISTIAN.

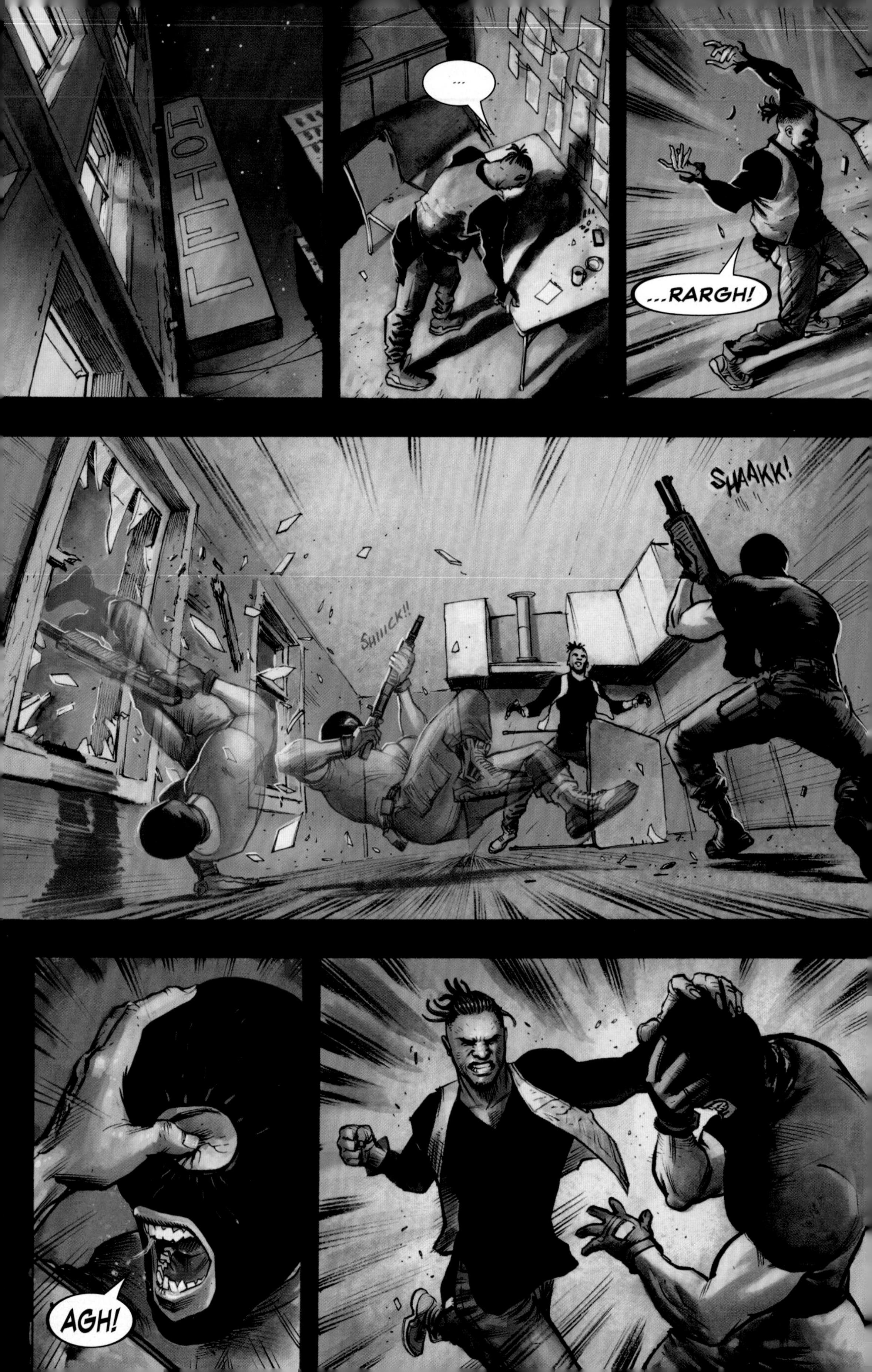
HOTEL
...
...RARGH!
SHAAKK!
SHIIICK!!
AGH!

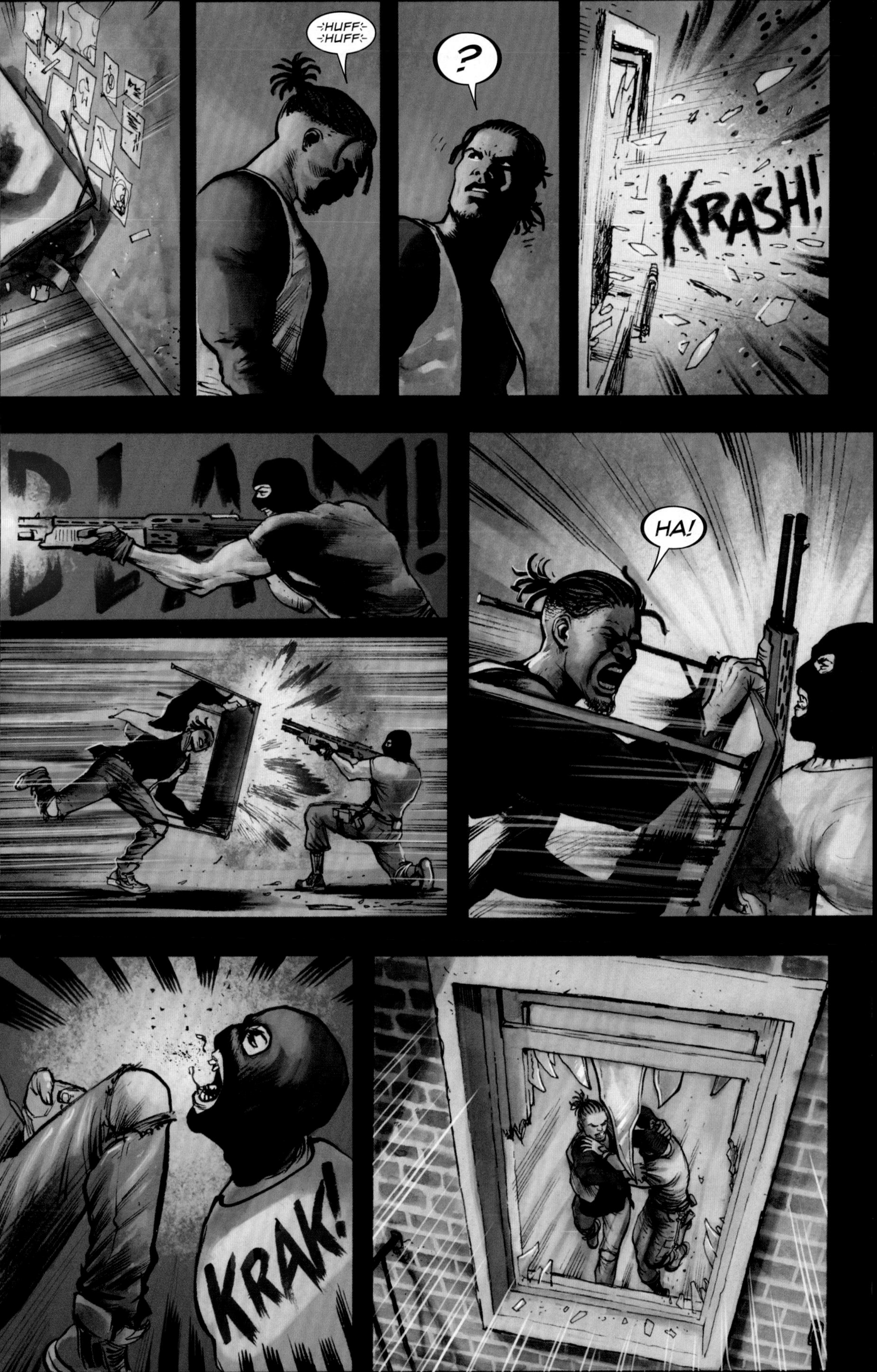
HUFF HUFF
?
KRASH!
HA!
KRAK!

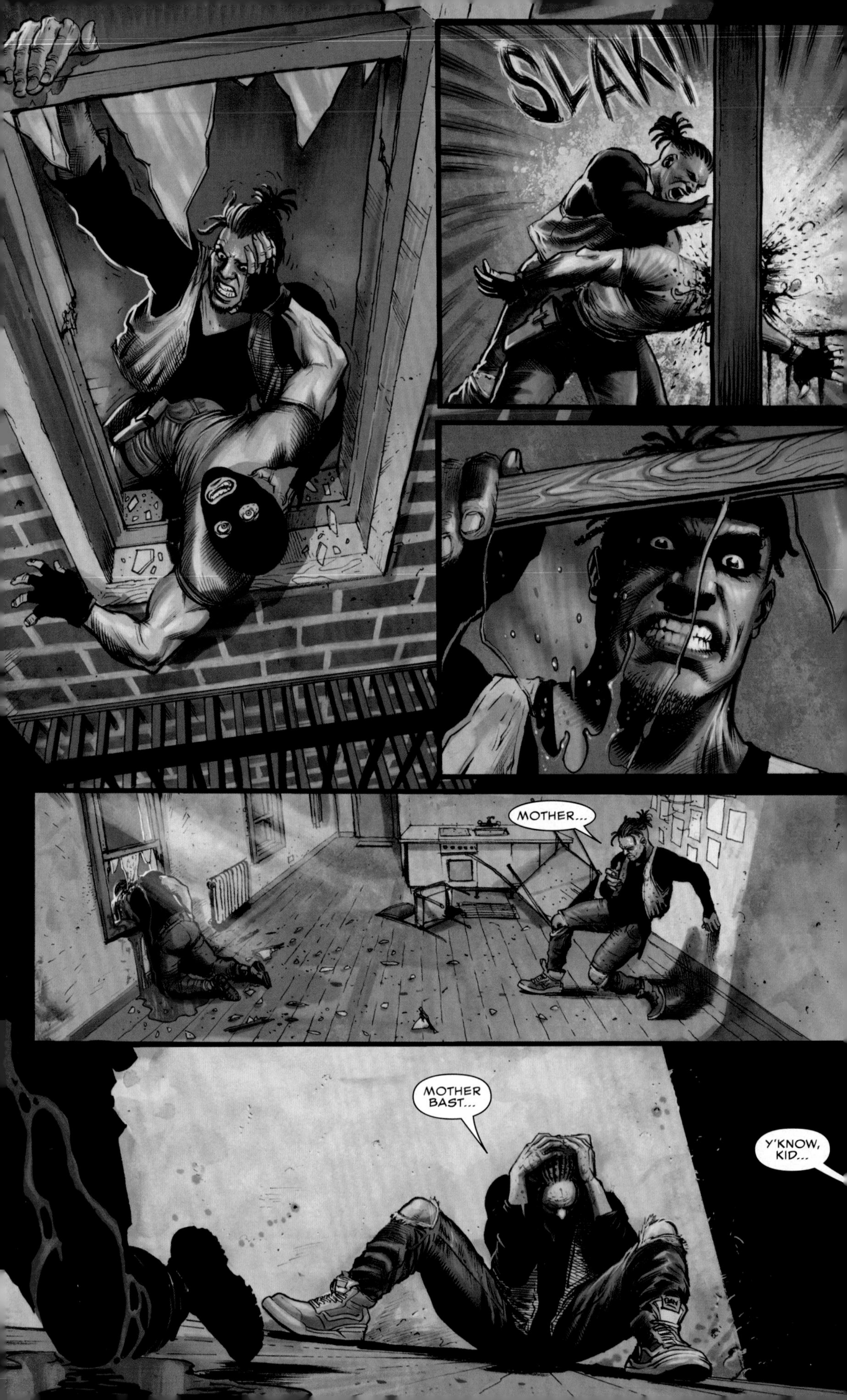
SLAK!
MOTHER...
MOTHER BAST...
Y'KNOW, KID...

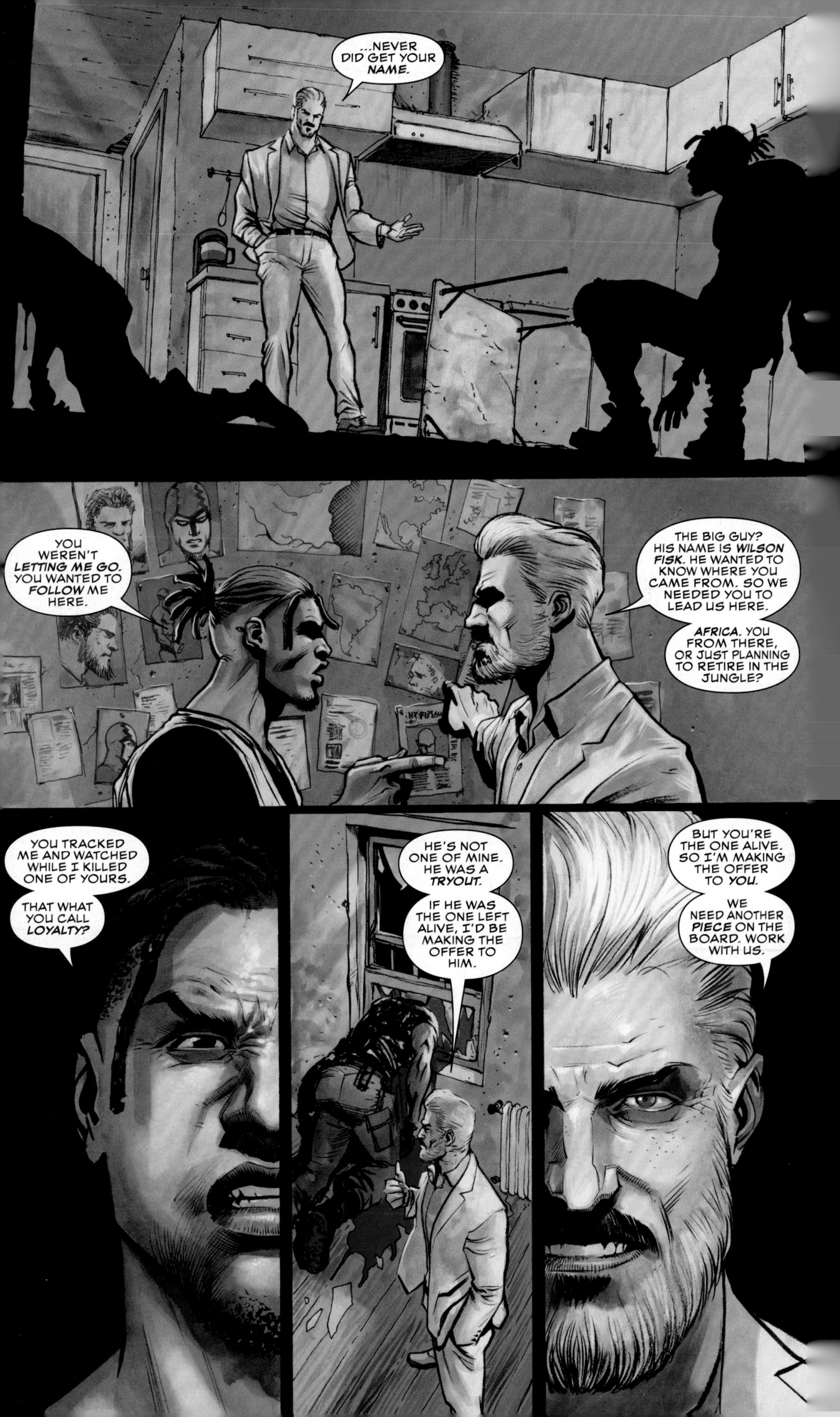
...NEVER DID GET YOUR NAME.
YOU WEREN'T LETTING ME GO. YOU WANTED TO FOLLOW ME HERE.
THE BIG GUY? HIS NAME IS WILSON FISK. HE WANTED TO KNOW WHERE YOU CAME FROM. SO WE NEEDED YOU TO LEAD US HERE.
AFRICA. YOU FROM THERE, OR JUST PLANNING TO RETIRE IN THE JUNGLE?
YOU TRACKED ME AND WATCHED WHILE I KILLED ONE OF YOURS.
THAT WHAT YOU CALL LOYALTY?
HE'S NOT ONE OF MINE. HE WAS A TRYOUT.
IF HE WAS THE ONE LEFT ALIVE, I'D BE MAKING THE OFFER TO HIM.
BUT YOU'RE THE ONE ALIVE. SO I'M MAKING THE OFFER TO YOU.
WE NEED ANOTHER PIECE ON THE BOARD. WORK WITH US.

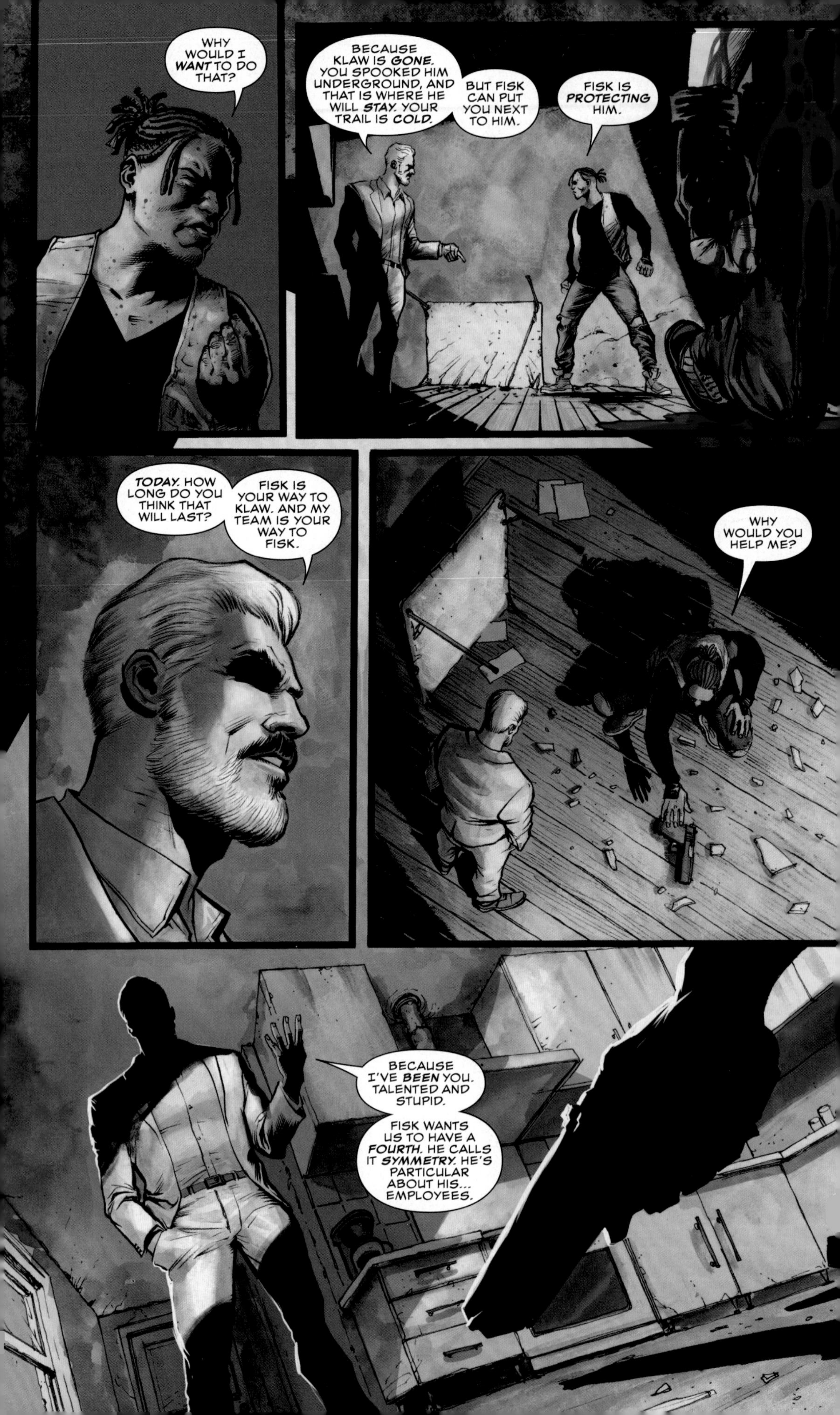
WHY WOULD I *WANT* TO DO THAT?
BECAUSE KLAW IS *GONE*. YOU SPOOKED HIM UNDERGROUND, AND THAT IS WHERE HE WILL *STAY*. YOUR TRAIL IS *COLD*.
BUT FISK CAN PUT YOU NEXT TO HIM.
FISK IS *PROTECTING* HIM.
TODAY. HOW LONG DO YOU THINK THAT WILL LAST?
FISK IS YOUR WAY TO KLAW. AND MY TEAM IS YOUR WAY TO FISK.
WHY WOULD YOU HELP ME?
BECAUSE I'VE *BEEN* YOU. TALENTED AND STUPID.
FISK WANTS US TO HAVE A *FOURTH*. HE CALLS IT *SYMMETRY*. HE'S PARTICULAR ABOUT HIS... EMPLOYEES.

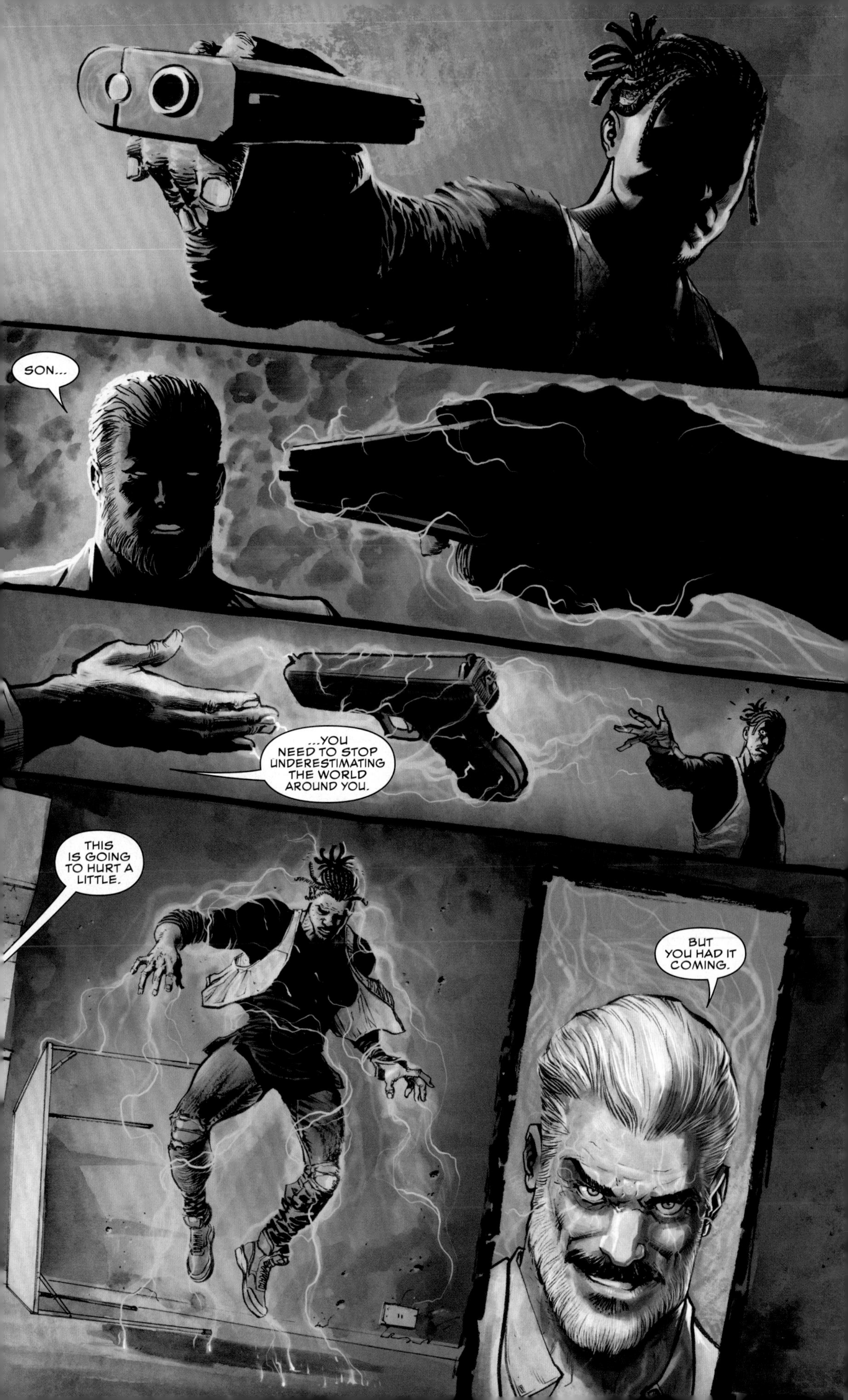
SON...
...YOU NEED TO STOP UNDERESTIMATING THE WORLD AROUND YOU.
THIS IS GOING TO HURT A LITTLE.
BUT YOU HAD IT COMING.

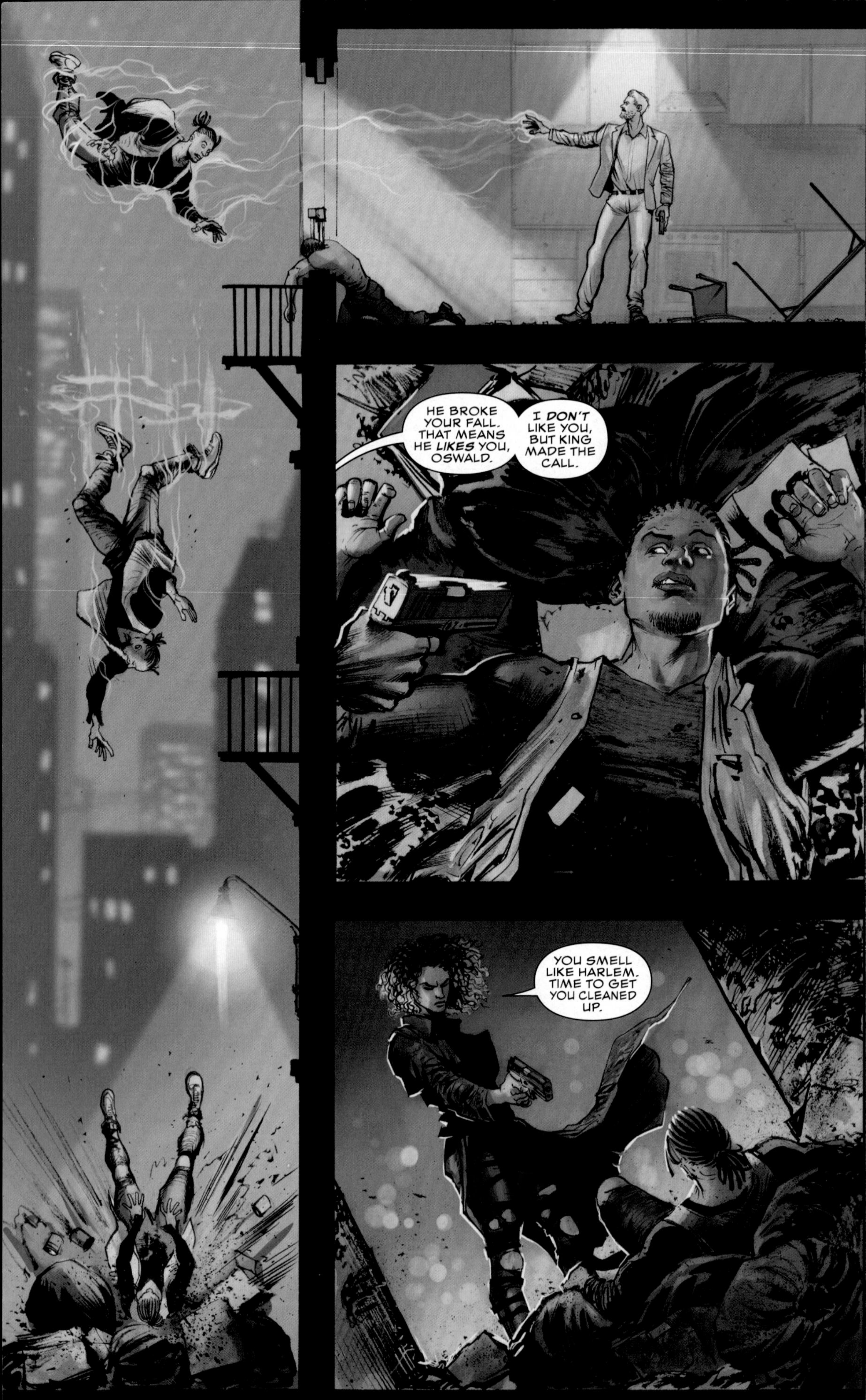
HE BROKE YOUR FALL. THAT MEANS HE *LIKES* YOU, OSWALD.
I *DON'T* LIKE YOU, BUT KING MADE THE CALL.
YOU SMELL LIKE HARLEM. TIME TO GET YOU CLEANED UP.

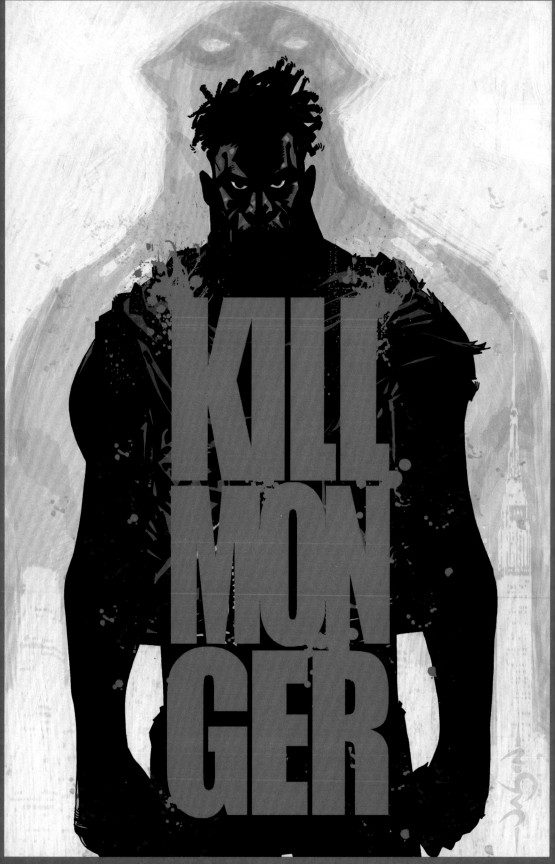

#1 VARIANT BY JASON PEARSON

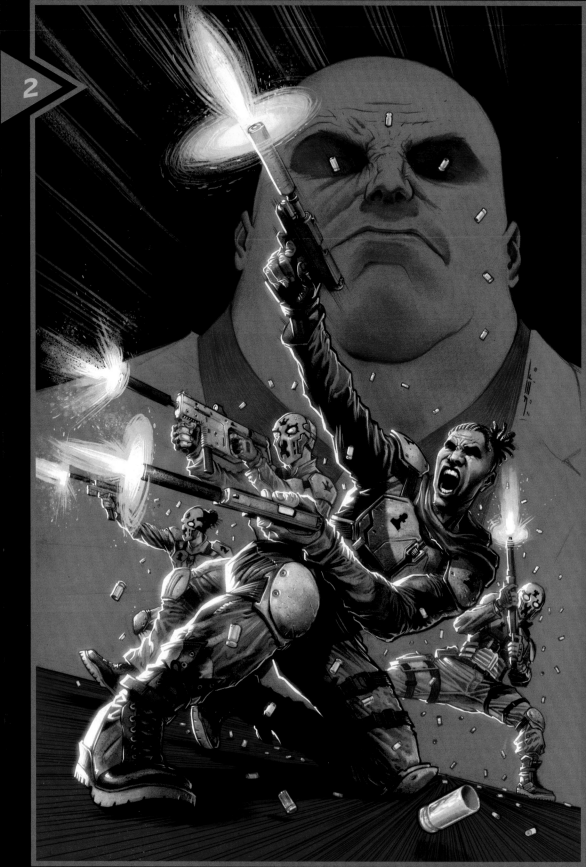

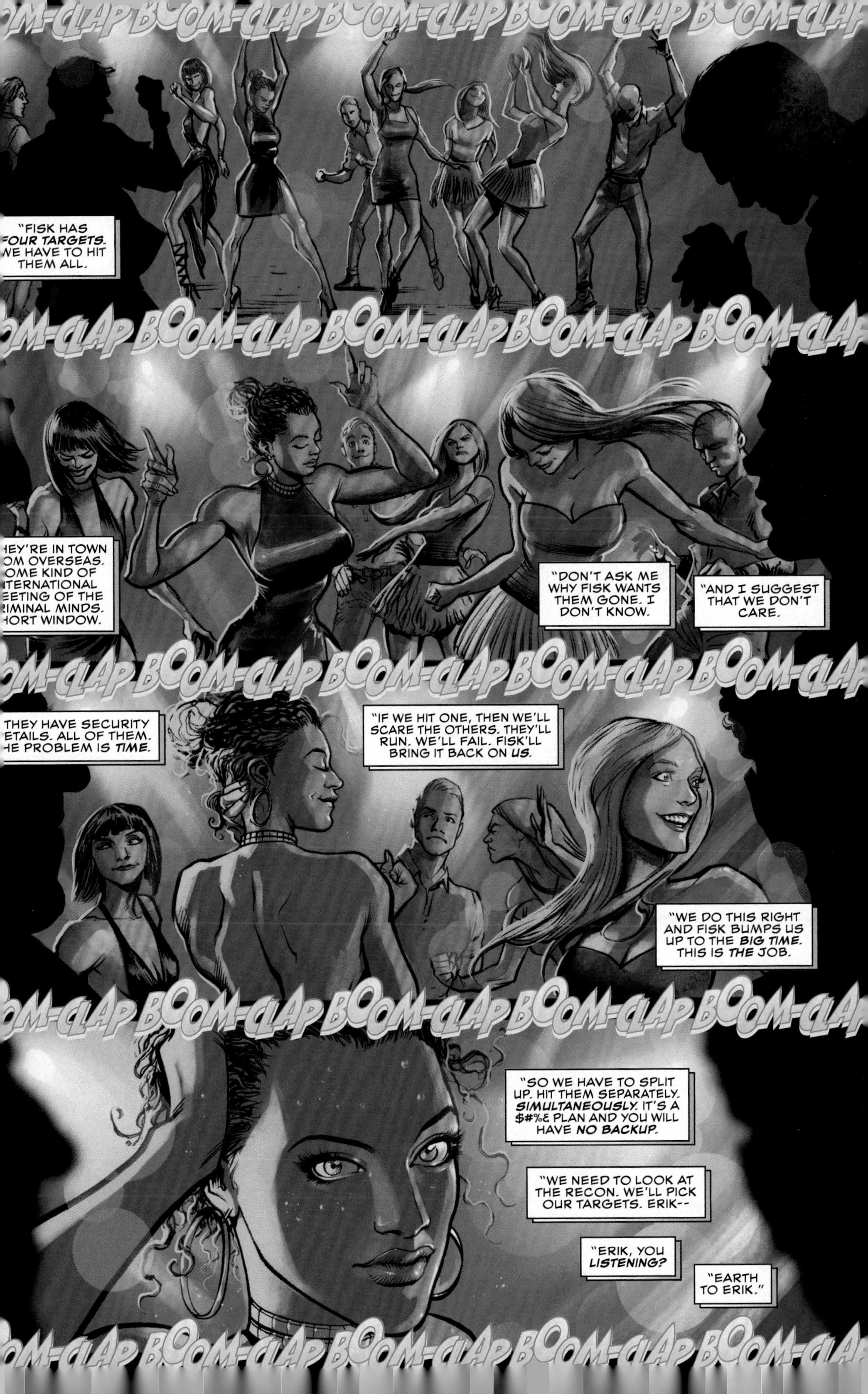
BOOM-CLAP BOOM-CLAP BOOM-CLAP BOOM-CLAP
"FISK HAS FOUR TARGETS. VE HAVE TO HIT THEM ALL.
BOOM-CLAP BOOM-CLAP BOOM-CLAP BOOM-CLAP
EY'RE IN TOWN OM OVERSEAS. OME KIND OF TERNATIONAL EETING OF THE RIMINAL MINDS. HORT WINDOW.
"DON'T ASK ME WHY FISK WANTS THEM GONE. I DON'T KNOW.
"AND I SUGGEST THAT WE DON'T CARE.
BOOM-CLAP BOOM-CLAP BOOM-CLAP BOOM-CLAP
THEY HAVE SECURITY ETAILS. ALL OF THEM. HE PROBLEM IS TIME.
"IF WE HIT ONE, THEN WE'LL SCARE THE OTHERS. THEY'LL RUN. WE'LL FAIL. FISK'LL BRING IT BACK ON US.
"WE DO THIS RIGHT AND FISK BUMPS US UP TO THE BIG TIME. THIS IS THE JOB.
BOOM-CLAP BOOM-CLAP BOOM-CLAP BOOM-CLAP
"SO WE HAVE TO SPLIT UP. HIT THEM SEPARATELY. SIMULTANEOUSLY. IT'S A $#%& PLAN AND YOU WILL HAVE NO BACKUP.
"WE NEED TO LOOK AT THE RECON. WE'LL PICK OUR TARGETS. ERIK--
"ERIK, YOU LISTENING?
"EARTH TO ERIK."
BOOM-CLAP BOOM-CLAP BOOM-CLAP BOOM-CLAP

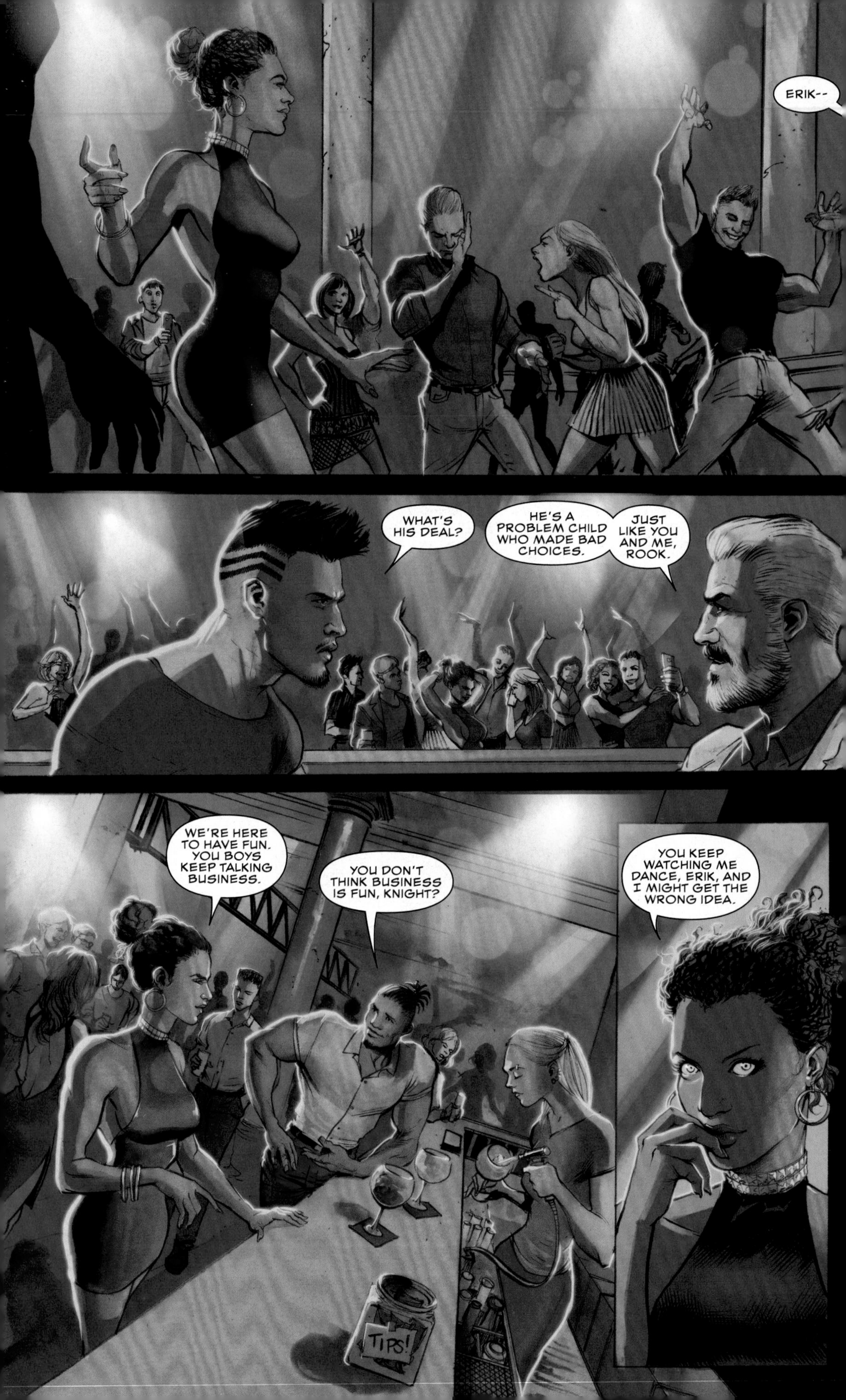
ERIK--
WHAT'S HIS DEAL?
HE'S A PROBLEM CHILD WHO MADE BAD CHOICES.
JUST LIKE YOU AND ME, ROOK.
WE'RE HERE TO HAVE FUN. YOU BOYS KEEP TALKING BUSINESS.
YOU DON'T THINK BUSINESS IS FUN, KNIGHT?
YOU KEEP WATCHING ME DANCE, ERIK, AND I MIGHT GET THE WRONG IDEA.
TIPS!

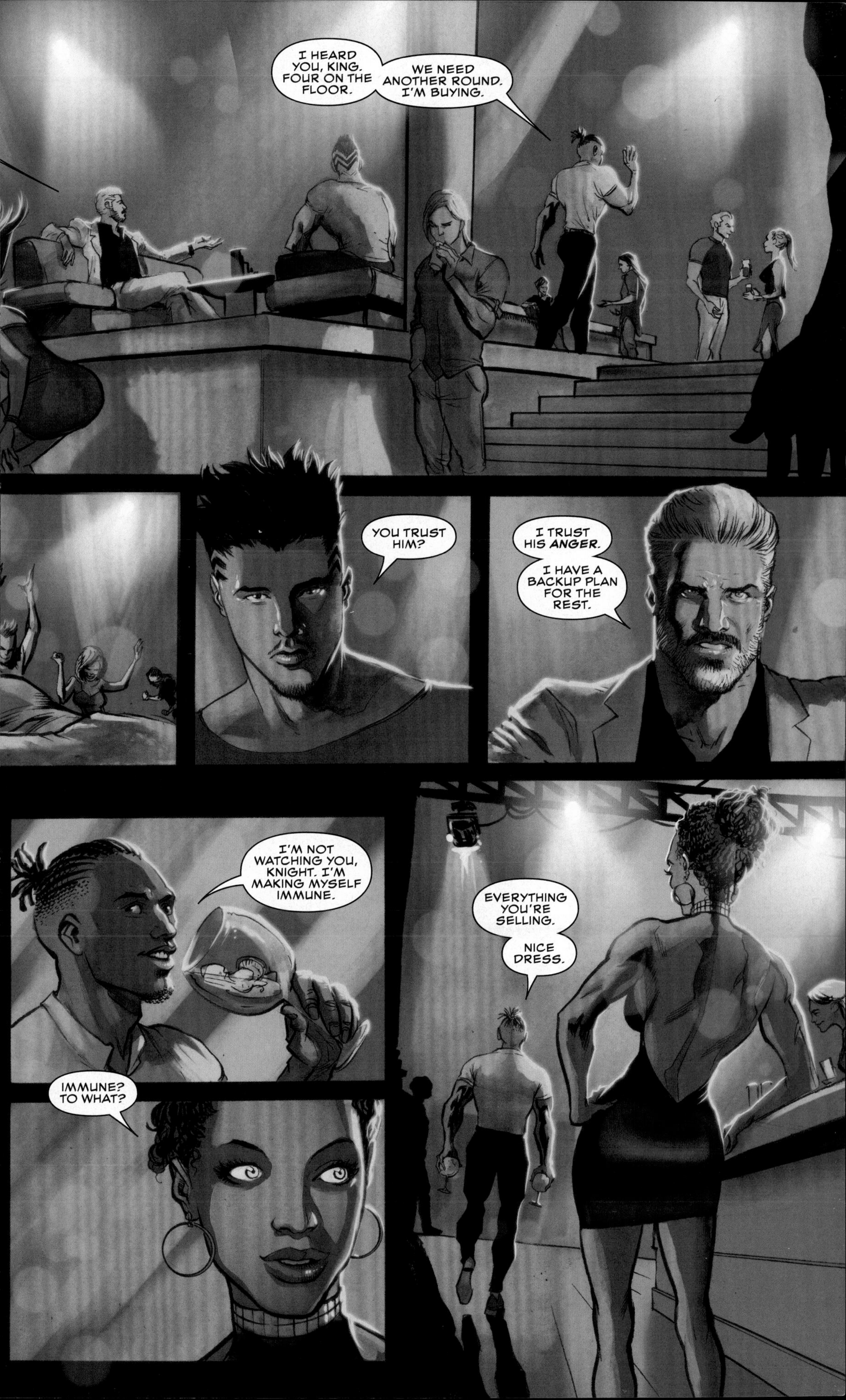
I HEARD YOU, KING. FOUR ON THE FLOOR.
WE NEED ANOTHER ROUND. I'M BUYING.
YOU TRUST HIM?
I TRUST HIS ANGER.
I HAVE A BACKUP PLAN FOR THE REST.
I'M NOT WATCHING YOU, KNIGHT. I'M MAKING MYSELF IMMUNE.
IMMUNE? TO WHAT?
EVERYTHING YOU'RE SELLING.
NICE DRESS.

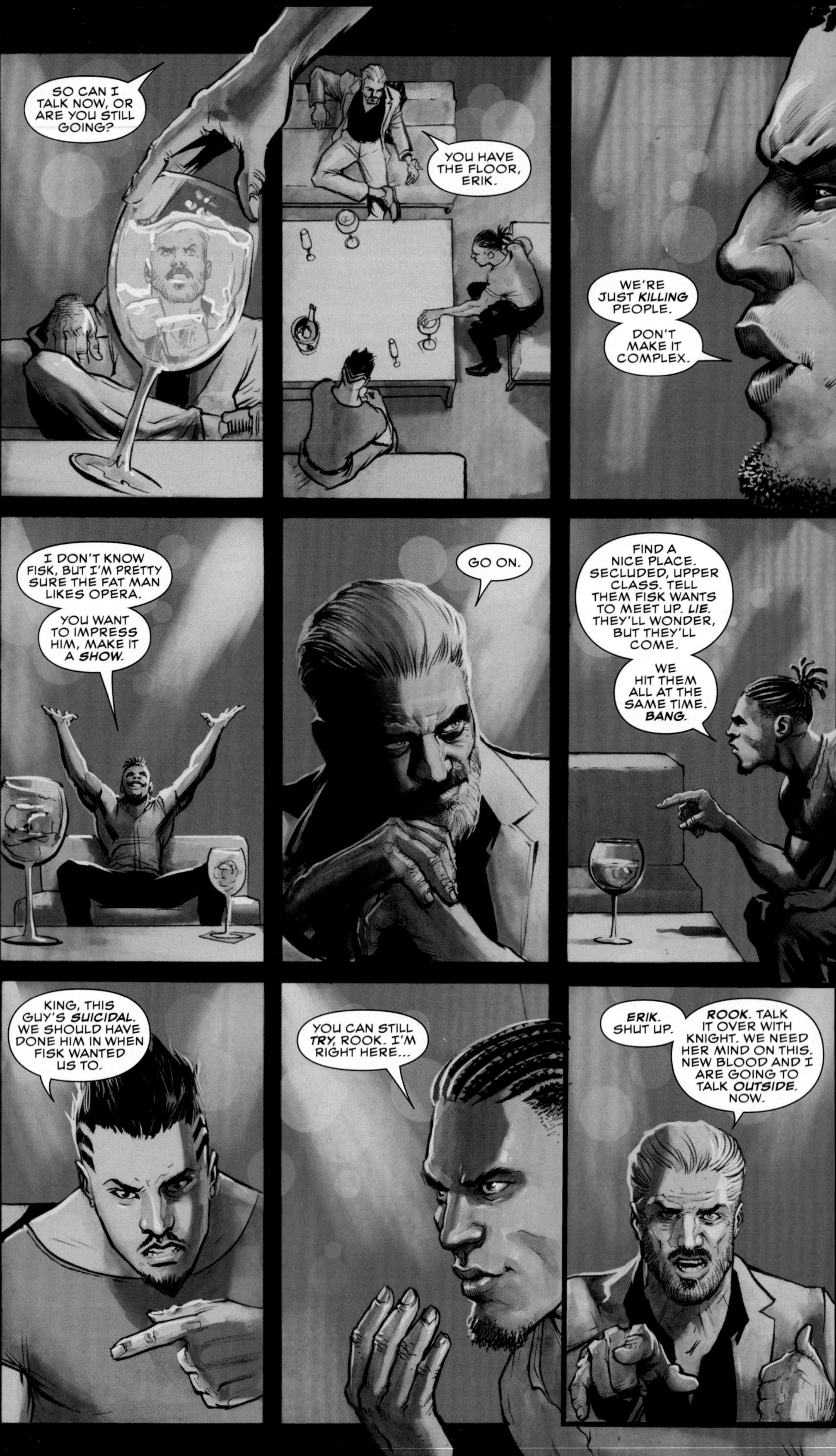
SO CAN I TALK NOW, OR ARE YOU STILL GOING?
YOU HAVE THE FLOOR, ERIK.
WE'RE JUST KILLING PEOPLE.
DON'T MAKE IT COMPLEX.
I DON'T KNOW FISK, BUT I'M PRETTY SURE THE FAT MAN LIKES OPERA.
YOU WANT TO IMPRESS HIM, MAKE IT A SHOW.
GO ON.
FIND A NICE PLACE. SECLUDED, UPPER CLASS. TELL THEM FISK WANTS TO MEET UP. LIE. THEY'LL WONDER, BUT THEY'LL COME.
WE HIT THEM ALL AT THE SAME TIME. BANG.
KING, THIS GUY'S SUICIDAL. WE SHOULD HAVE DONE HIM IN WHEN FISK WANTED US TO.
YOU CAN STILL TRY, ROOK. I'M RIGHT HERE...
ERIK. SHUT UP.
ROOK. TALK IT OVER WITH KNIGHT. WE NEED HER MIND ON THIS. NEW BLOOD AND I ARE GOING TO TALK OUTSIDE. NOW.

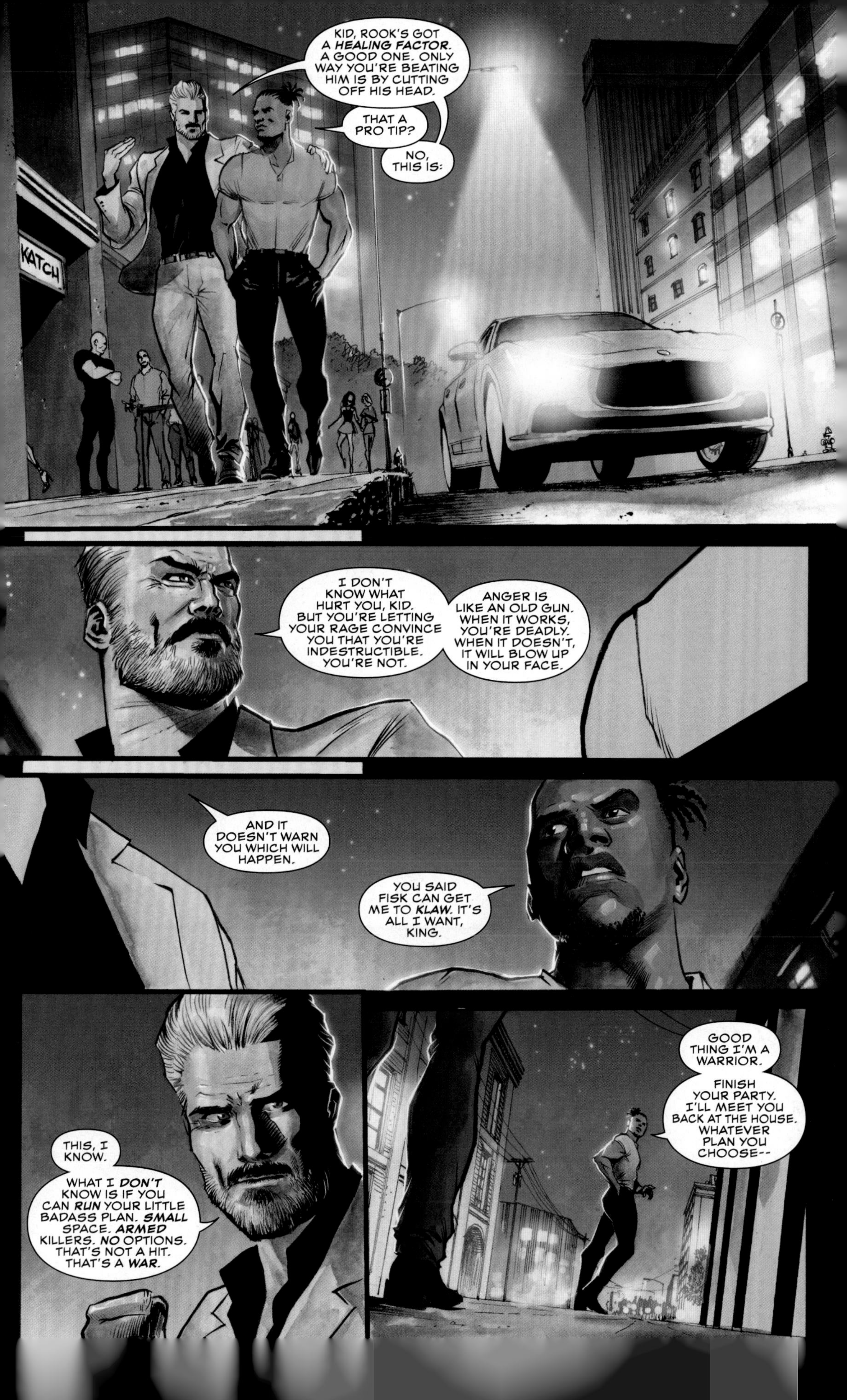
KID, ROOK'S GOT A HEALING FACTOR. A GOOD ONE. ONLY WAY YOU'RE BEATING HIM IS BY CUTTING OFF HIS HEAD.
THAT A PRO TIP?
NO, THIS IS:
KATCH
I DON'T KNOW WHAT HURT YOU, KID. BUT YOU'RE LETTING YOUR RAGE CONVINCE YOU THAT YOU'RE INDESTRUCTIBLE. YOU'RE NOT.
ANGER IS LIKE AN OLD GUN. WHEN IT WORKS, YOU'RE DEADLY. WHEN IT DOESN'T, IT WILL BLOW UP IN YOUR FACE.
AND IT DOESN'T WARN YOU WHICH WILL HAPPEN.
YOU SAID FISK CAN GET ME TO KLAW. IT'S ALL I WANT, KING.
THIS, I KNOW.
WHAT I DON'T KNOW IS IF YOU CAN RUN YOUR LITTLE BADASS PLAN. SMALL SPACE. ARMED KILLERS. NO OPTIONS. THAT'S NOT A HIT. THAT'S A WAR.
GOOD THING I'M A WARRIOR.
FINISH YOUR PARTY. I'LL MEET YOU BACK AT THE HOUSE. WHATEVER PLAN YOU CHOOSE--

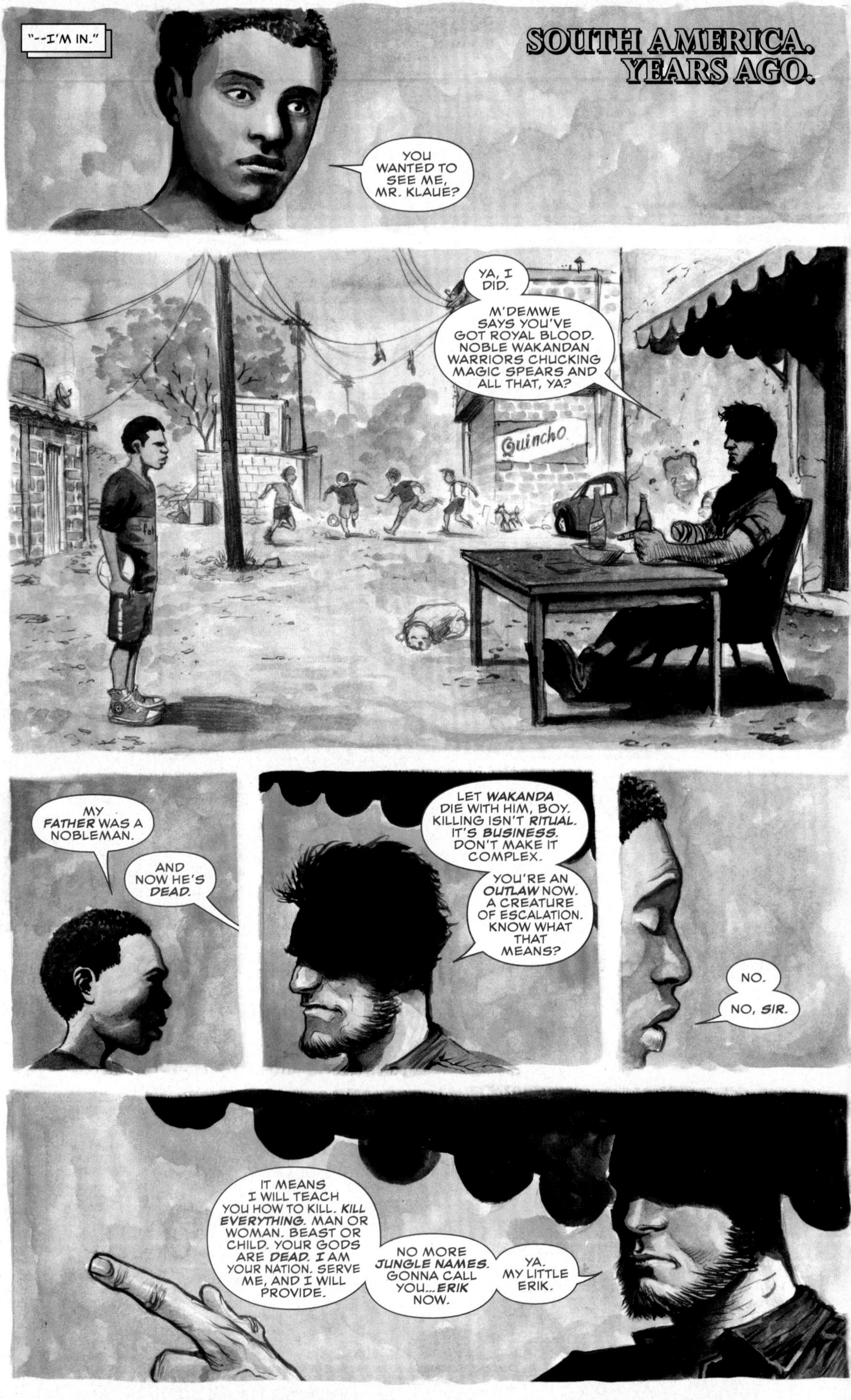
"--I'M IN."
SOUTH AMERICA. YEARS AGO.
YOU WANTED TO SEE ME, MR. KLAUE?
YA, I DID.
M'DEMWE SAYS YOU'VE GOT ROYAL BLOOD. NOBLE WAKANDAN WARRIORS CHUCKING MAGIC SPEARS AND ALL THAT, YA?
Quincho
MY FATHER WAS A NOBLEMAN.
AND NOW HE'S DEAD.
LET WAKANDA DIE WITH HIM, BOY. KILLING ISN'T RITUAL. IT'S BUSINESS. DON'T MAKE IT COMPLEX.
YOU'RE AN OUTLAW NOW. A CREATURE OF ESCALATION. KNOW WHAT THAT MEANS?
NO.
NO, SIR.
IT MEANS I WILL TEACH YOU HOW TO KILL. KILL EVERYTHING. MAN OR WOMAN. BEAST OR CHILD. YOUR GODS ARE DEAD. I AM YOUR NATION. SERVE ME, AND I WILL PROVIDE.
NO MORE JUNGLE NAMES. GONNA CALL YOU...ERIK NOW.
YA. MY LITTLE ERIK.

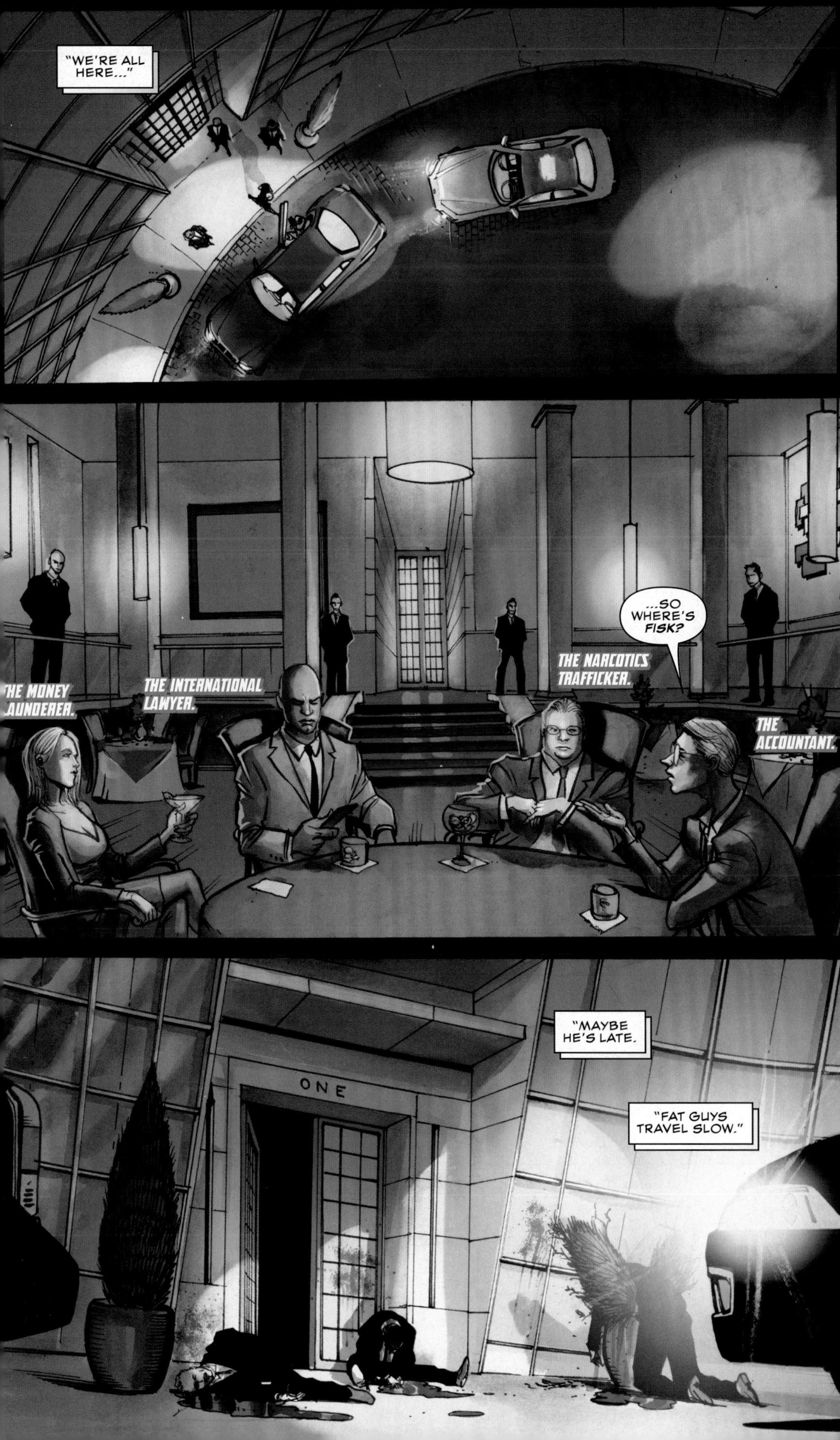
"WE'RE ALL HERE..."
THE MONEY LAUNDERER.
THE INTERNATIONAL LAWYER.
THE NARCOTICS TRAFFICKER.
...SO WHERE'S FISK?
THE ACCOUNTANT.
"MAYBE HE'S LATE.
ONE
"FAT GUYS TRAVEL SLOW."

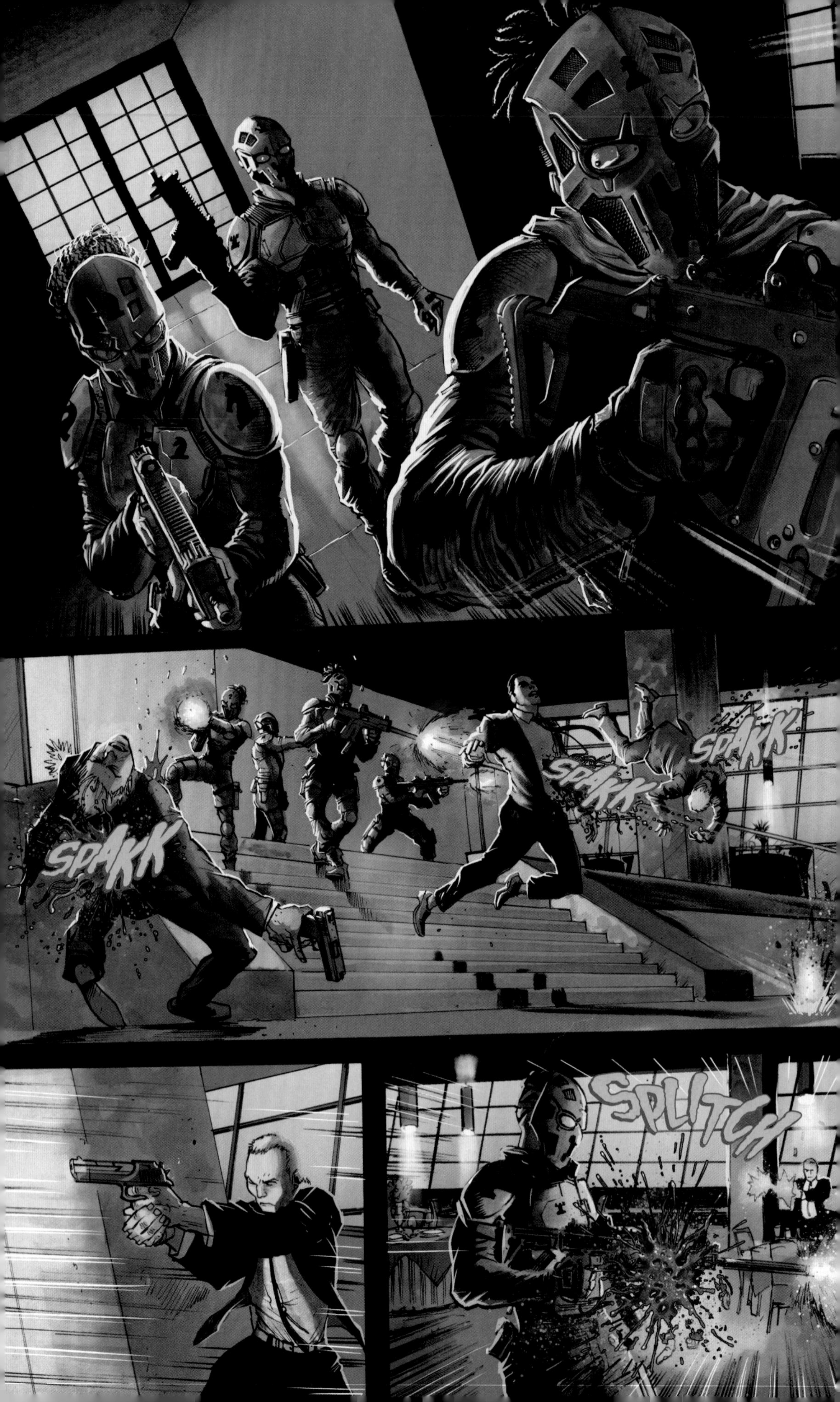
SPAKK
SPAKK
SPAKK
SPLITCH

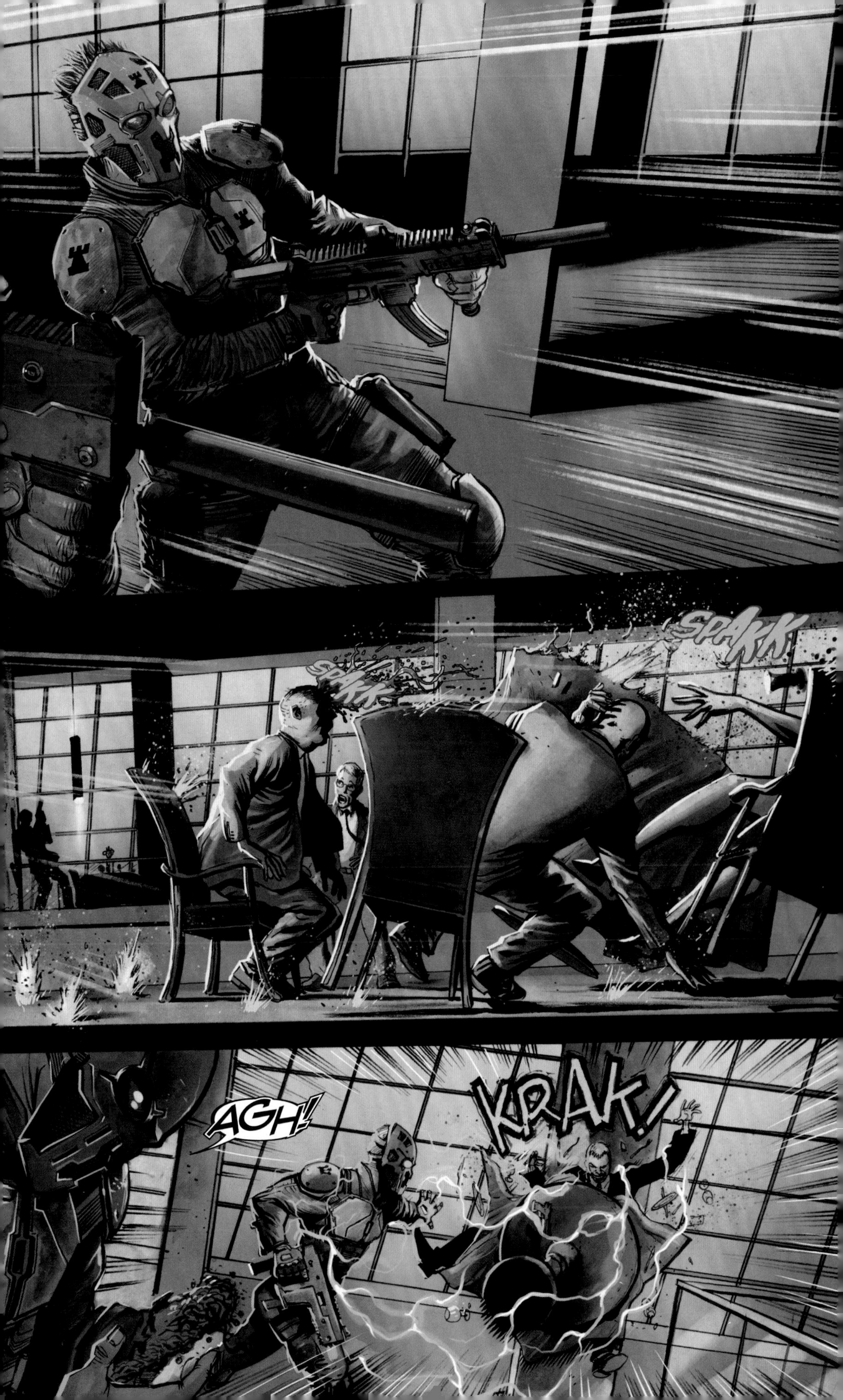

SPAKK
SPAKK
AGH!
KRAK!

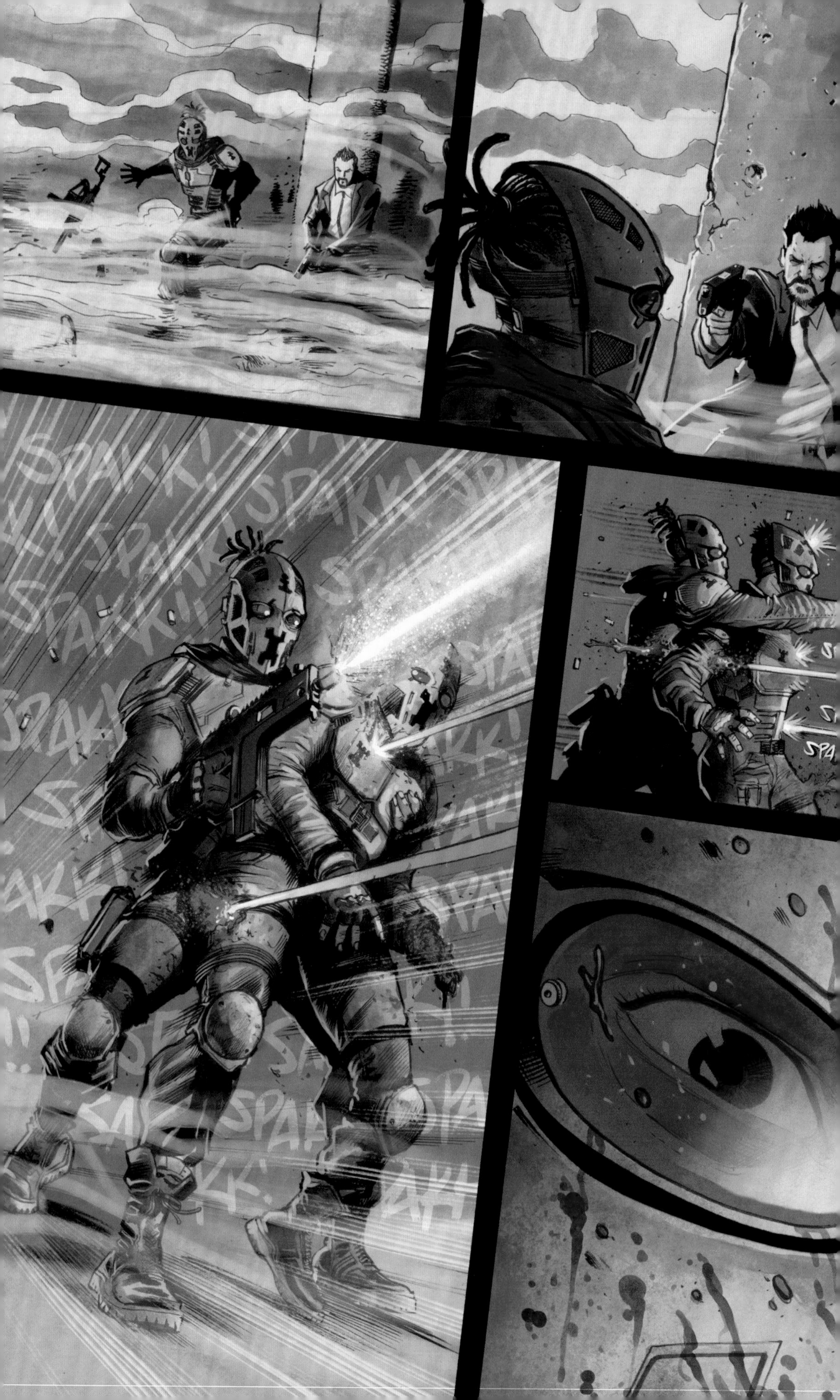

SPAKK!

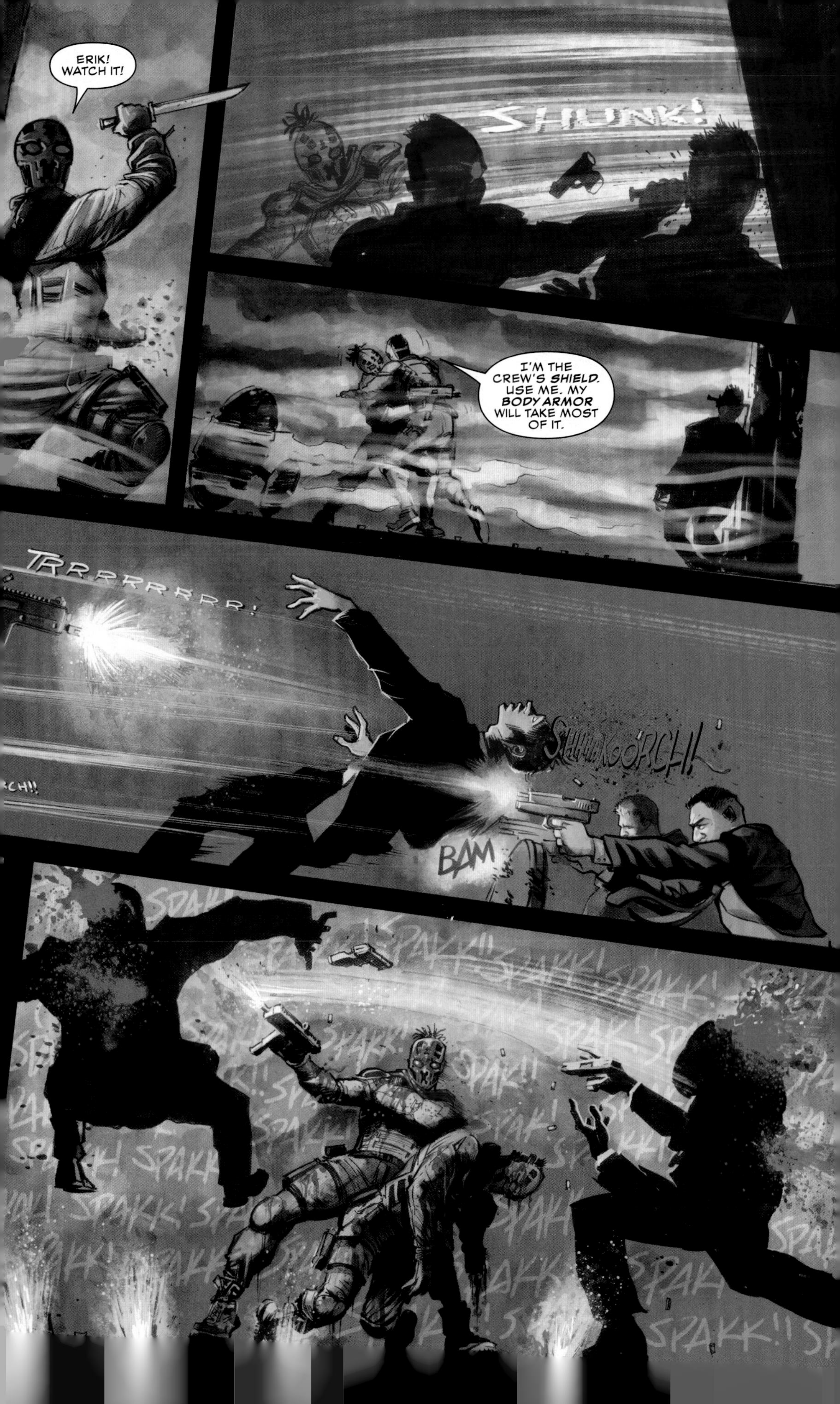

ERIK! WATCH IT!
SHUNK!
I'M THE CREW'S SHIELD. USE ME. MY BODY ARMOR WILL TAKE MOST OF IT.
TRRRRRRRRRRR!
SHHHKOOORCH!
CH!!
BAM
SPAKK! SPAKK! SPAKK!

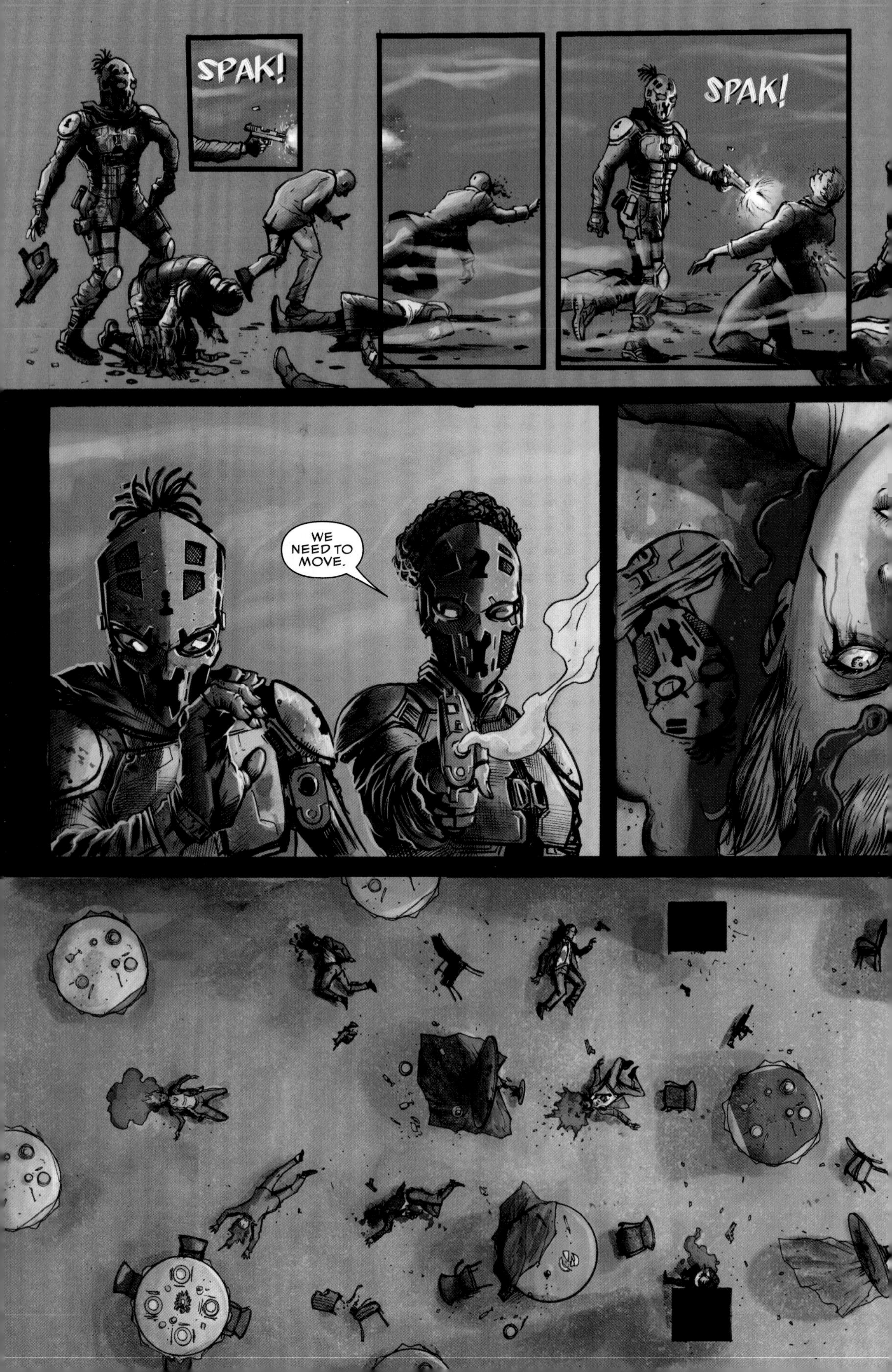
SPAK!
SPAK!
WE NEED TO MOVE.

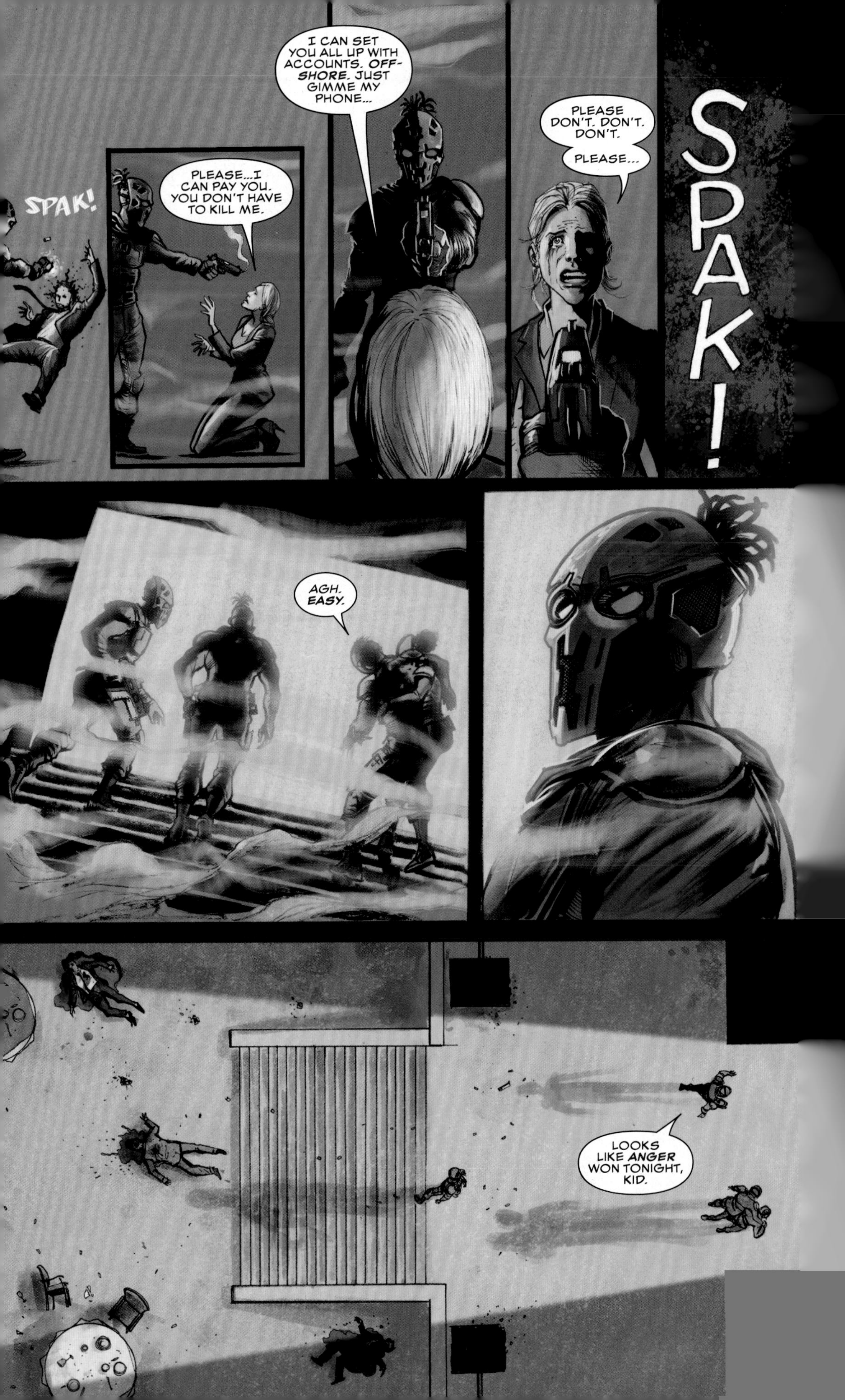
SPAK!
PLEASE...I CAN PAY YOU. YOU DON'T HAVE TO KILL ME.
I CAN SET YOU ALL UP WITH ACCOUNTS. OFF-SHORE. JUST GIMME MY PHONE...
PLEASE DON'T. DON'T. DON'T.
PLEASE...
SPAK!
AGH. EASY.
LOOKS LIKE ANGER WON TONIGHT, KID.

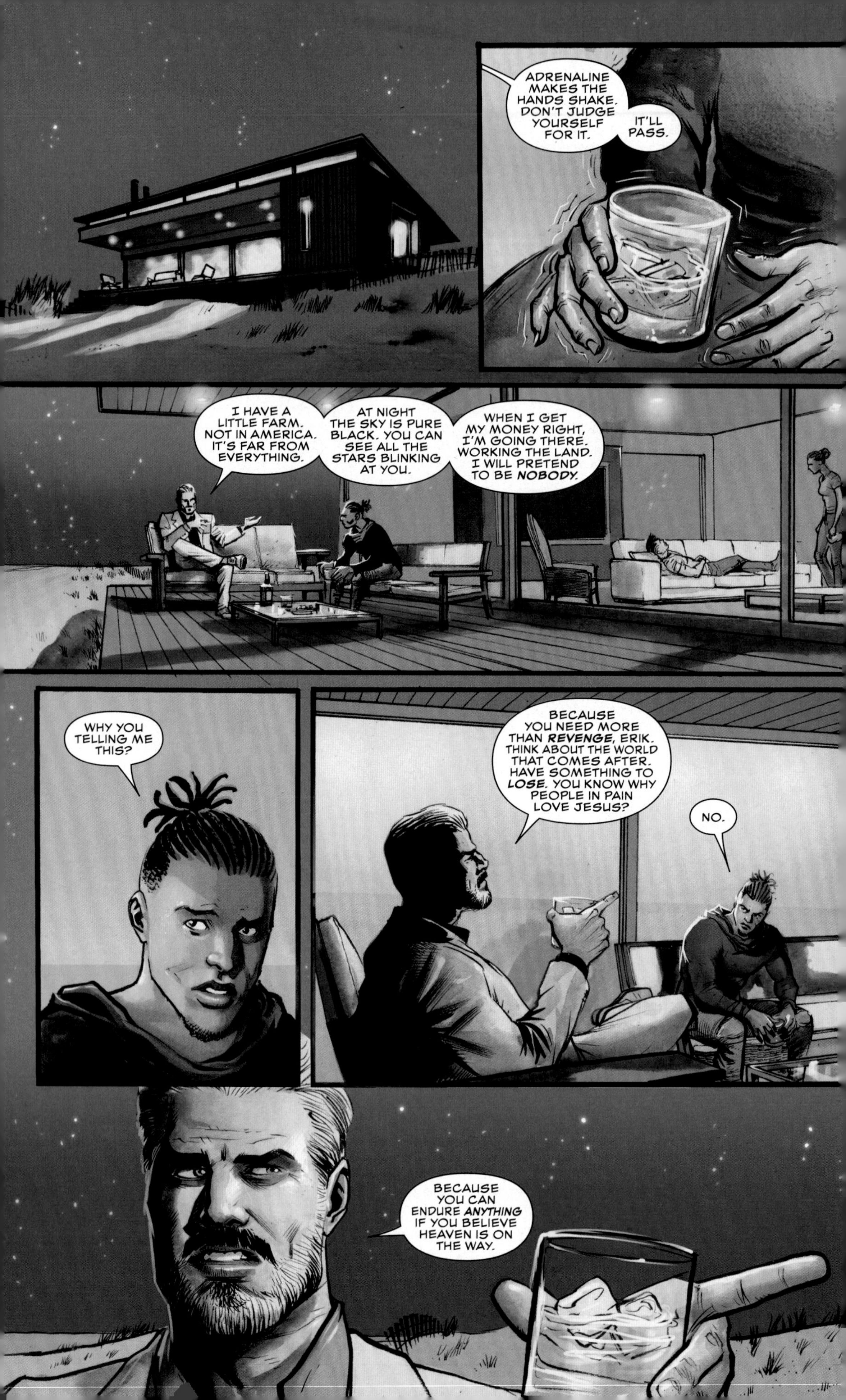
ADRENALINE MAKES THE HANDS SHAKE. DON'T JUDGE YOURSELF FOR IT.
IT'LL PASS.
I HAVE A LITTLE FARM. NOT IN AMERICA. IT'S FAR FROM EVERYTHING.
AT NIGHT THE SKY IS PURE BLACK. YOU CAN SEE ALL THE STARS BLINKING AT YOU.
WHEN I GET MY MONEY RIGHT, I'M GOING THERE. WORKING THE LAND. I WILL PRETEND TO BE ***NOBODY***.
WHY YOU TELLING ME THIS?
BECAUSE YOU NEED MORE THAN ***REVENGE***, ERIK. THINK ABOUT THE WORLD THAT COMES AFTER. HAVE SOMETHING TO ***LOSE***. YOU KNOW WHY PEOPLE IN PAIN LOVE JESUS?
NO.
BECAUSE YOU CAN ENDURE ***ANYTHING*** IF YOU BELIEVE HEAVEN IS ON THE WAY.

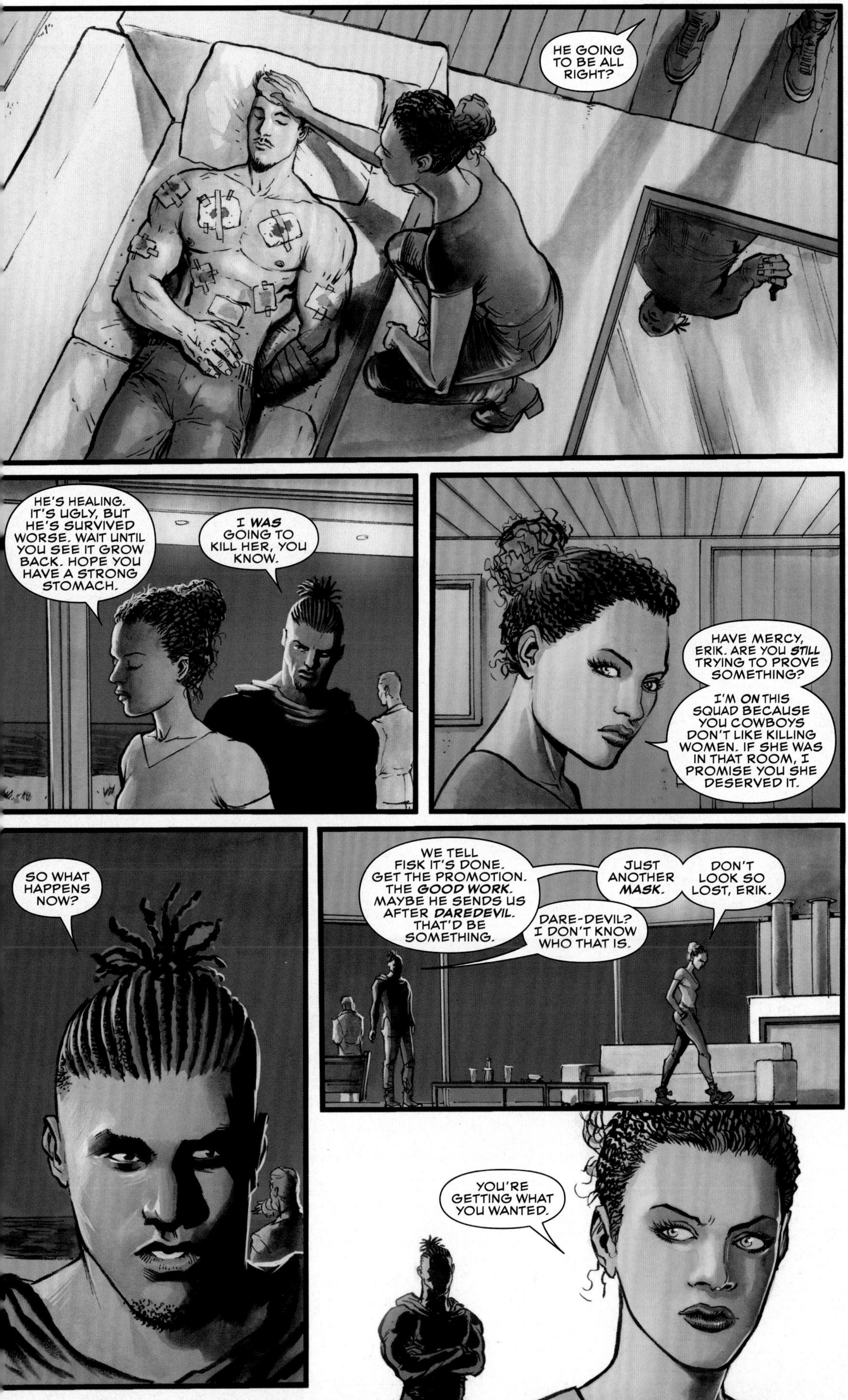

HE GOING TO BE ALL RIGHT?
HE'S HEALING. IT'S UGLY, BUT HE'S SURVIVED WORSE. WAIT UNTIL YOU SEE IT GROW BACK. HOPE YOU HAVE A STRONG STOMACH.
I WAS GOING TO KILL HER, YOU KNOW.
HAVE MERCY, ERIK. ARE YOU STILL TRYING TO PROVE SOMETHING?
I'M ON THIS SQUAD BECAUSE YOU COWBOYS DON'T LIKE KILLING WOMEN. IF SHE WAS IN THAT ROOM, I PROMISE YOU SHE DESERVED IT.
SO WHAT HAPPENS NOW?
WE TELL FISK IT'S DONE. GET THE PROMOTION. THE GOOD WORK. MAYBE HE SENDS US AFTER DAREDEVIL. THAT'D BE SOMETHING.
JUST ANOTHER MASK.
DON'T LOOK SO LOST, ERIK.
DARE-DEVIL? I DON'T KNOW WHO THAT IS.
YOU'RE GETTING WHAT YOU WANTED.

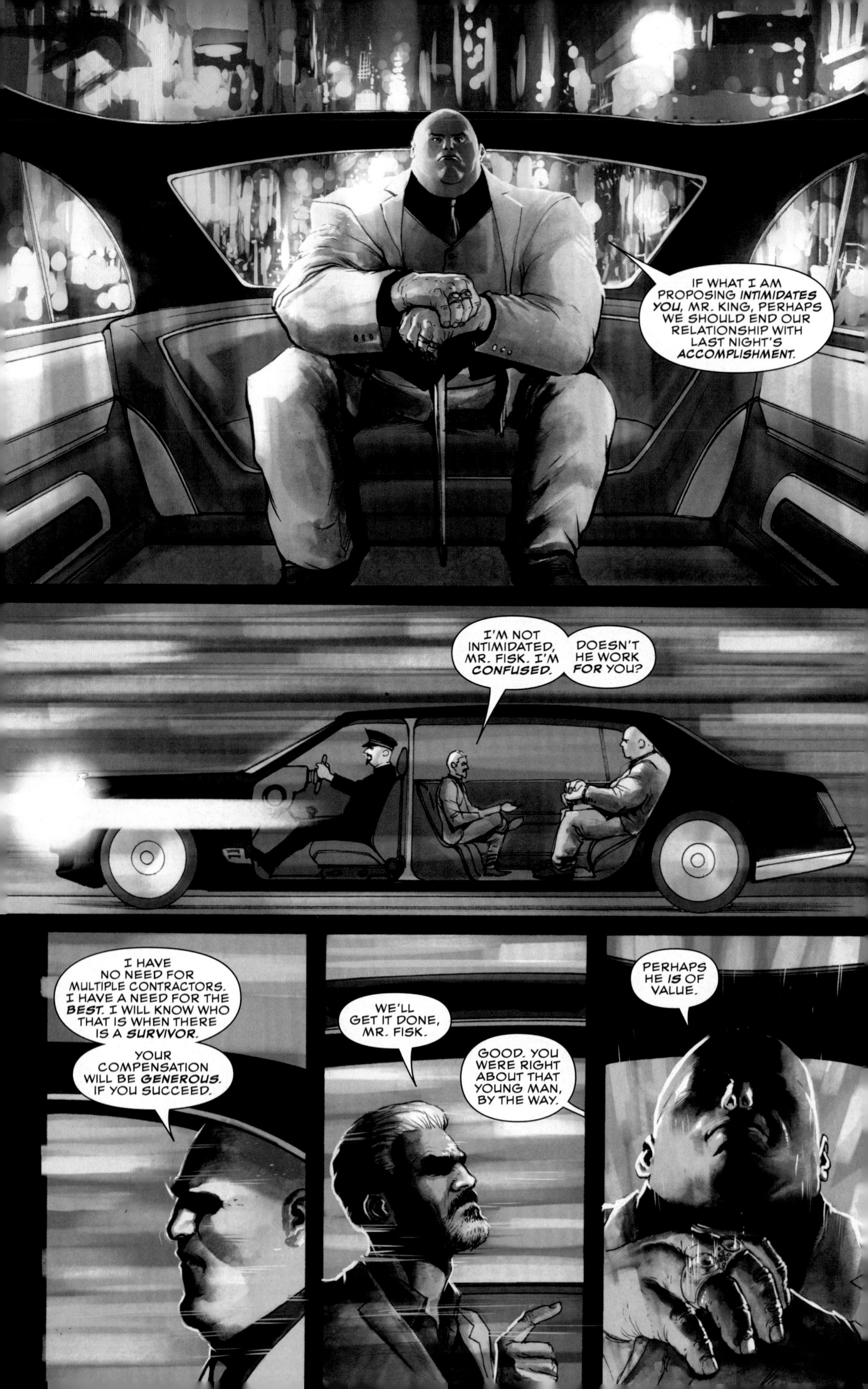
IF WHAT I AM PROPOSING INTIMIDATES YOU, MR. KING, PERHAPS WE SHOULD END OUR RELATIONSHIP WITH LAST NIGHT'S ACCOMPLISHMENT.
I'M NOT INTIMIDATED, MR. FISK. I'M CONFUSED.
DOESN'T HE WORK FOR YOU?
I HAVE NO NEED FOR MULTIPLE CONTRACTORS. I HAVE A NEED FOR THE BEST. I WILL KNOW WHO THAT IS WHEN THERE IS A SURVIVOR.
YOUR COMPENSATION WILL BE GENEROUS. IF YOU SUCCEED.
WE'LL GET IT DONE, MR. FISK.
GOOD. YOU WERE RIGHT ABOUT THAT YOUNG MAN, BY THE WAY.
PERHAPS HE IS OF VALUE.

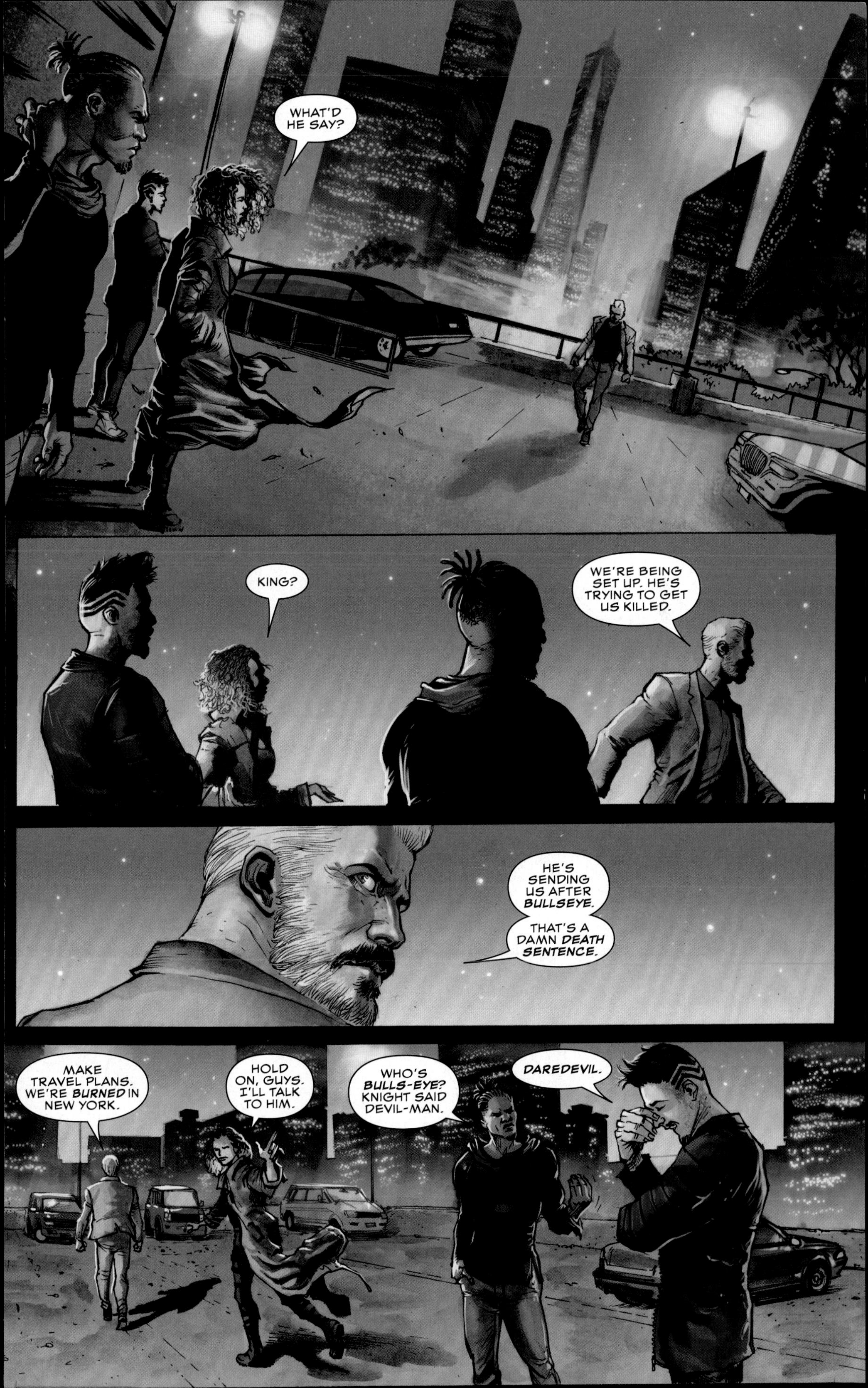
WHAT'D HE SAY?
KING?
WE'RE BEING SET UP. HE'S TRYING TO GET US KILLED.
HE'S SENDING US AFTER BULLSEYE.
THAT'S A DAMN DEATH SENTENCE.
MAKE TRAVEL PLANS. WE'RE BURNED IN NEW YORK.
HOLD ON, GUYS. I'LL TALK TO HIM.
WHO'S BULLS-EYE? KNIGHT SAID DEVIL-MAN.
DAREDEVIL.

KING! TALK TO ME.

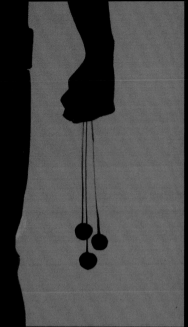

WE CAN'T BEAT BULLSEYE. NO ONE HAS.

THIS IS THE *EXIT STRATEGY*, KING. YOU DON'T WANT TO WORK FOR FISK FOREVER. YOU WANT TO *RETIRE*, RIGHT? SO TELL FISK WE WANT *TRIPLE*.

WE GET IT DONE AND THEN IT'S HAPPILY EVER AFTER.

WHMMMMMM

IT'S A *TRAP*, KNIGHT! FISK *DOESN'T* WANT US.

MAYBE IT'S BECAUSE WE LEFT ERIK ALIVE. MAYBE "THE KINGPIN" JUST CHANGED HIS MIND. DOESN'T MATTER. WE LEAVE. WE SURVIVE. *THAT* IS THE CALL.

ROOK. YOU SAVED MY LIFE LAST NIGHT.

I OWE YOU.

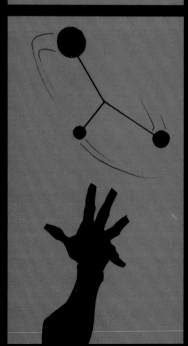

WE'RE GOOD.

WHATEVER PROBLEM WE HAD--

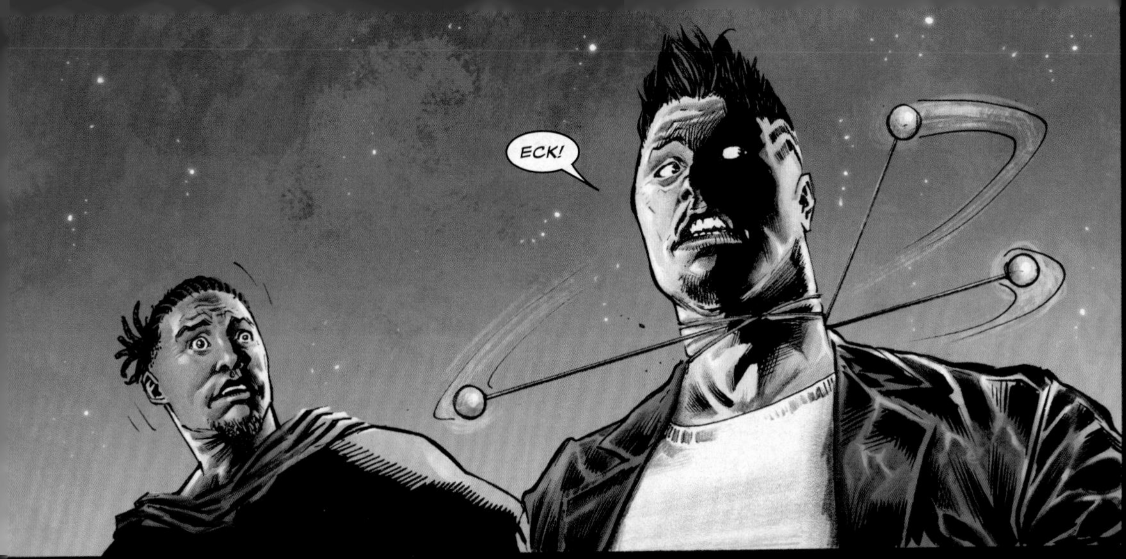
ECK!

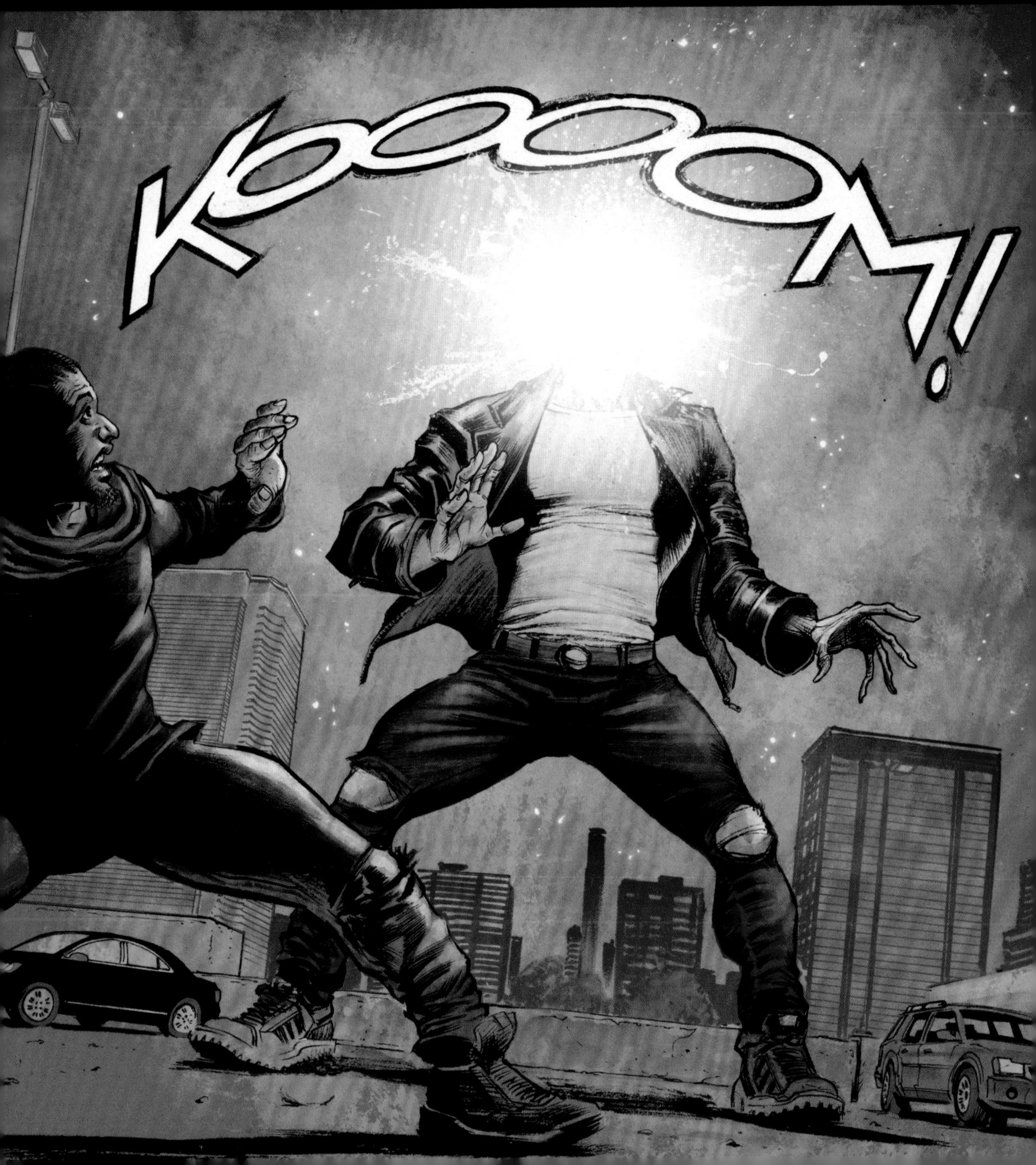
KOOOOOM!!

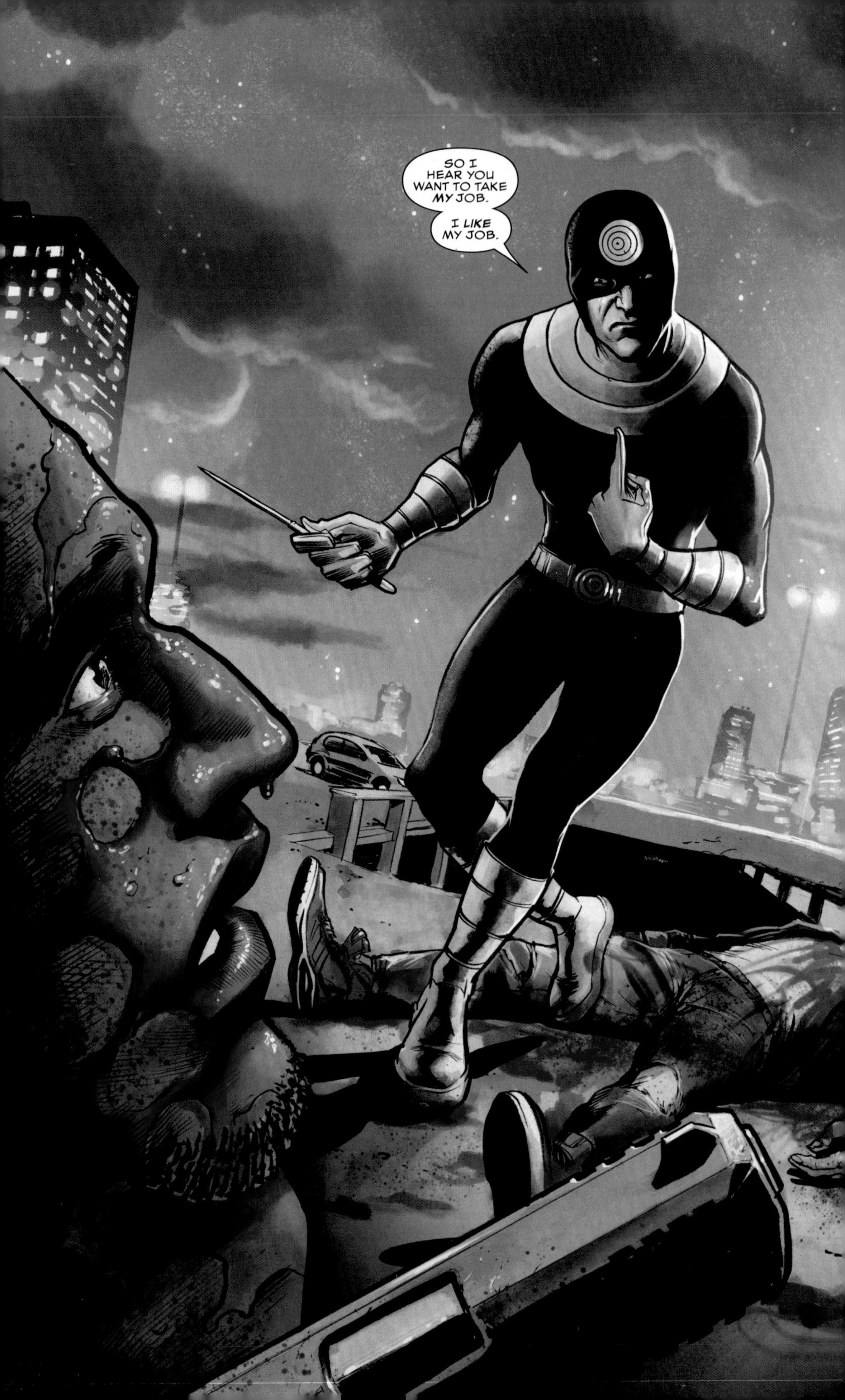
SO I HEAR YOU WANT TO TAKE *MY* JOB.
I *LIKE* MY JOB.

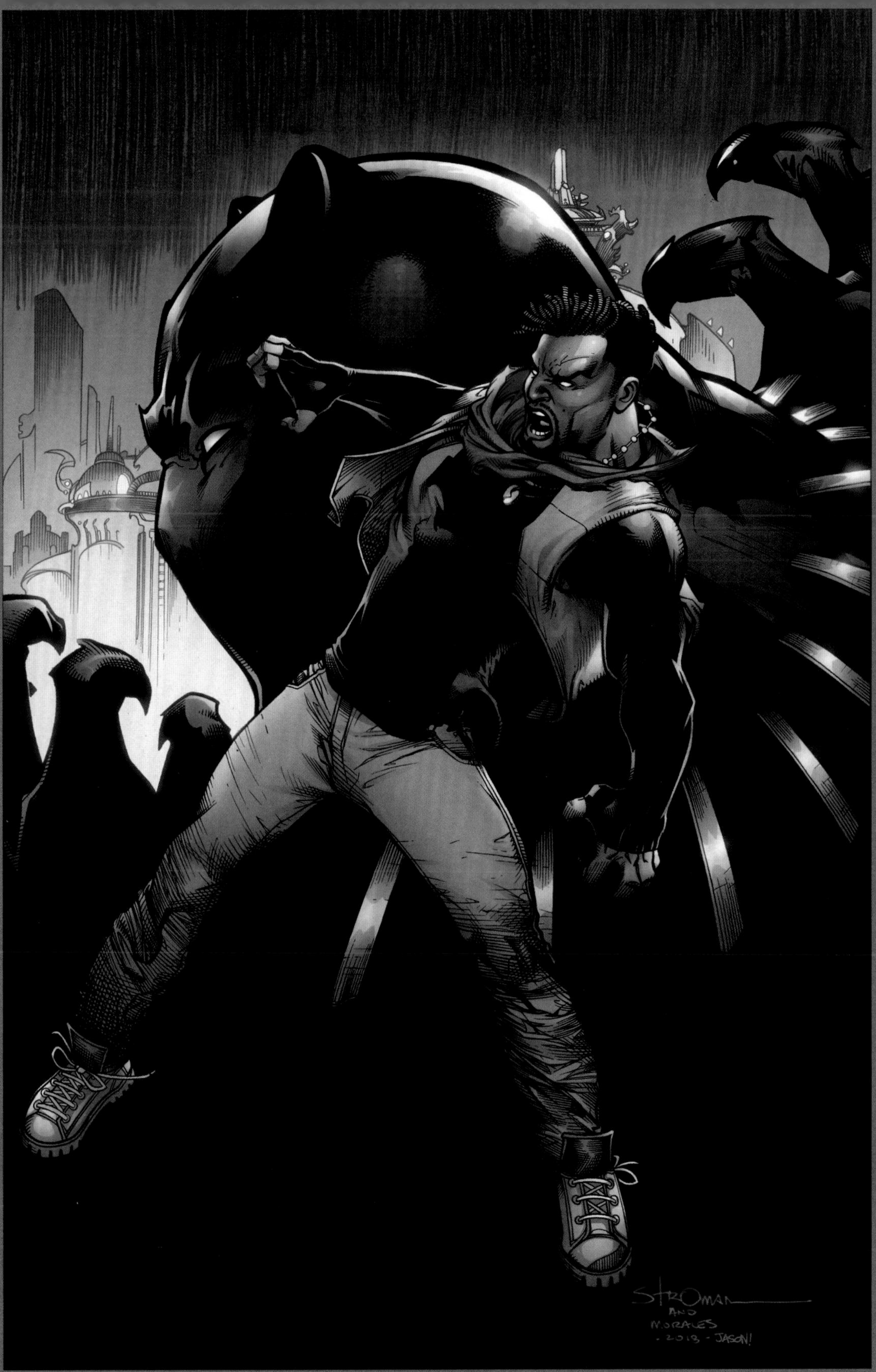
STROMAN
AND
MORALES
-2018- JASON!
#1 VARIANT BY LARRY STROMAN, MARK MORALES & JASON KEITH

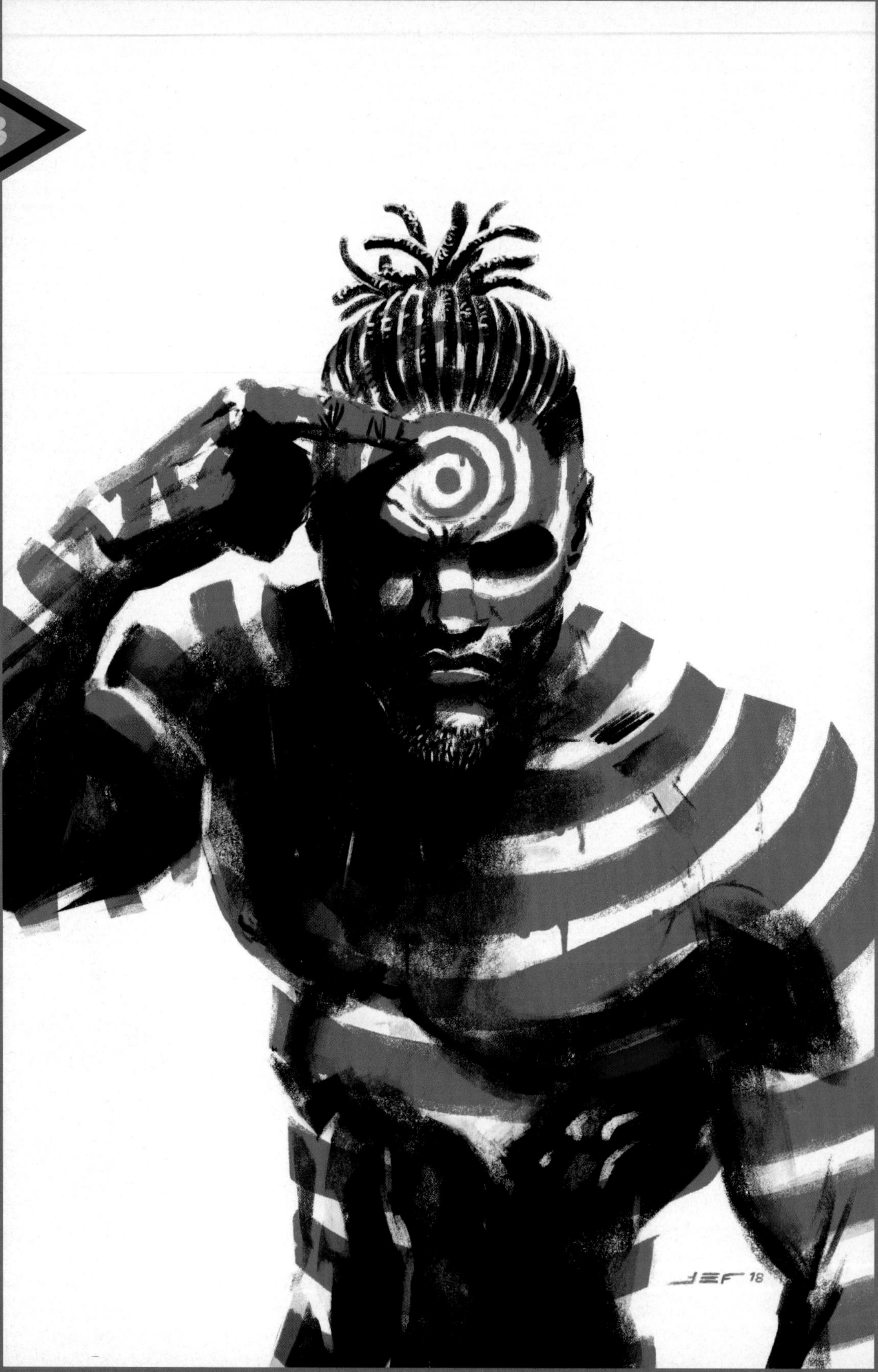

3

BLAM

BLAM

MISSED. MY TURN.

FVOOSH

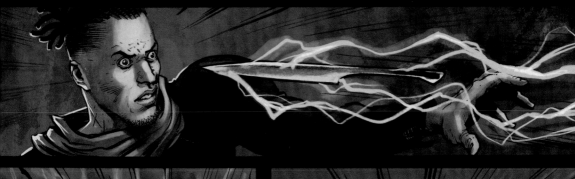

ERIK! RUN!

I'M NOT SCARED OF HIM.

BLAM BLAM

BLAM

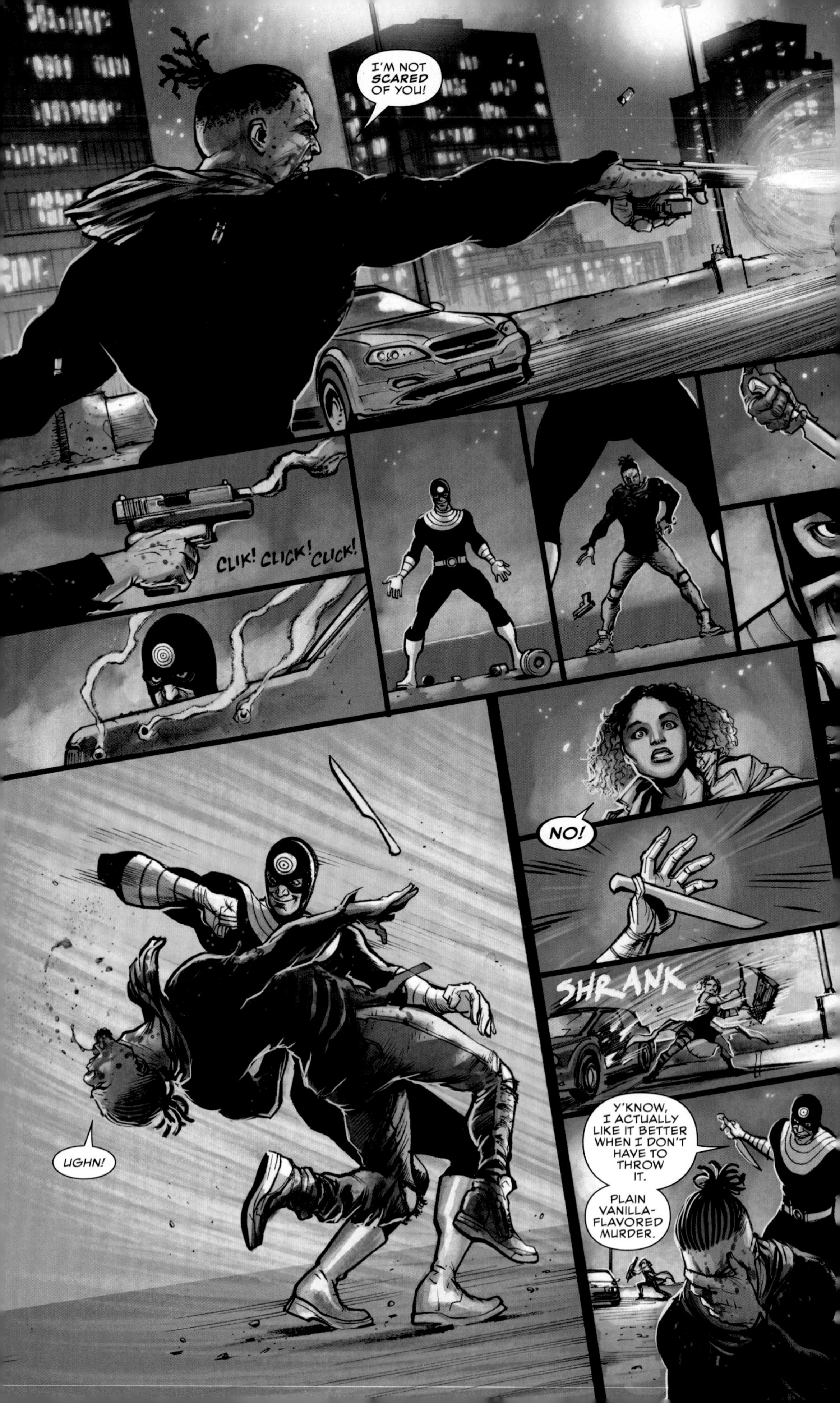
I'M NOT SCARED OF YOU!
CLIK! CLICK! CLICK!
NO!
SHRANK
UGHN!
Y'KNOW, I ACTUALLY LIKE IT BETTER WHEN I DON'T HAVE TO THROW IT.
PLAIN VANILLA-FLAVORED MURDER.

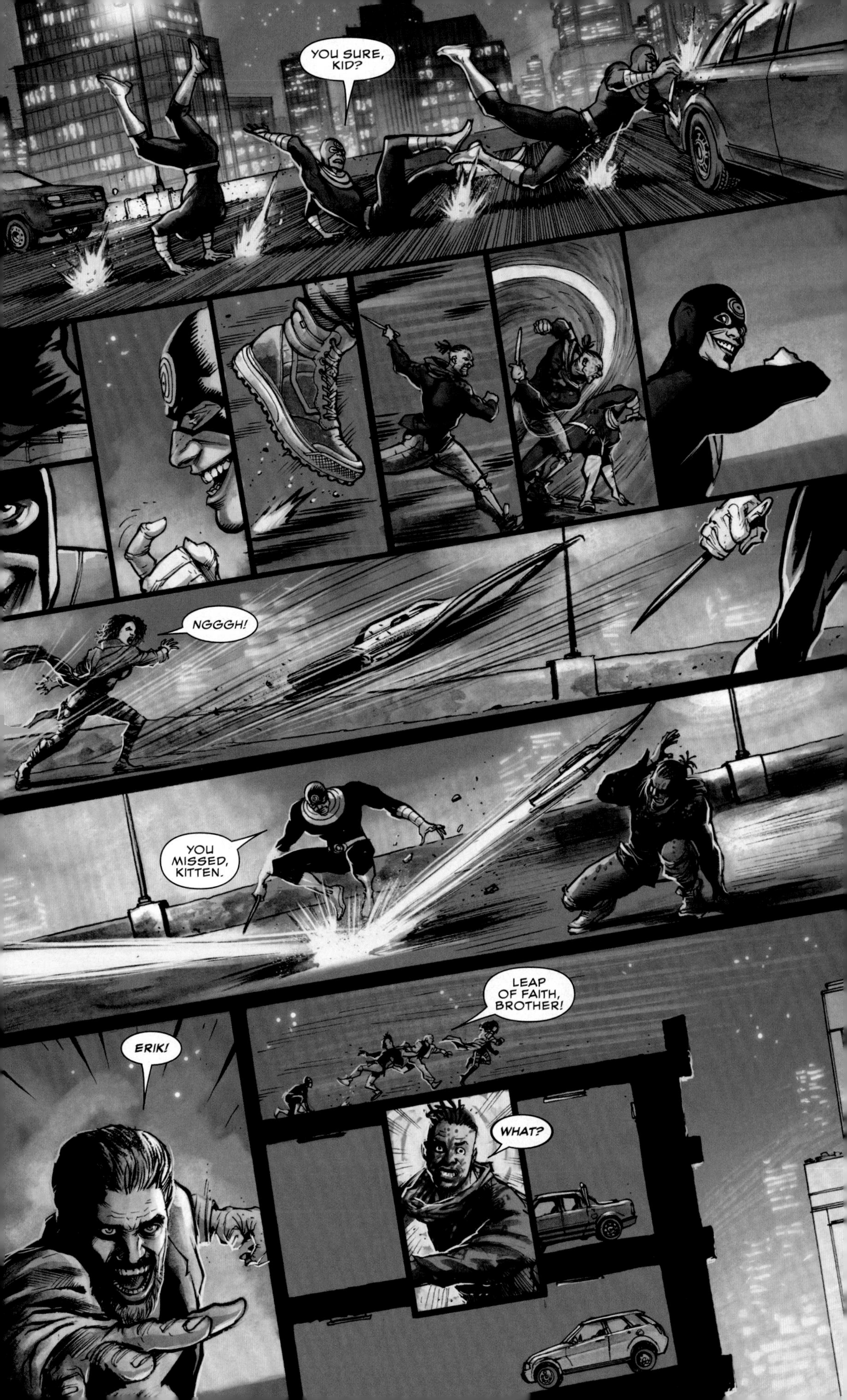
YOU SURE, KID?
NGGGH!
YOU MISSED, KITTEN.
LEAP OF FAITH, BROTHER!
ERIK!
WHAT?

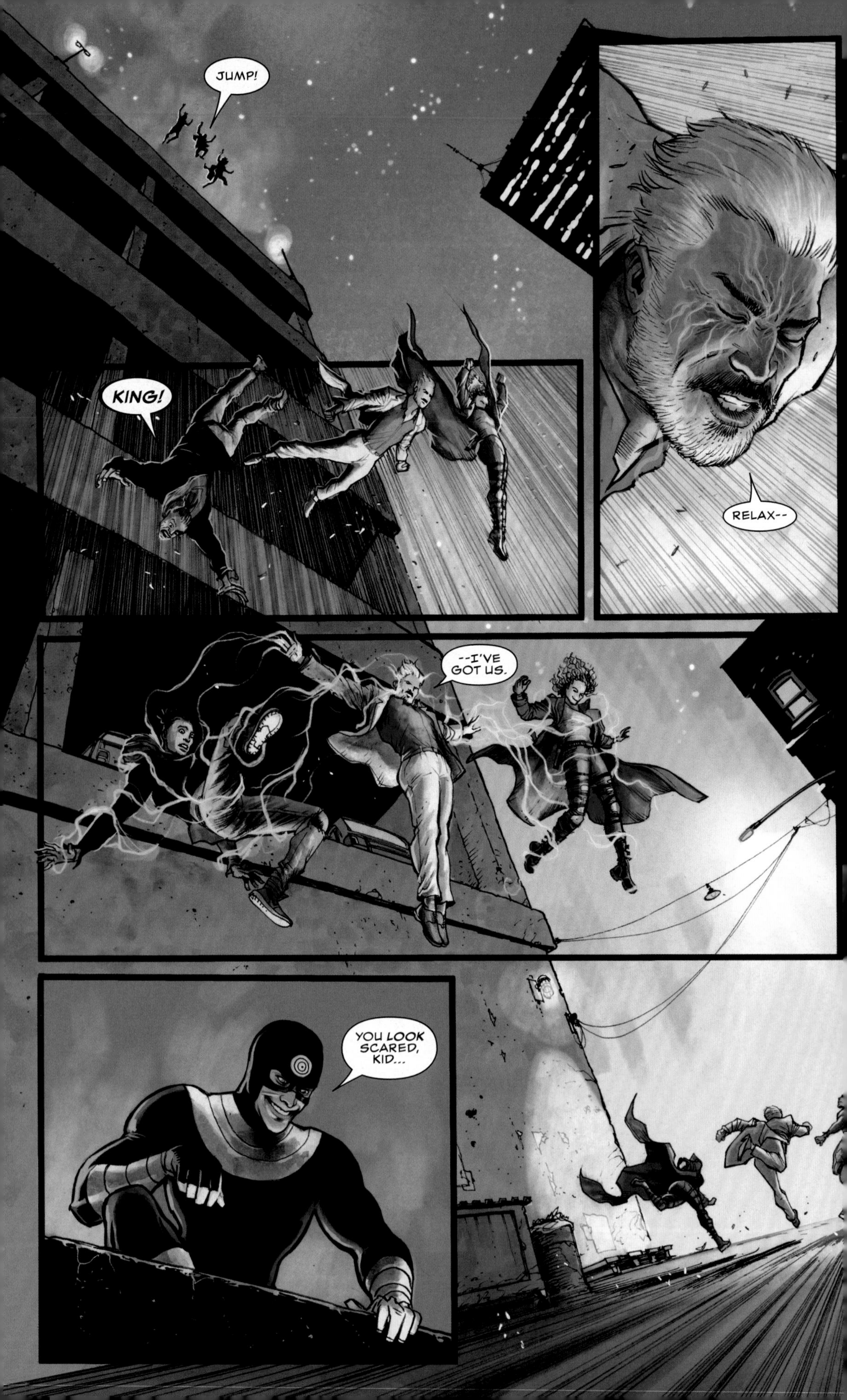
JUMP!
KING!
RELAX--
--I'VE GOT US.
YOU LOOK SCARED, KID...

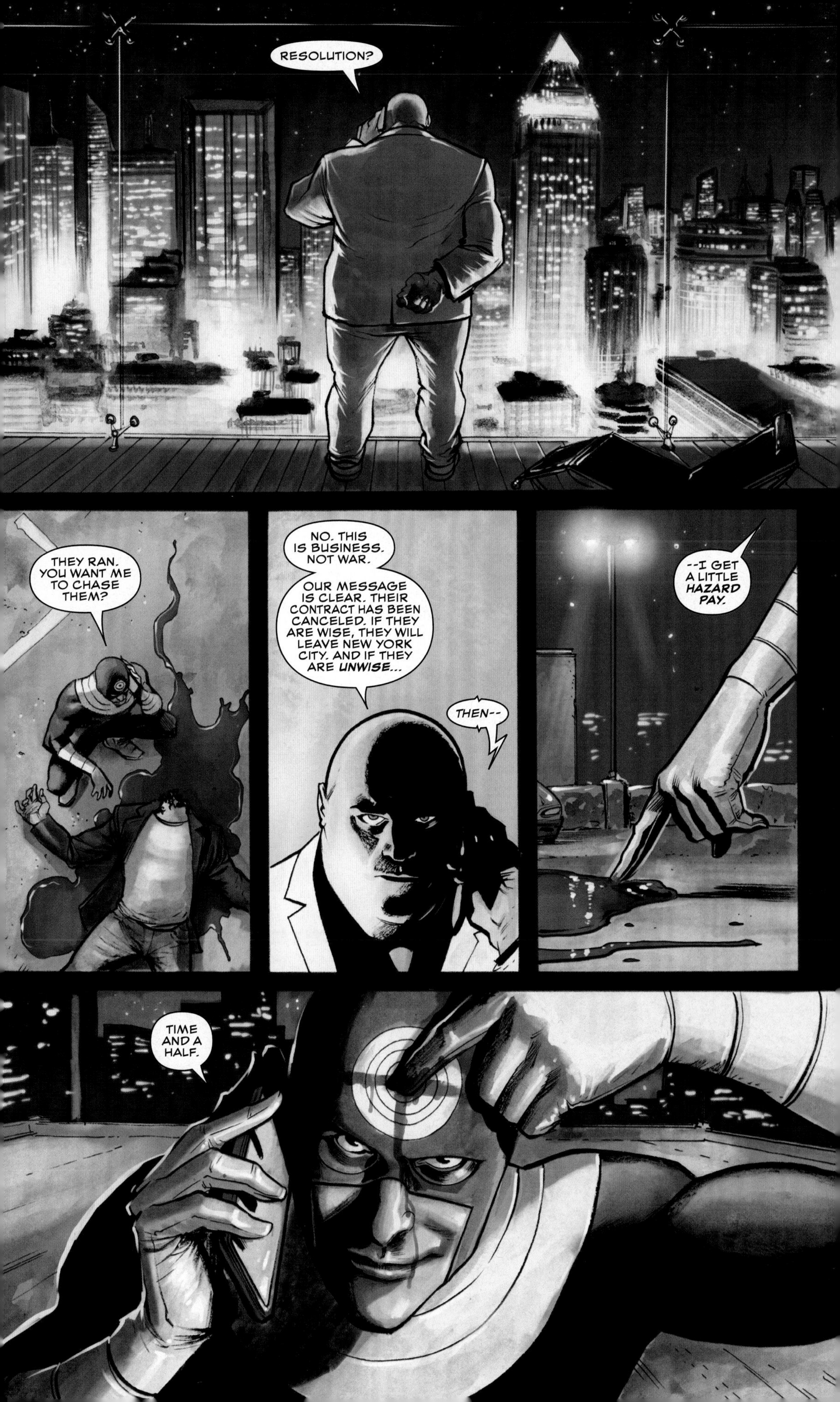
RESOLUTION?
THEY RAN. YOU WANT ME TO CHASE THEM?
NO. THIS IS BUSINESS. NOT WAR.
OUR MESSAGE IS CLEAR. THEIR CONTRACT HAS BEEN CANCELED. IF THEY ARE WISE, THEY WILL LEAVE NEW YORK CITY. AND IF THEY ARE UNWISE...
THEN--
--I GET A LITTLE HAZARD PAY.
TIME AND A HALF.

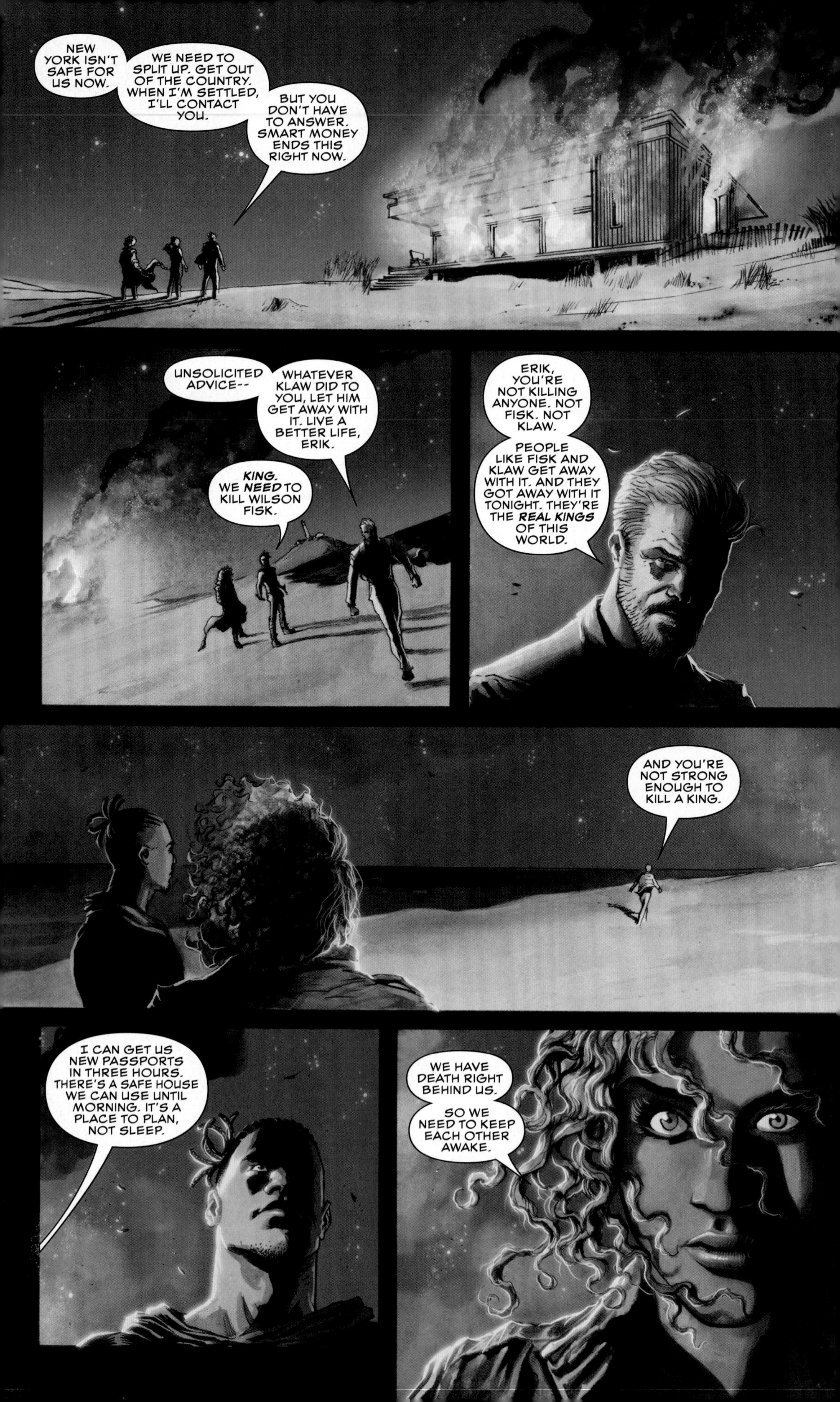
NEW YORK ISN'T SAFE FOR US NOW.
WE NEED TO SPLIT UP. GET OUT OF THE COUNTRY. WHEN I'M SETTLED, I'LL CONTACT YOU.
BUT YOU DON'T HAVE TO ANSWER. SMART MONEY ENDS THIS RIGHT NOW.
UNSOLICITED ADVICE--
WHATEVER KLAW DID TO YOU, LET HIM GET AWAY WITH IT. LIVE A BETTER LIFE, ERIK.
KING. WE NEED TO KILL WILSON FISK.
ERIK, YOU'RE NOT KILLING ANYONE. NOT FISK. NOT KLAW.
PEOPLE LIKE FISK AND KLAW GET AWAY WITH IT. AND THEY GOT AWAY WITH IT TONIGHT. THEY'RE THE REAL KINGS OF THIS WORLD.
AND YOU'RE NOT STRONG ENOUGH TO KILL A KING.
I CAN GET US NEW PASSPORTS IN THREE HOURS. THERE'S A SAFE HOUSE WE CAN USE UNTIL MORNING. IT'S A PLACE TO PLAN, NOT SLEEP.
WE HAVE DEATH RIGHT BEHIND US.
SO WE NEED TO KEEP EACH OTHER AWAKE.

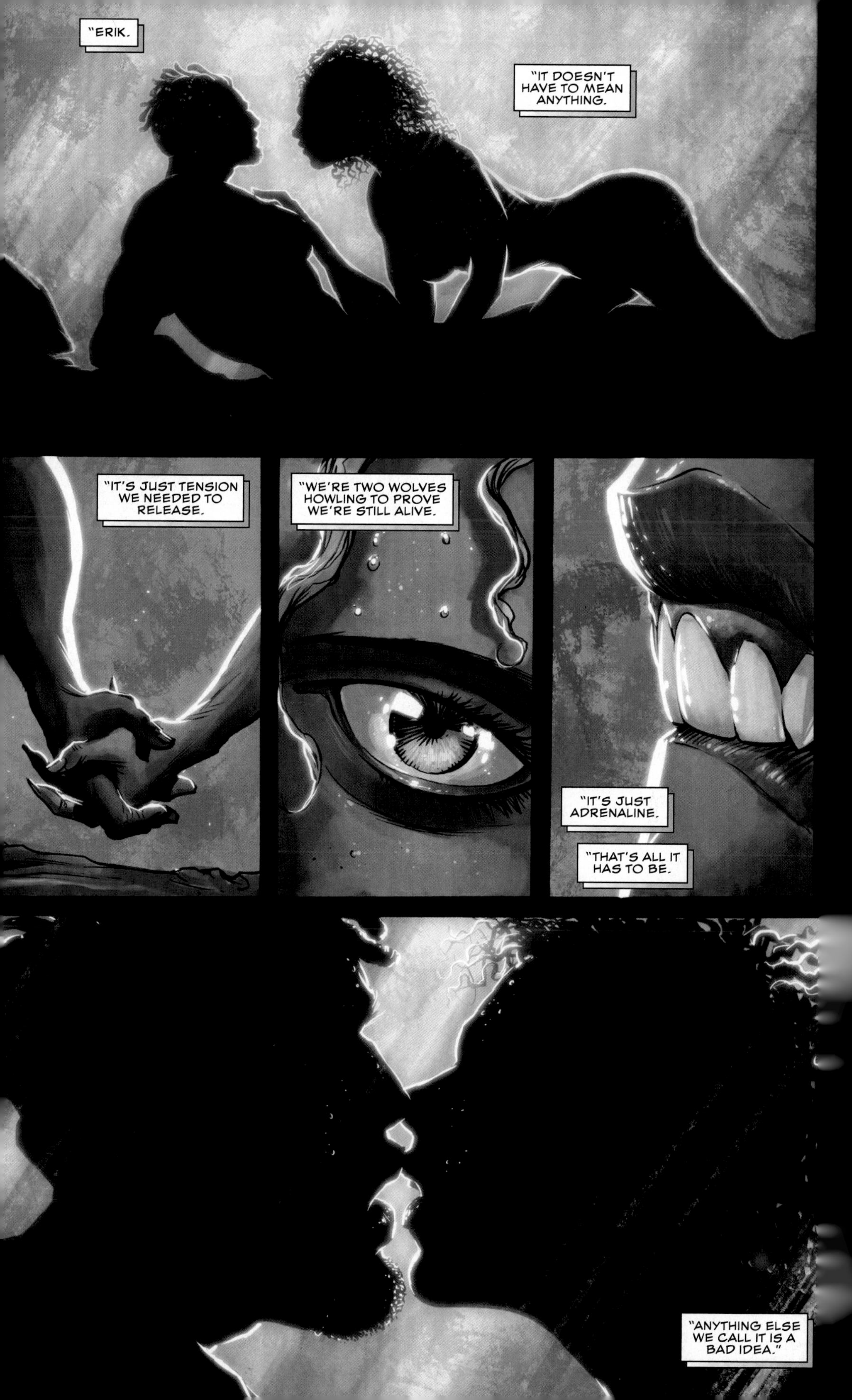
"ERIK.
"IT DOESN'T HAVE TO MEAN ANYTHING.
"IT'S JUST TENSION WE NEEDED TO RELEASE.
"WE'RE TWO WOLVES HOWLING TO PROVE WE'RE STILL ALIVE.
"IT'S JUST ADRENALINE.
"THAT'S ALL IT HAS TO BE.
"ANYTHING ELSE WE CALL IT IS A BAD IDEA."

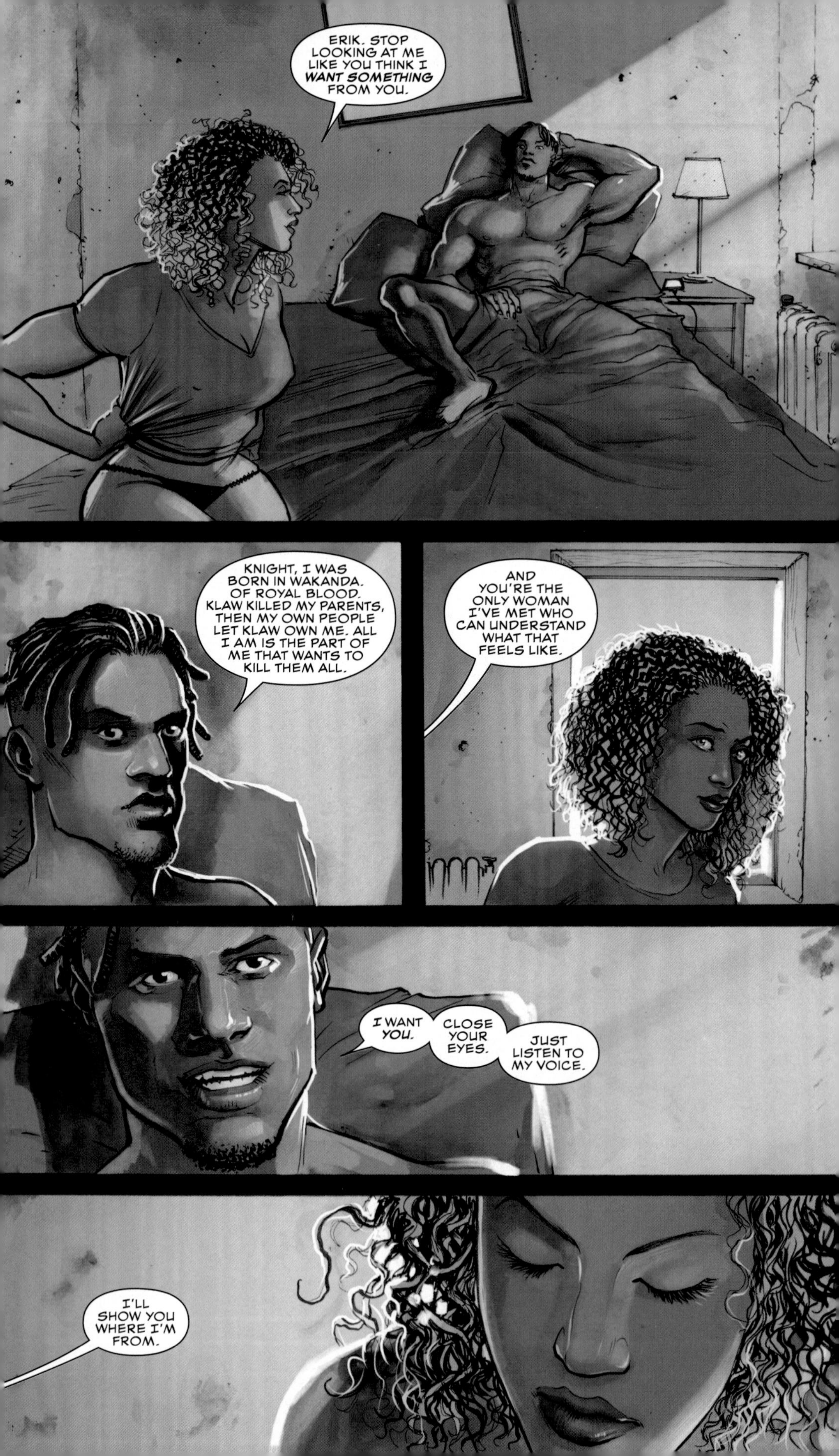
ERIK. STOP LOOKING AT ME LIKE YOU THINK I *WANT SOMETHING* FROM YOU.
KNIGHT, I WAS BORN IN WAKANDA. OF ROYAL BLOOD. KLAW KILLED MY PARENTS, THEN MY OWN PEOPLE LET KLAW OWN ME. ALL I AM IS THE PART OF ME THAT WANTS TO KILL THEM ALL.
AND YOU'RE THE ONLY WOMAN I'VE MET WHO CAN UNDERSTAND WHAT THAT FEELS LIKE.
I WANT *YOU.*
CLOSE YOUR EYES.
JUST LISTEN TO MY VOICE.
I'LL SHOW YOU WHERE I'M FROM.

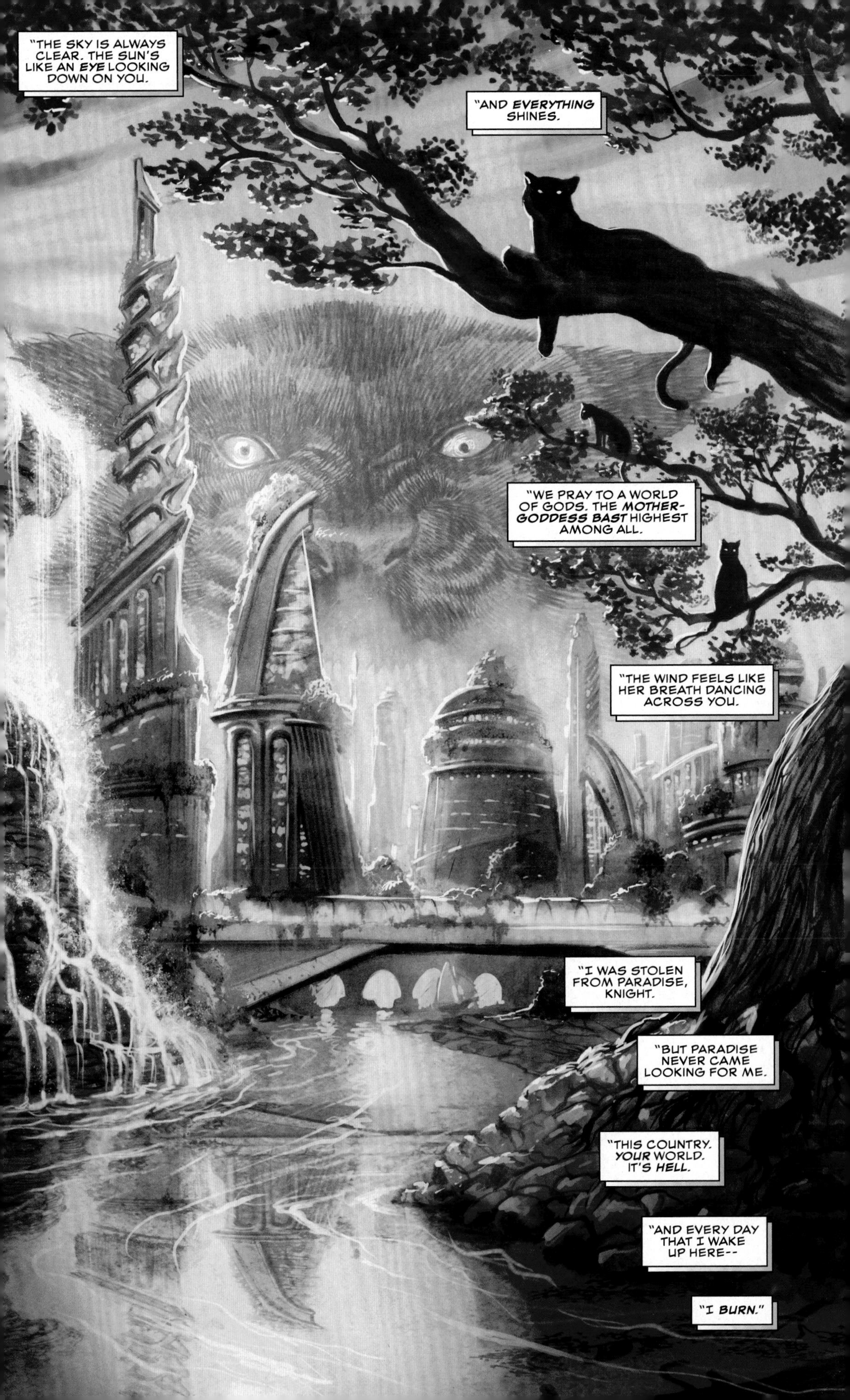
"THE SKY IS ALWAYS CLEAR. THE SUN'S LIKE AN *EYE* LOOKING DOWN ON YOU.
"AND *EVERYTHING* SHINES.
"WE PRAY TO A WORLD OF GODS. THE *MOTHER-GODDESS BAST* HIGHEST AMONG ALL.
"THE WIND FEELS LIKE HER BREATH DANCING ACROSS YOU.
"I WAS STOLEN FROM PARADISE, KNIGHT.
"BUT PARADISE NEVER CAME LOOKING FOR ME.
"THIS COUNTRY. *YOUR* WORLD. IT'S *HELL*.
"AND EVERY DAY THAT I WAKE UP HERE--
"I *BURN*."

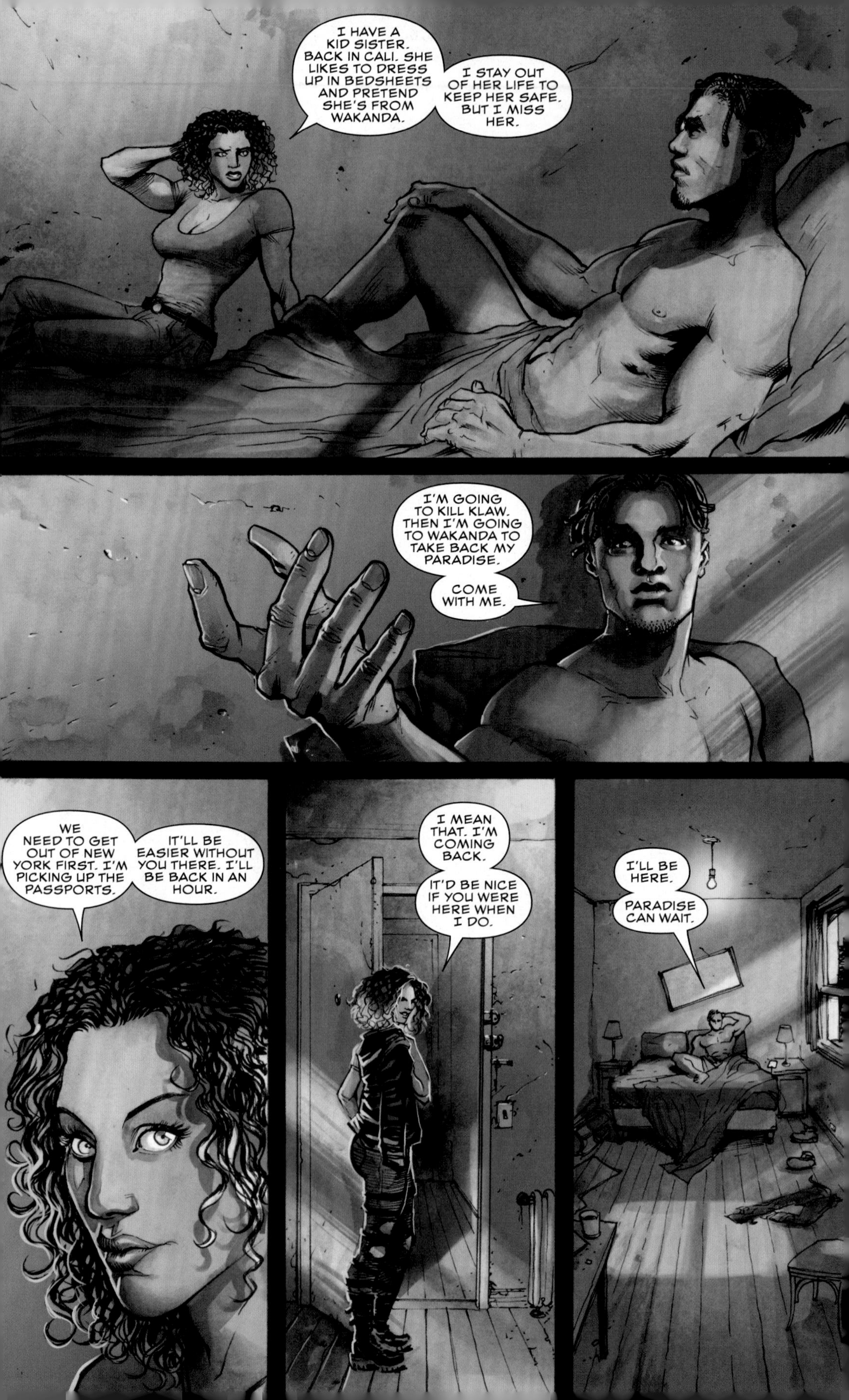
I HAVE A KID SISTER. BACK IN CALI. SHE LIKES TO DRESS UP IN BEDSHEETS AND PRETEND SHE'S FROM WAKANDA.
I STAY OUT OF HER LIFE TO KEEP HER SAFE. BUT I MISS HER.
I'M GOING TO KILL KLAW. THEN I'M GOING TO WAKANDA TO TAKE BACK MY PARADISE.
COME WITH ME.
WE NEED TO GET OUT OF NEW YORK FIRST. I'M PICKING UP THE PASSPORTS.
IT'LL BE EASIER WITHOUT YOU THERE. I'LL BE BACK IN AN HOUR.
I MEAN THAT. I'M COMING BACK.
IT'D BE NICE IF YOU WERE HERE WHEN I DO.
I'LL BE HERE.
PARADISE CAN WAIT.

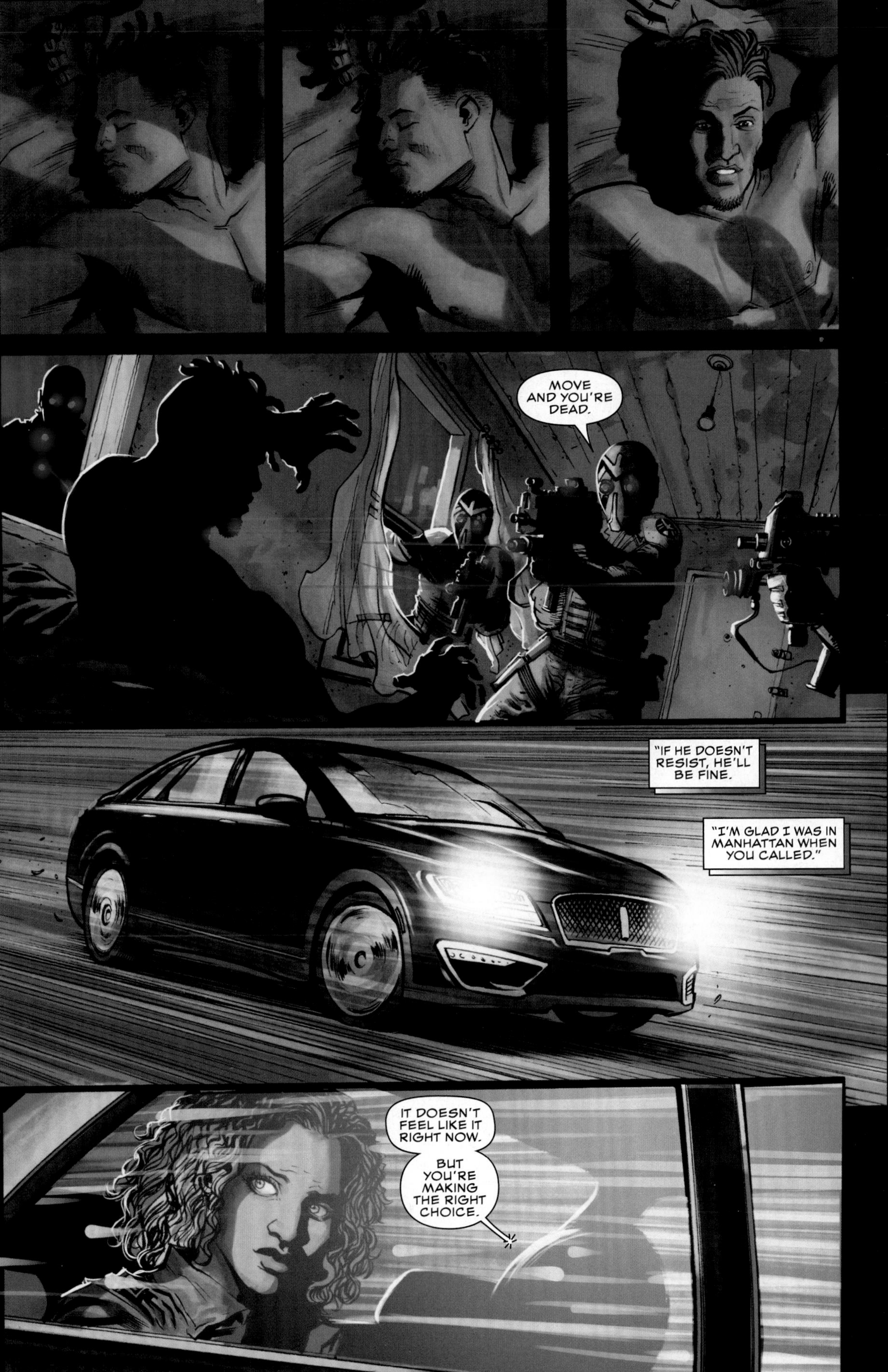
MOVE AND YOU'RE DEAD.
"IF HE DOESN'T RESIST, HE'LL BE FINE.
"I'M GLAD I WAS IN MANHATTAN WHEN YOU CALLED."
IT DOESN'T FEEL LIKE IT RIGHT NOW.
BUT YOU'RE MAKING THE RIGHT CHOICE.

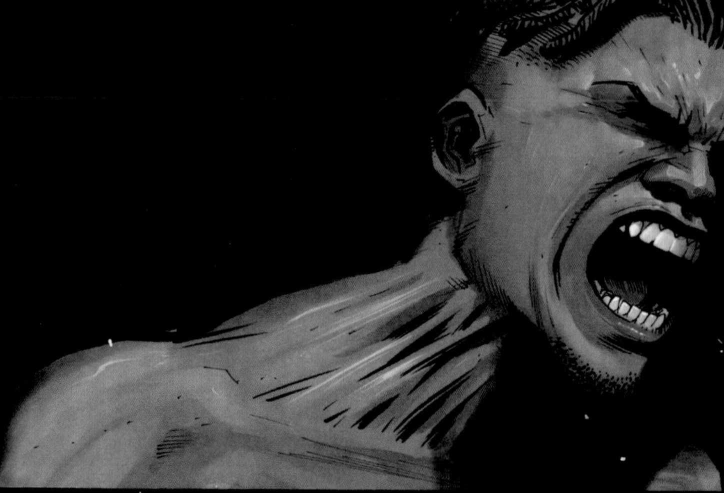
HEY!

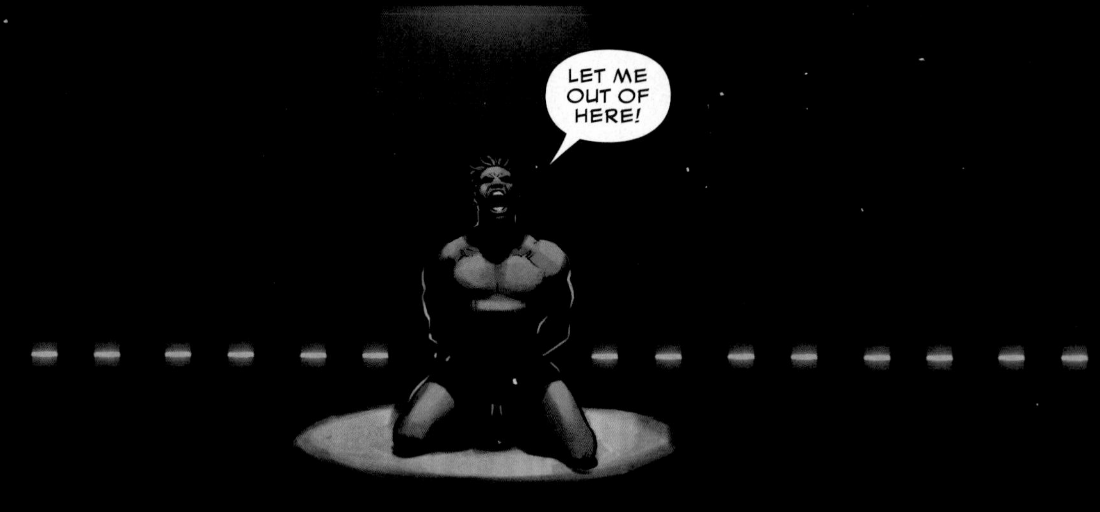
LET ME OUT OF HERE!

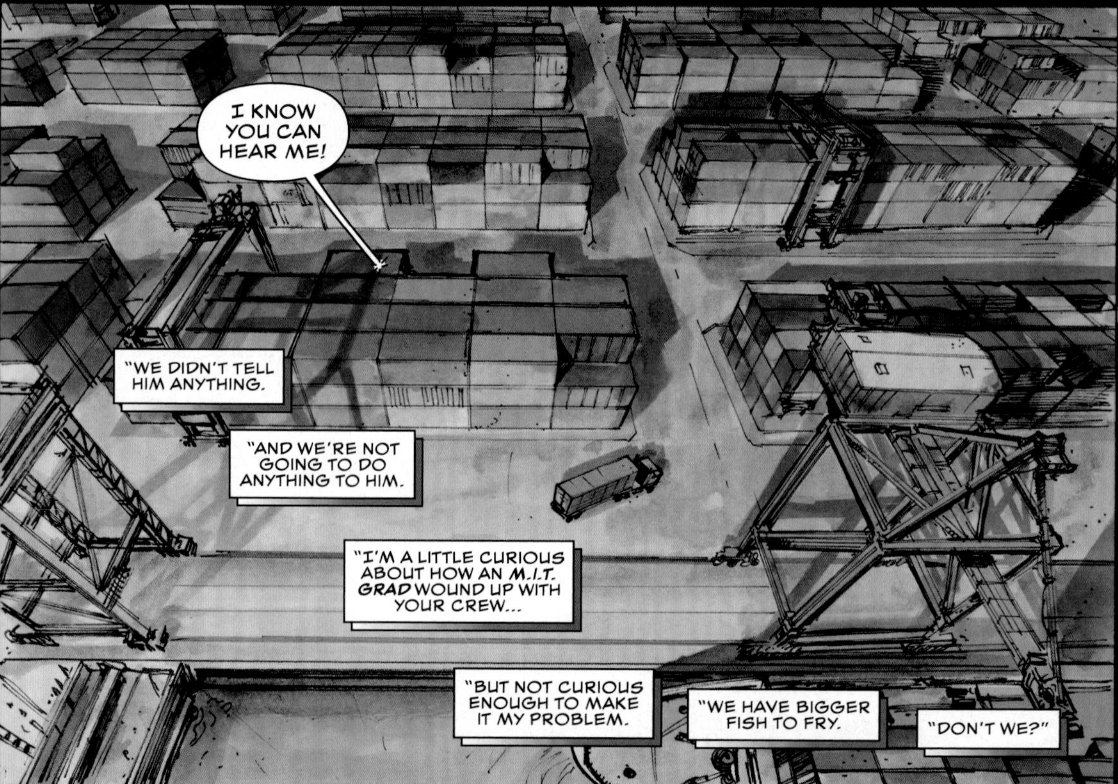
I KNOW YOU CAN HEAR ME!
"WE DIDN'T TELL HIM ANYTHING.
"AND WE'RE NOT GOING TO DO ANYTHING TO HIM.
"I'M A LITTLE CURIOUS ABOUT HOW AN M.I.T. GRAD WOUND UP WITH YOUR CREW...
"BUT NOT CURIOUS ENOUGH TO MAKE IT MY PROBLEM.
"WE HAVE BIGGER FISH TO FRY.
"DON'T WE?"

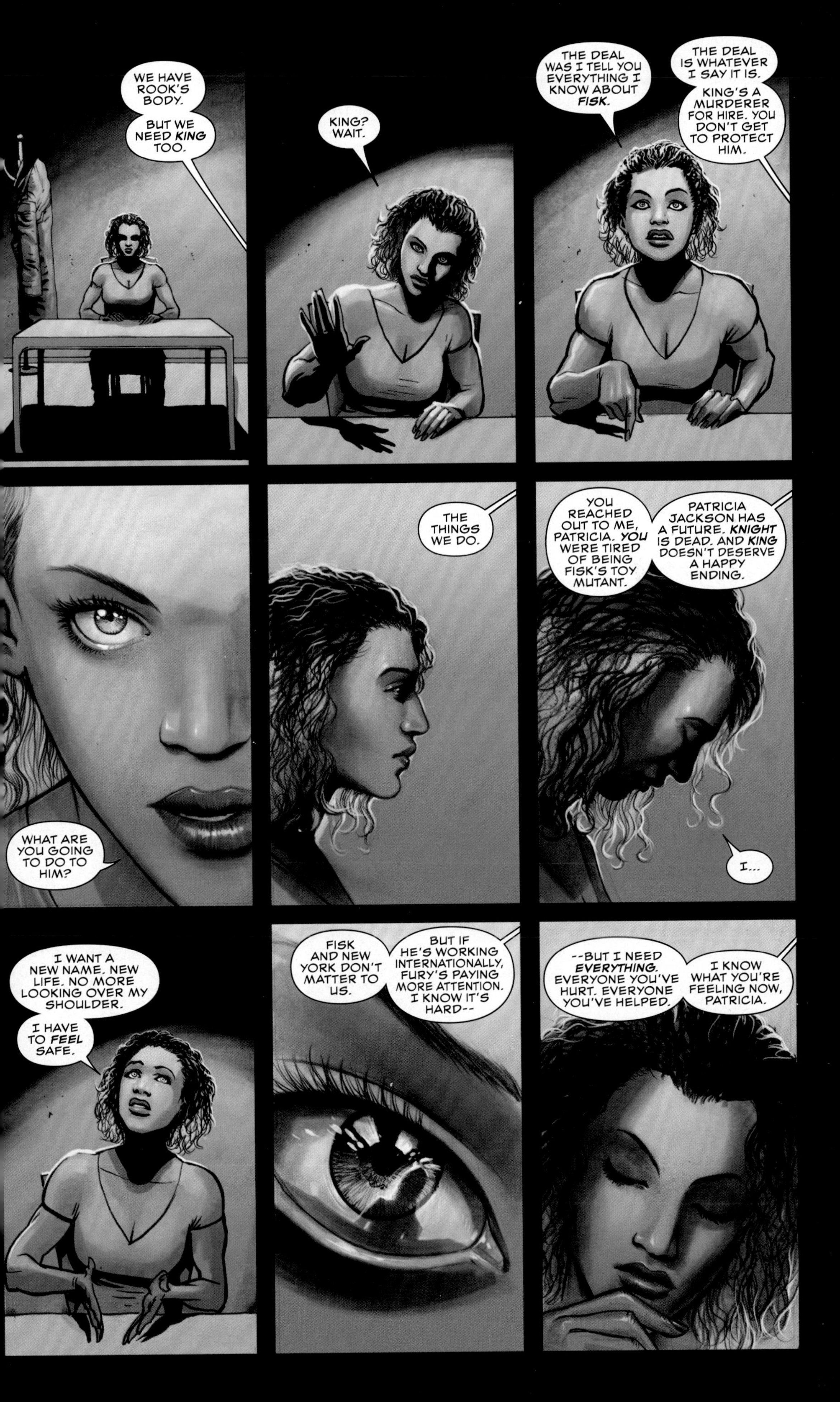
WE HAVE ROOK'S BODY.
BUT WE NEED KING TOO.
KING? WAIT.
THE DEAL WAS I TELL YOU EVERYTHING I KNOW ABOUT FISK.
THE DEAL IS WHATEVER I SAY IT IS.
KING'S A MURDERER FOR HIRE. YOU DON'T GET TO PROTECT HIM.
WHAT ARE YOU GOING TO DO TO HIM?
THE THINGS WE DO.
YOU REACHED OUT TO ME, PATRICIA. YOU WERE TIRED OF BEING FISK'S TOY MUTANT.
PATRICIA JACKSON HAS A FUTURE. KNIGHT IS DEAD. AND KING DOESN'T DESERVE A HAPPY ENDING.
I...
I WANT A NEW NAME. NEW LIFE. NO MORE LOOKING OVER MY SHOULDER.
I HAVE TO FEEL SAFE.
FISK AND NEW YORK DON'T MATTER TO US.
BUT IF HE'S WORKING INTERNATIONALLY, FURY'S PAYING MORE ATTENTION. I KNOW IT'S HARD--
--BUT I NEED EVERYTHING. EVERYONE YOU'VE HURT. EVERYONE YOU'VE HELPED.
I KNOW WHAT YOU'RE FEELING NOW, PATRICIA.

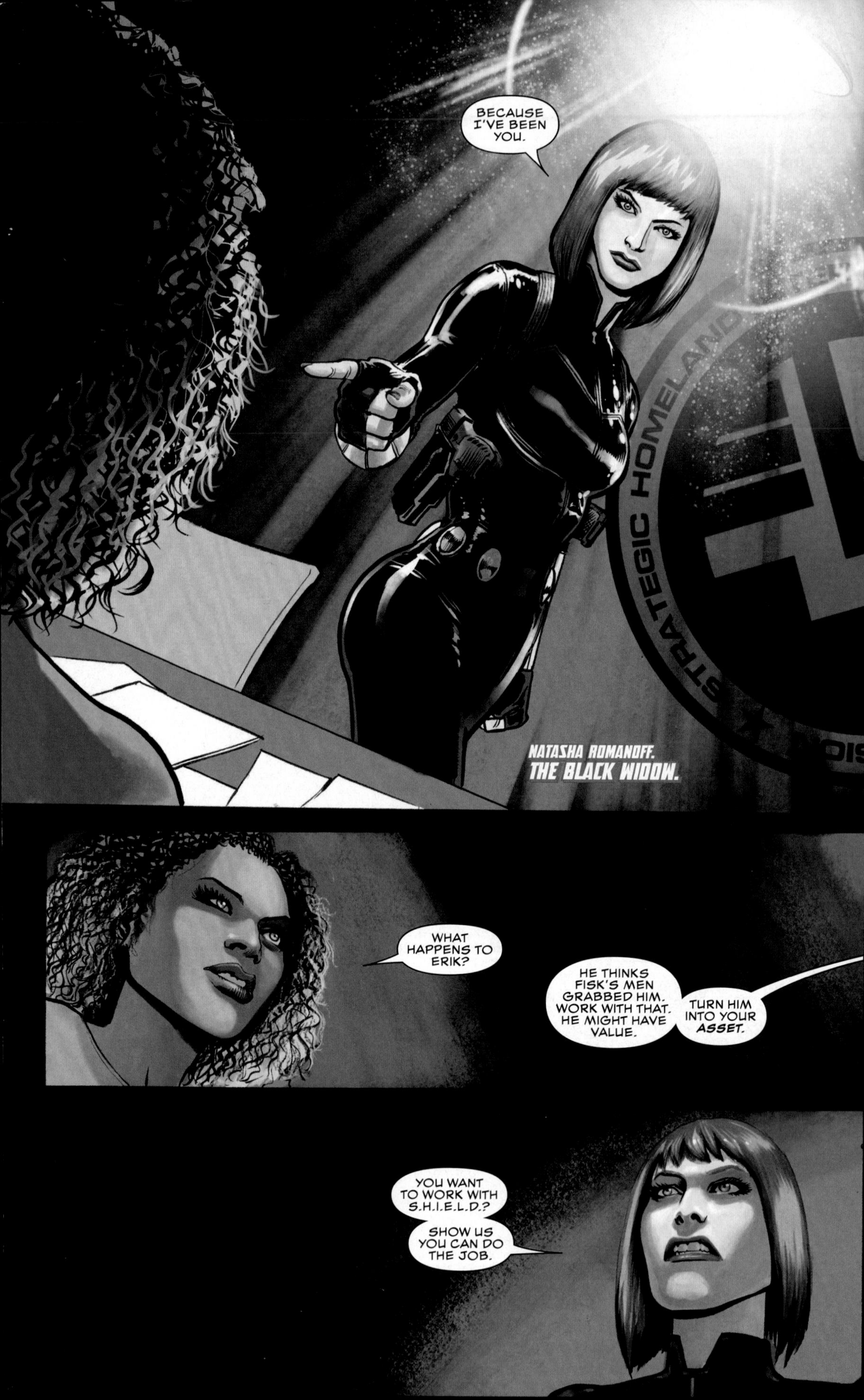
BECAUSE I'VE BEEN YOU.
STRATEGIC HOMELAND
NATASHA ROMANOFF.
THE BLACK WIDOW.
WHAT HAPPENS TO ERIK?
HE THINKS FISK'S MEN GRABBED HIM. WORK WITH THAT. HE MIGHT HAVE VALUE.
TURN HIM INTO YOUR ASSET.
YOU WANT TO WORK WITH S.H.I.E.L.D.?
SHOW US YOU CAN DO THE JOB.

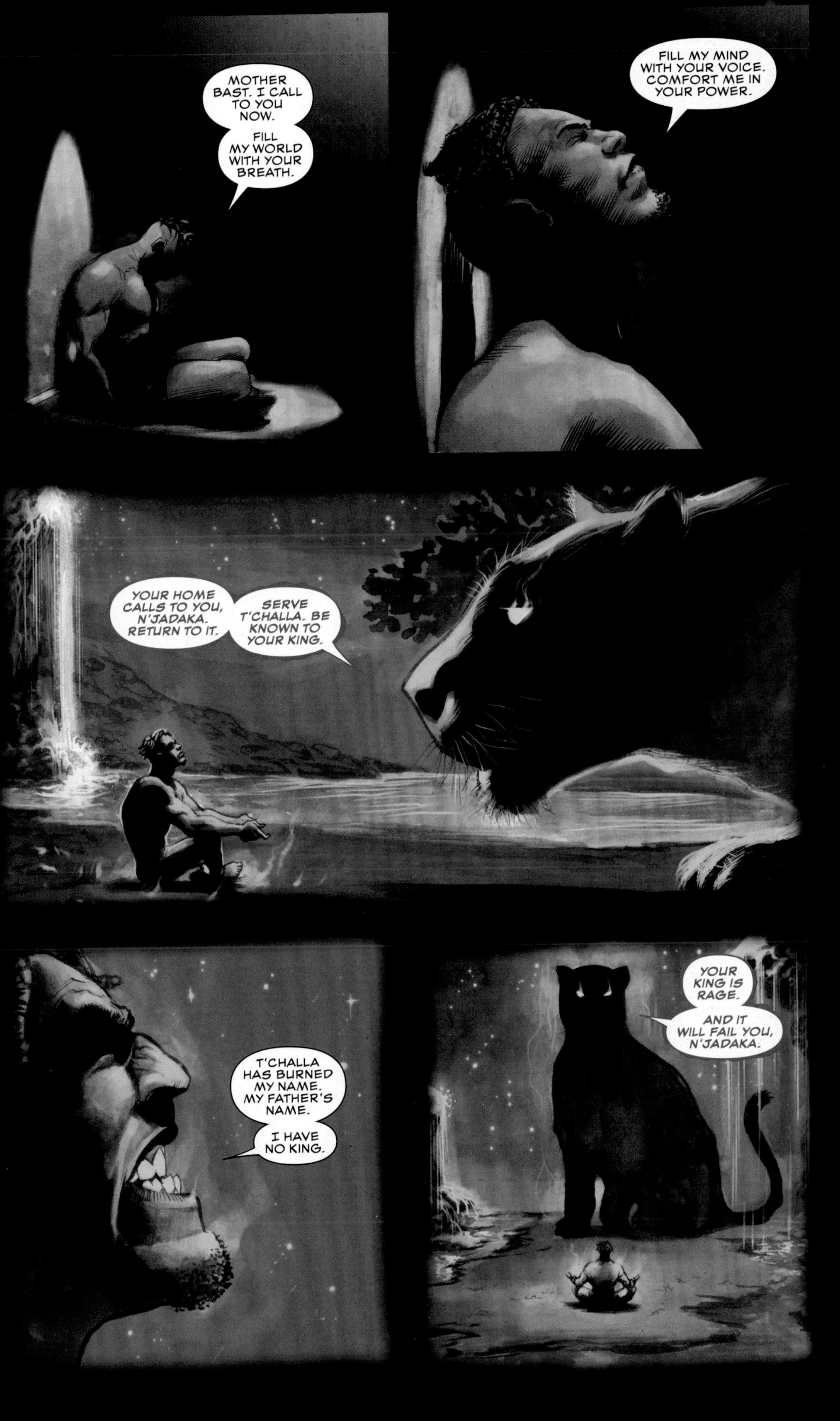
MOTHER BAST. I CALL TO YOU NOW.
FILL MY WORLD WITH YOUR BREATH.
FILL MY MIND WITH YOUR VOICE. COMFORT ME IN YOUR POWER.
YOUR HOME CALLS TO YOU, N'JADAKA. RETURN TO IT.
SERVE T'CHALLA. BE KNOWN TO YOUR KING.
T'CHALLA HAS BURNED MY NAME. MY FATHER'S NAME.
I HAVE NO KING.
YOUR KING IS RAGE.
AND IT WILL FAIL YOU, N'JADAKA.

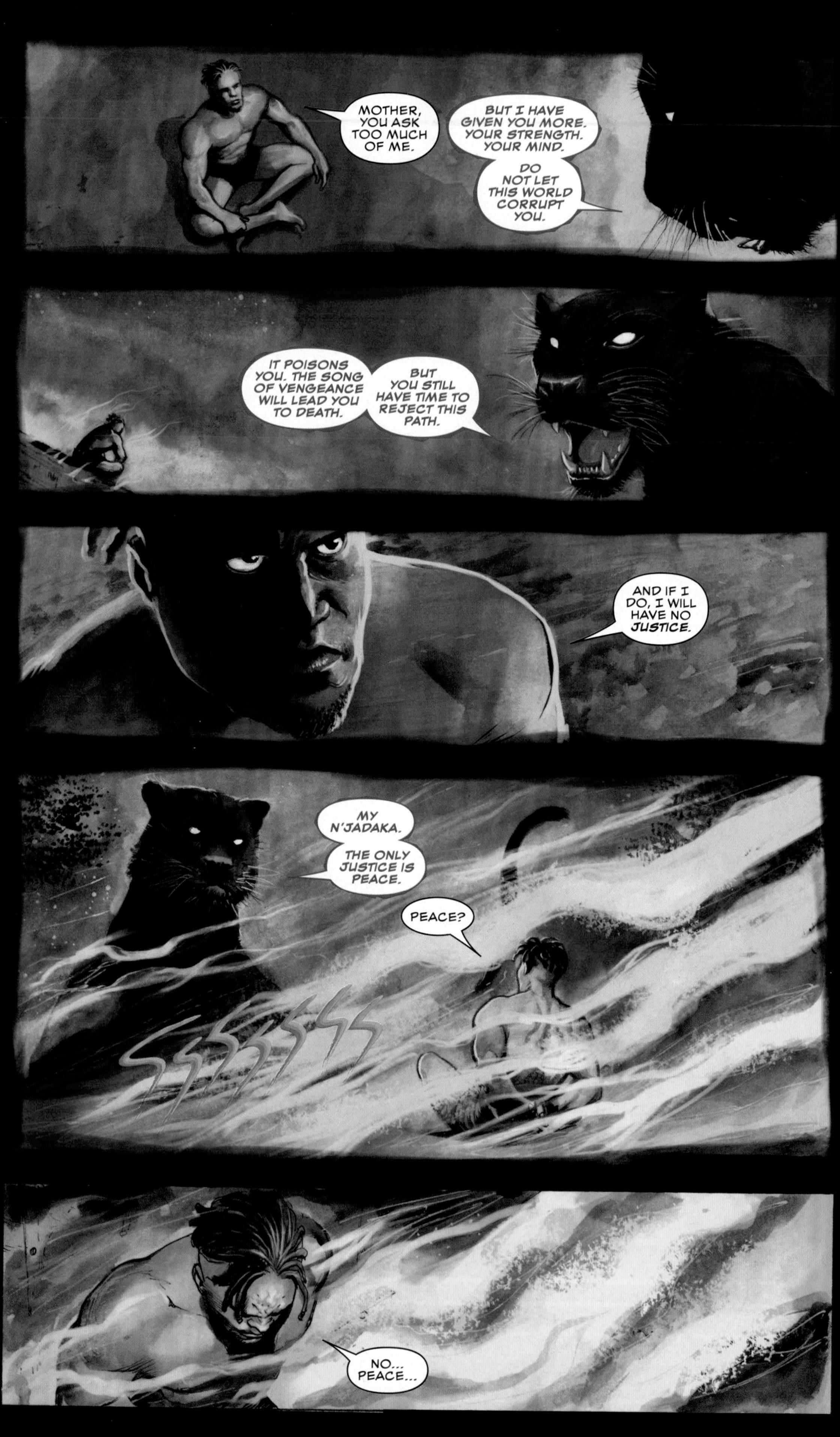
MOTHER, YOU ASK TOO MUCH OF ME.
BUT I HAVE GIVEN YOU MORE. YOUR STRENGTH. YOUR MIND.
DO NOT LET THIS WORLD CORRUPT YOU.
IT POISONS YOU. THE SONG OF VENGEANCE WILL LEAD YOU TO DEATH.
BUT YOU STILL HAVE TIME TO REJECT THIS PATH.
AND IF I DO, I WILL HAVE NO JUSTICE.
MY N'JADAKA.
THE ONLY JUSTICE IS PEACE.
PEACE?
SSSSSSS
NO... PEACE...

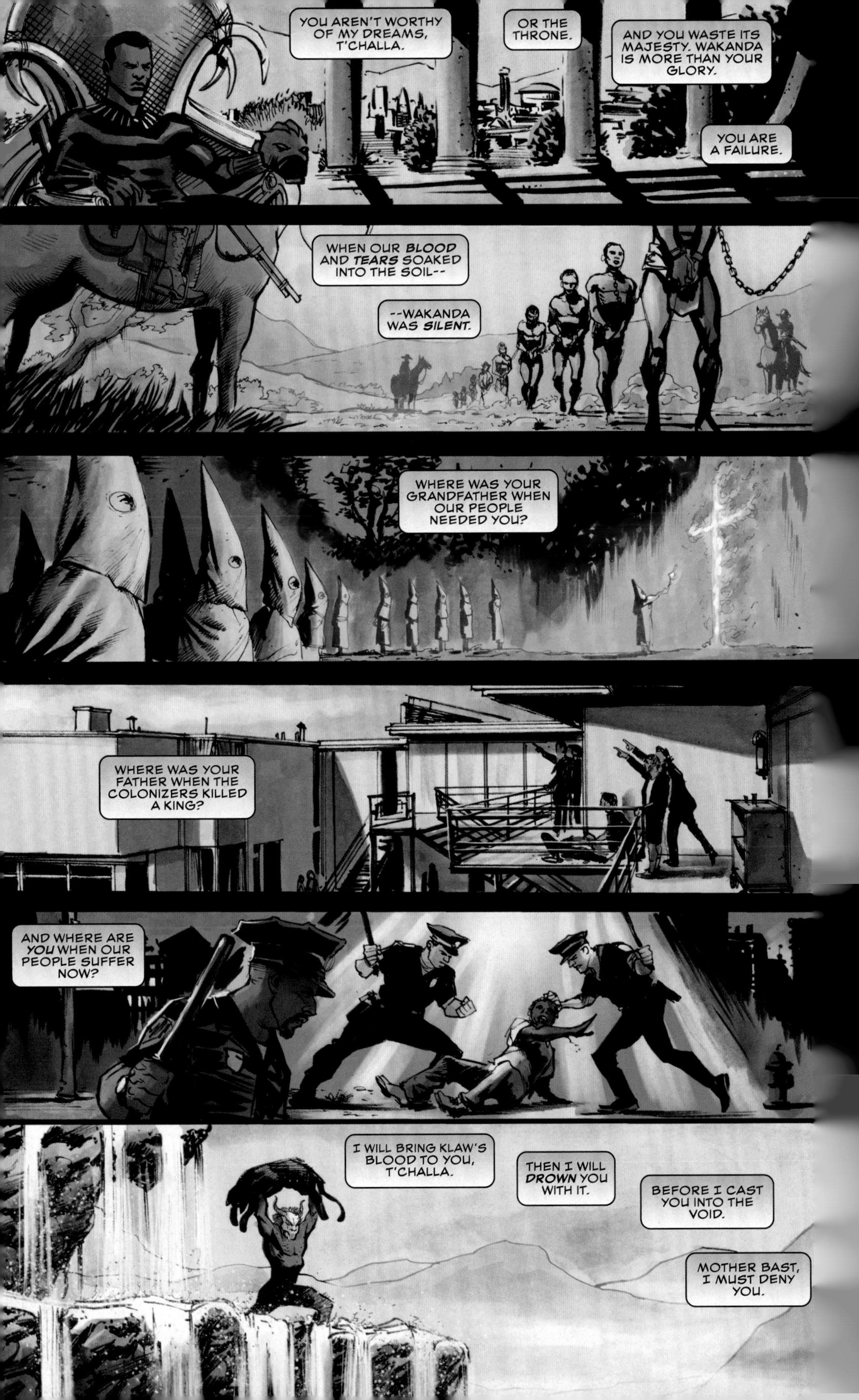
YOU AREN'T WORTHY OF MY DREAMS, T'CHALLA.
OR THE THRONE.
AND YOU WASTE ITS MAJESTY. WAKANDA IS MORE THAN YOUR GLORY.
YOU ARE A FAILURE.
WHEN OUR BLOOD AND TEARS SOAKED INTO THE SOIL--
--WAKANDA WAS SILENT.
WHERE WAS YOUR GRANDFATHER WHEN OUR PEOPLE NEEDED YOU?
WHERE WAS YOUR FATHER WHEN THE COLONIZERS KILLED A KING?
AND WHERE ARE YOU WHEN OUR PEOPLE SUFFER NOW?
I WILL BRING KLAW'S BLOOD TO YOU, T'CHALLA.
THEN I WILL DROWN YOU WITH IT.
BEFORE I CAST YOU INTO THE VOID.
MOTHER BAST, I MUST DENY YOU.

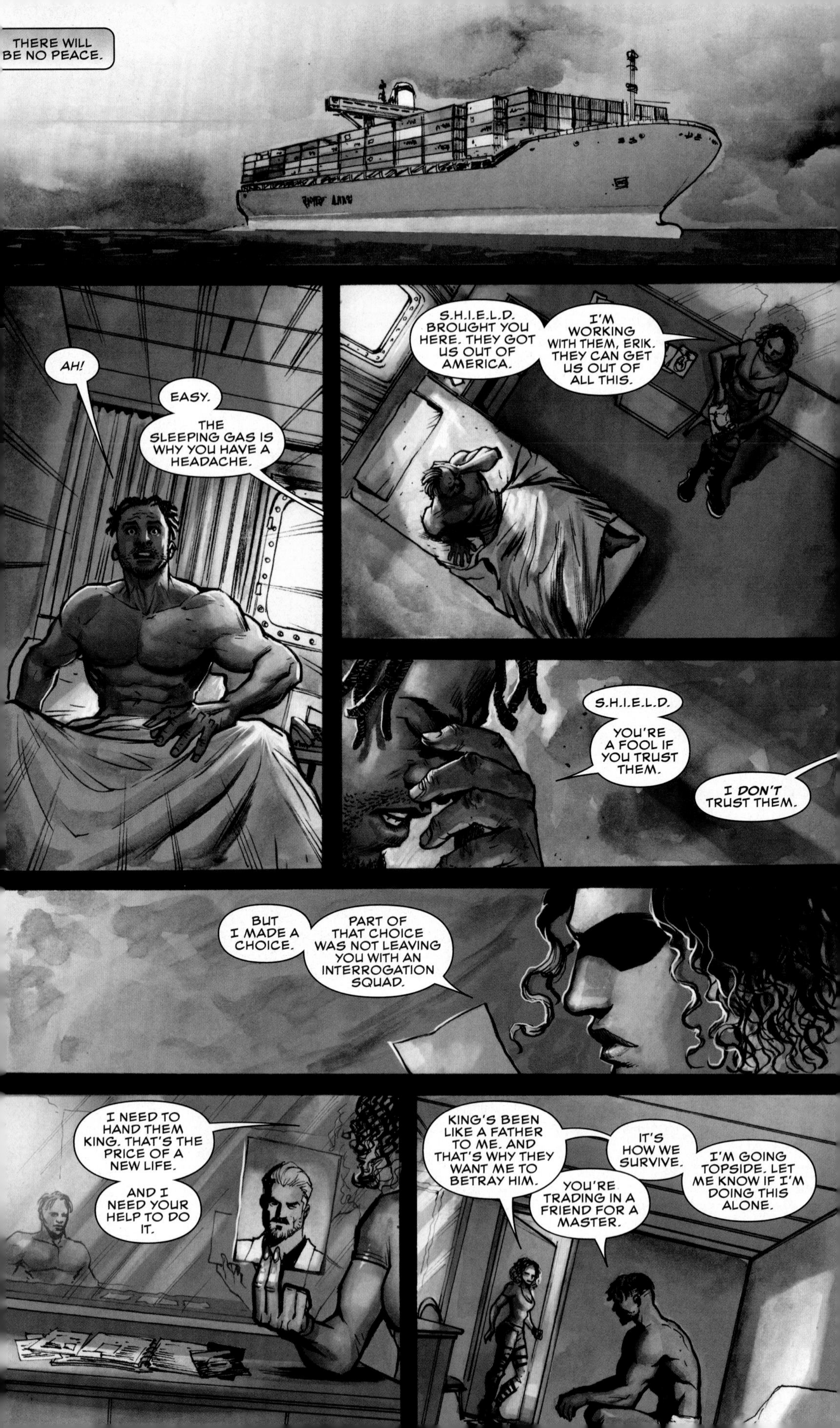
THERE WILL BE NO PEACE.
AH!
EASY.
THE SLEEPING GAS IS WHY YOU HAVE A HEADACHE.
S.H.I.E.L.D. BROUGHT YOU HERE. THEY GOT US OUT OF AMERICA.
I'M WORKING WITH THEM, ERIK. THEY CAN GET US OUT OF ALL THIS.
S.H.I.E.L.D.
YOU'RE A FOOL IF YOU TRUST THEM.
I DON'T TRUST THEM.
BUT I MADE A CHOICE.
PART OF THAT CHOICE WAS NOT LEAVING YOU WITH AN INTERROGATION SQUAD.
I NEED TO HAND THEM KING. THAT'S THE PRICE OF A NEW LIFE.
AND I NEED YOUR HELP TO DO IT.
KING'S BEEN LIKE A FATHER TO ME. AND THAT'S WHY THEY WANT ME TO BETRAY HIM.
IT'S HOW WE SURVIVE.
YOU'RE TRADING IN A FRIEND FOR A MASTER.
I'M GOING TOPSIDE. LET ME KNOW IF I'M DOING THIS ALONE.

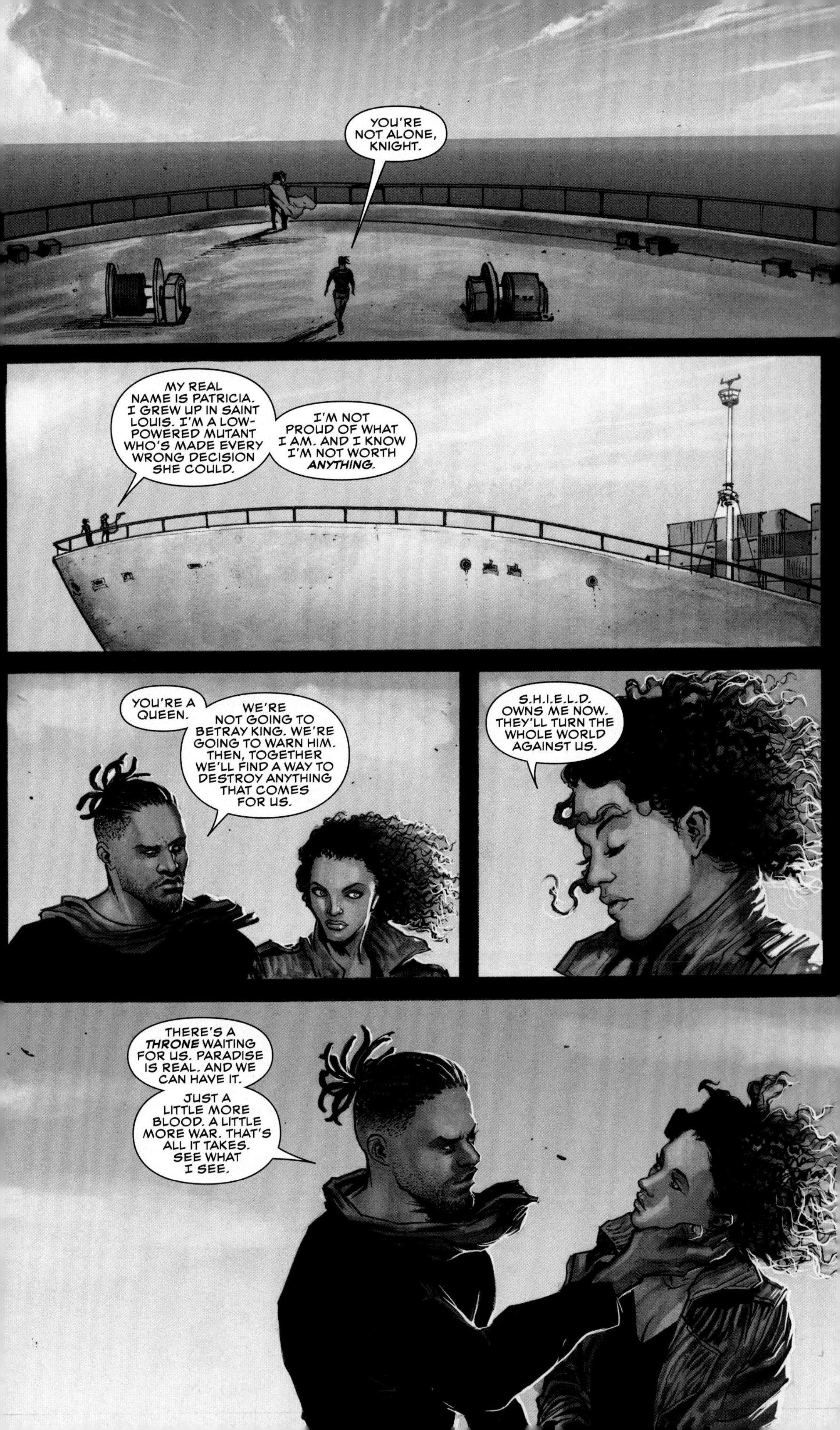
YOU'RE NOT ALONE, KNIGHT.
MY REAL NAME IS PATRICIA. I GREW UP IN SAINT LOUIS. I'M A LOW-POWERED MUTANT WHO'S MADE EVERY WRONG DECISION SHE COULD.
I'M NOT PROUD OF WHAT I AM. AND I KNOW I'M NOT WORTH *ANYTHING.*
YOU'RE A QUEEN.
WE'RE NOT GOING TO BETRAY KING. WE'RE GOING TO WARN HIM. THEN, TOGETHER WE'LL FIND A WAY TO DESTROY ANYTHING THAT COMES FOR US.
S.H.I.E.L.D. OWNS ME NOW. THEY'LL TURN THE WHOLE WORLD AGAINST US.
THERE'S A *THRONE* WAITING FOR US. PARADISE IS REAL. AND WE CAN HAVE IT.
JUST A LITTLE MORE BLOOD. A LITTLE MORE WAR. THAT'S ALL IT TAKES. SEE WHAT I SEE.

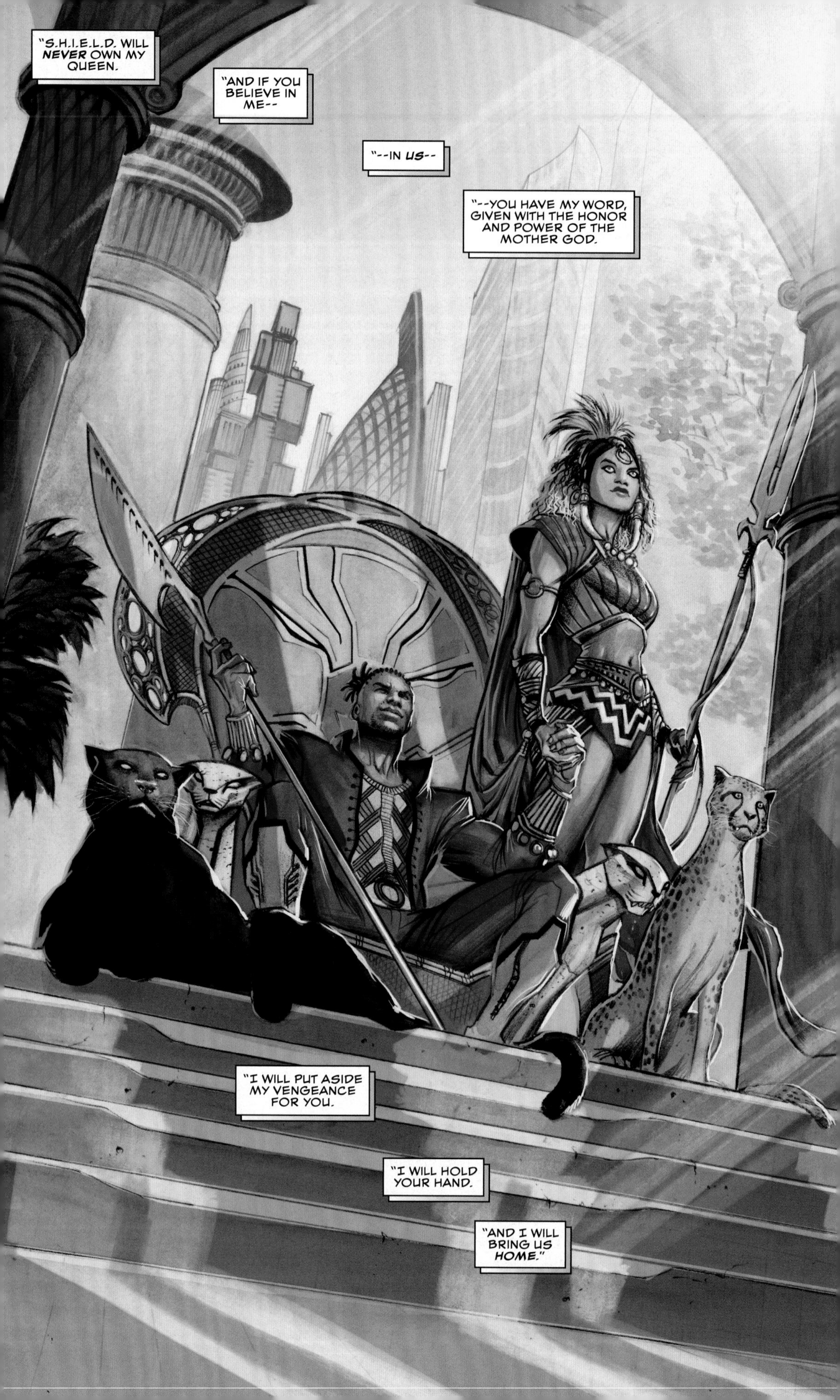
"S.H.I.E.L.D. WILL NEVER OWN MY QUEEN.
"AND IF YOU BELIEVE IN ME--
"--IN US--
"--YOU HAVE MY WORD, GIVEN WITH THE HONOR AND POWER OF THE MOTHER GOD.
"I WILL PUT ASIDE MY VENGEANCE FOR YOU.
"I WILL HOLD YOUR HAND.
"AND I WILL BRING US HOME."

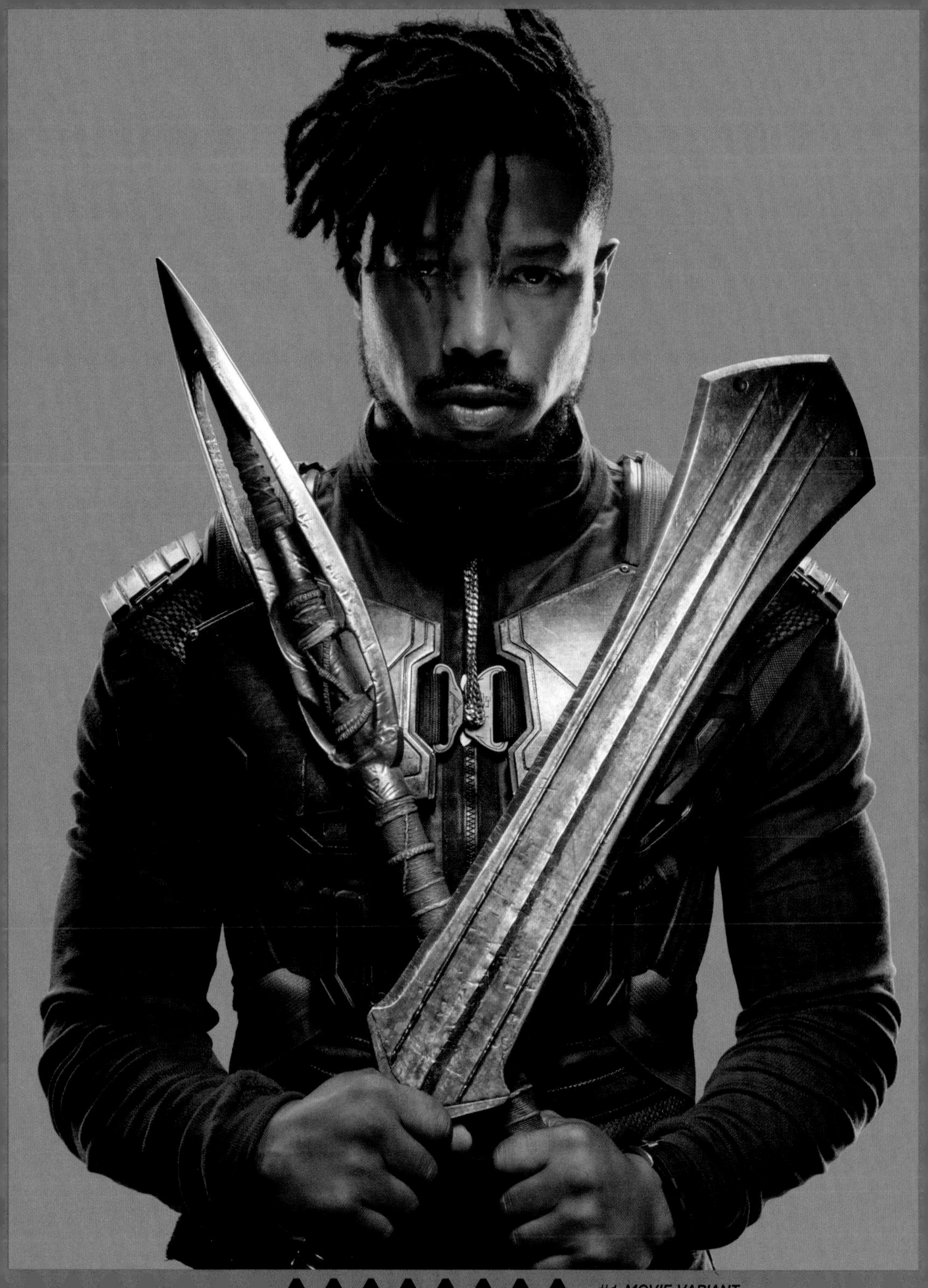

#1 MOVIE VARIANT

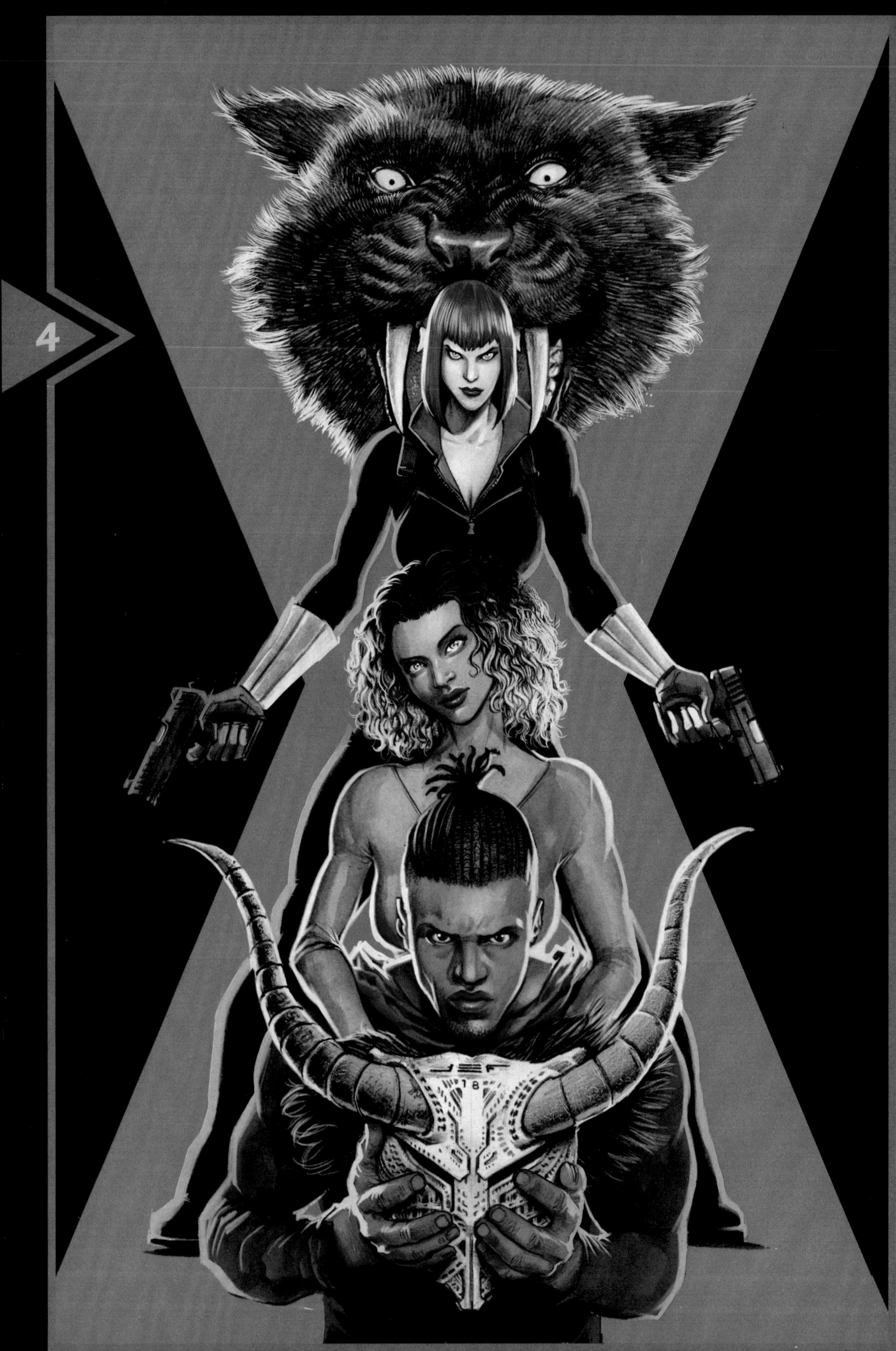
4

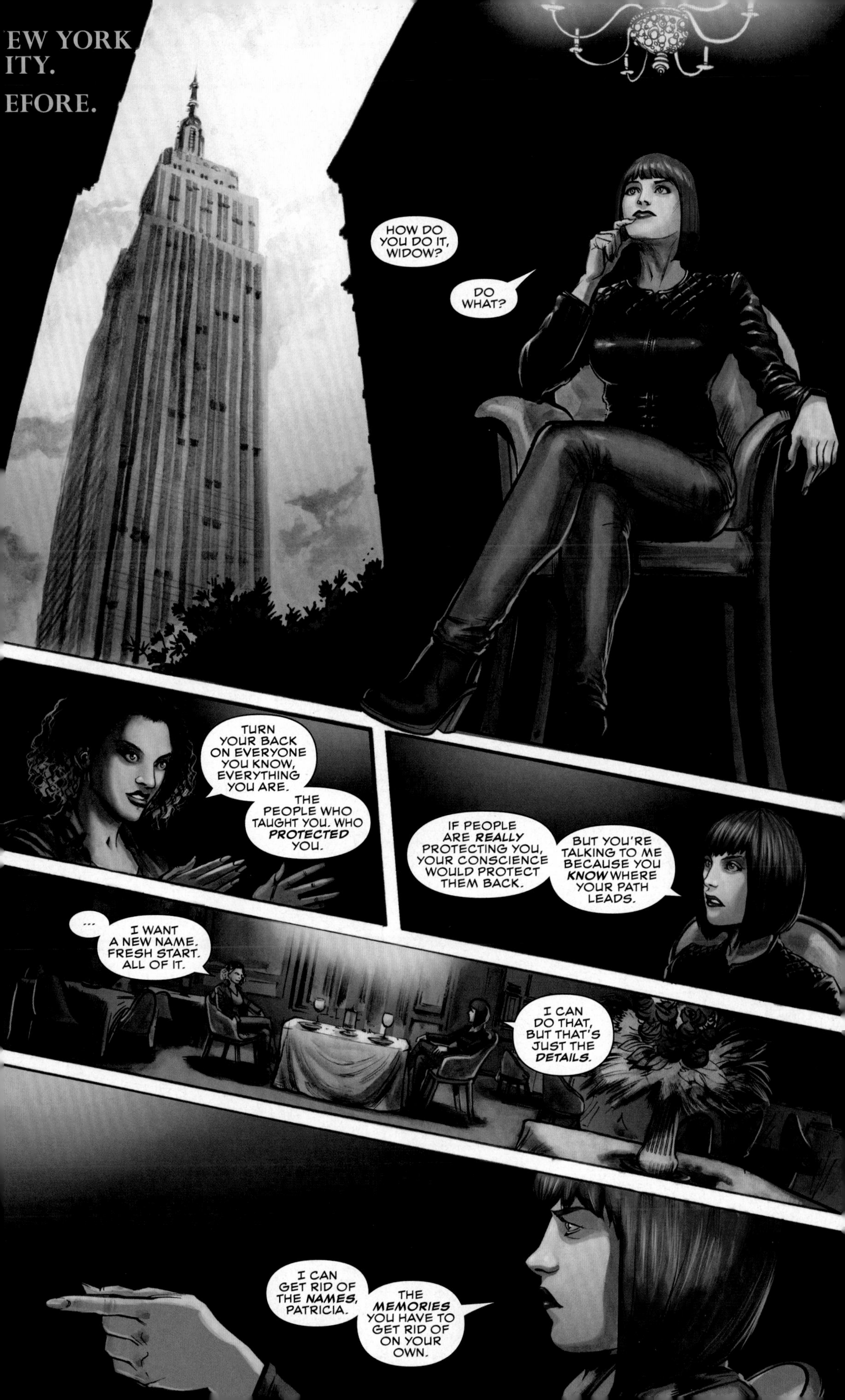
EW YORK
ITY.
EFORE.
HOW DO YOU DO IT, WIDOW?
DO WHAT?
TURN YOUR BACK ON EVERYONE YOU KNOW, EVERYTHING YOU ARE.
THE PEOPLE WHO TAUGHT YOU. WHO PROTECTED YOU.
IF PEOPLE ARE REALLY PROTECTING YOU, YOUR CONSCIENCE WOULD PROTECT THEM BACK.
BUT YOU'RE TALKING TO ME BECAUSE YOU KNOW WHERE YOUR PATH LEADS.
...
I WANT A NEW NAME. FRESH START. ALL OF IT.
I CAN DO THAT, BUT THAT'S JUST THE DETAILS.
I CAN GET RID OF THE NAMES, PATRICIA.
THE MEMORIES YOU HAVE TO GET RID OF ON YOUR OWN.

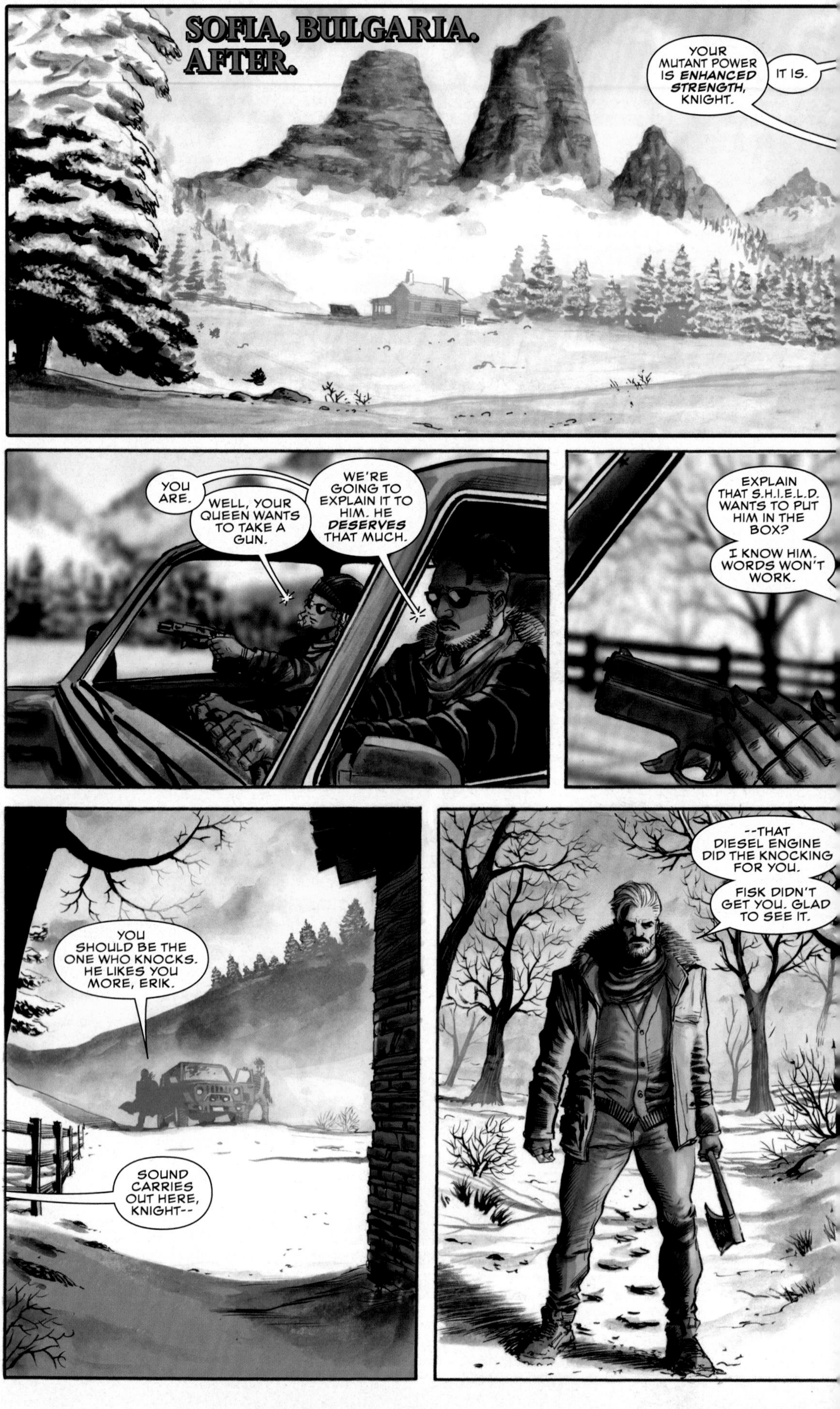
SOFIA, BULGARIA. AFTER.
YOUR MUTANT POWER IS ENHANCED STRENGTH, KNIGHT.
IT IS.
YOU ARE.
WELL, YOUR QUEEN WANTS TO TAKE A GUN.
WE'RE GOING TO EXPLAIN IT TO HIM. HE DESERVES THAT MUCH.
EXPLAIN THAT S.H.I.E.L.D. WANTS TO PUT HIM IN THE BOX?
I KNOW HIM. WORDS WON'T WORK.
YOU SHOULD BE THE ONE WHO KNOCKS. HE LIKES YOU MORE, ERIK.
SOUND CARRIES OUT HERE, KNIGHT--
--THAT DIESEL ENGINE DID THE KNOCKING FOR YOU.
FISK DIDN'T GET YOU. GLAD TO SEE IT.

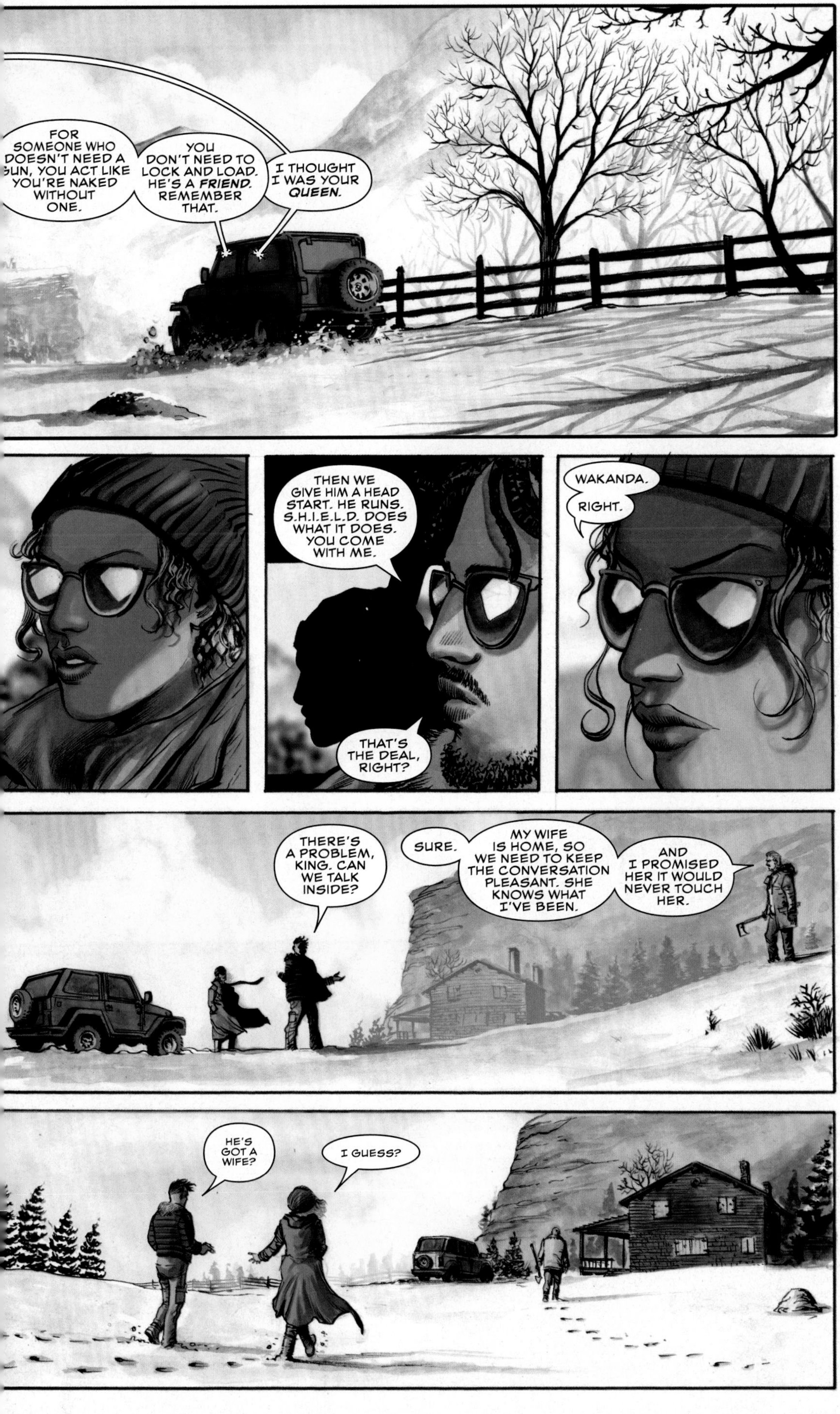
FOR SOMEONE WHO DOESN'T NEED A GUN, YOU ACT LIKE YOU'RE NAKED WITHOUT ONE.
YOU DON'T NEED TO LOCK AND LOAD. HE'S A *FRIEND*. REMEMBER THAT.
I THOUGHT I WAS YOUR *QUEEN*.
THEN WE GIVE HIM A HEAD START. HE RUNS. S.H.I.E.L.D. DOES WHAT IT DOES. YOU COME WITH ME.
THAT'S THE DEAL, RIGHT?
WAKANDA.
RIGHT.
THERE'S A PROBLEM, KING. CAN WE TALK INSIDE?
SURE.
MY WIFE IS HOME, SO WE NEED TO KEEP THE CONVERSATION PLEASANT. SHE KNOWS WHAT I'VE BEEN.
AND I PROMISED HER IT WOULD NEVER TOUCH HER.
HE'S GOT A WIFE?
I GUESS?

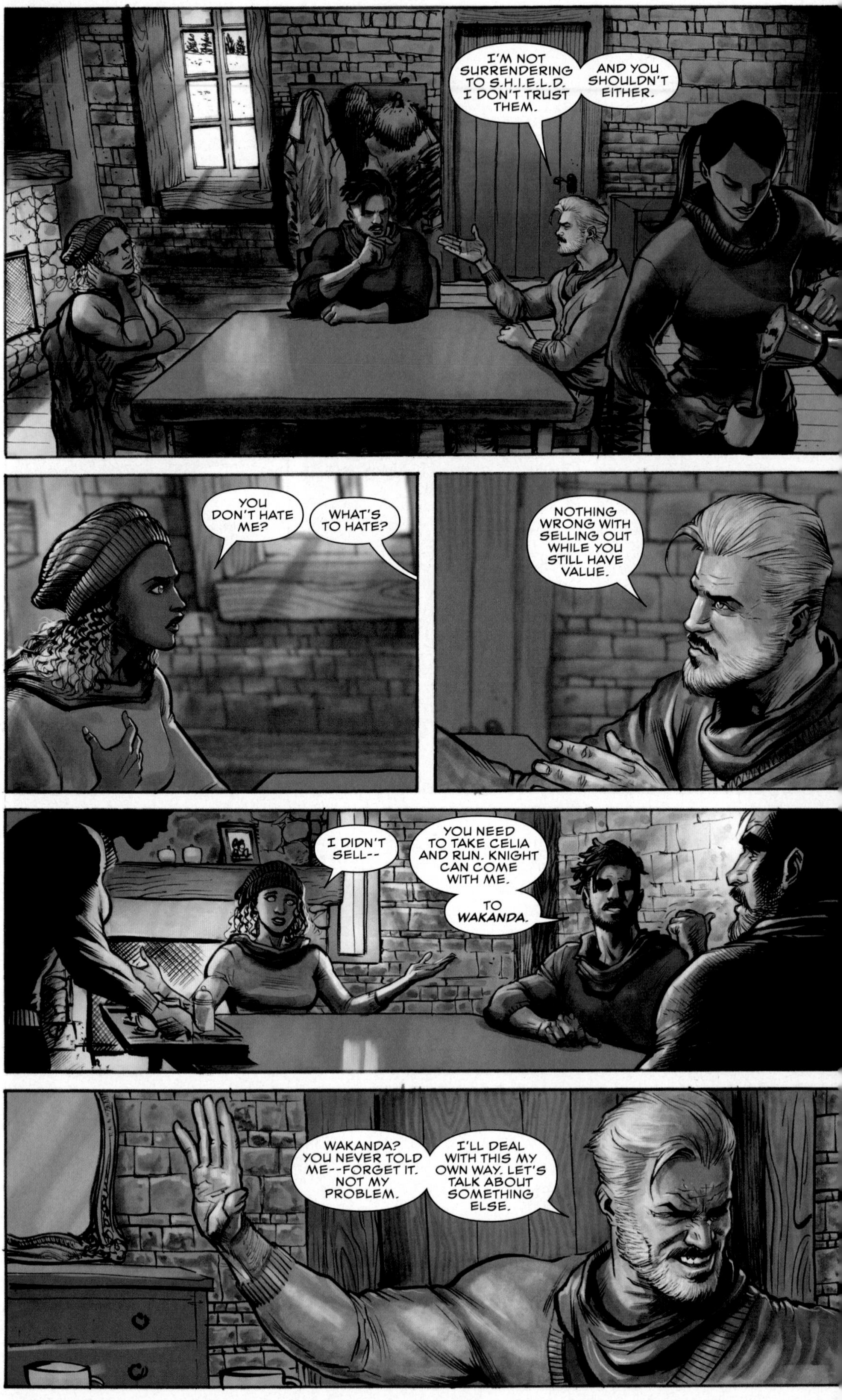
I'M NOT SURRENDERING TO S.H.I.E.L.D. I DON'T TRUST THEM.
AND YOU SHOULDN'T EITHER.
YOU DON'T HATE ME?
WHAT'S TO HATE?
NOTHING WRONG WITH SELLING OUT WHILE YOU STILL HAVE VALUE.
I DIDN'T SELL--
YOU NEED TO TAKE CELIA AND RUN. KNIGHT CAN COME WITH ME.
TO *WAKANDA.*
WAKANDA? YOU NEVER TOLD ME--FORGET IT. NOT MY PROBLEM.
I'LL DEAL WITH THIS MY OWN WAY. LET'S TALK ABOUT SOMETHING ELSE.

YOU'RE TOO DAMN STUBBORN. THEY CAN *HELP* YOU. THEY'RE HELPING *ME*.

THEY'RE *USING* YOU, KNIGHT! YOU CAN *HATE* YOURSELF AS MUCH AS YOU WANT, BUT I'M NOT YOU!

ROBERT--

--NOT IN THE HOUSE.

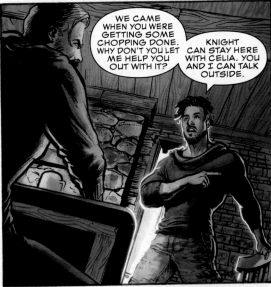

WE CAME WHEN YOU WERE GETTING SOME CHOPPING DONE. WHY DON'T YOU LET ME HELP YOU OUT WITH IT?

KNIGHT CAN STAY HERE WITH CELIA. YOU AND I CAN TALK OUTSIDE.

FINE.

WHAT DID I TELL YOU ABOUT *WORDS?*

JUST STAY HERE. I CAN GET THROUGH TO HIM.

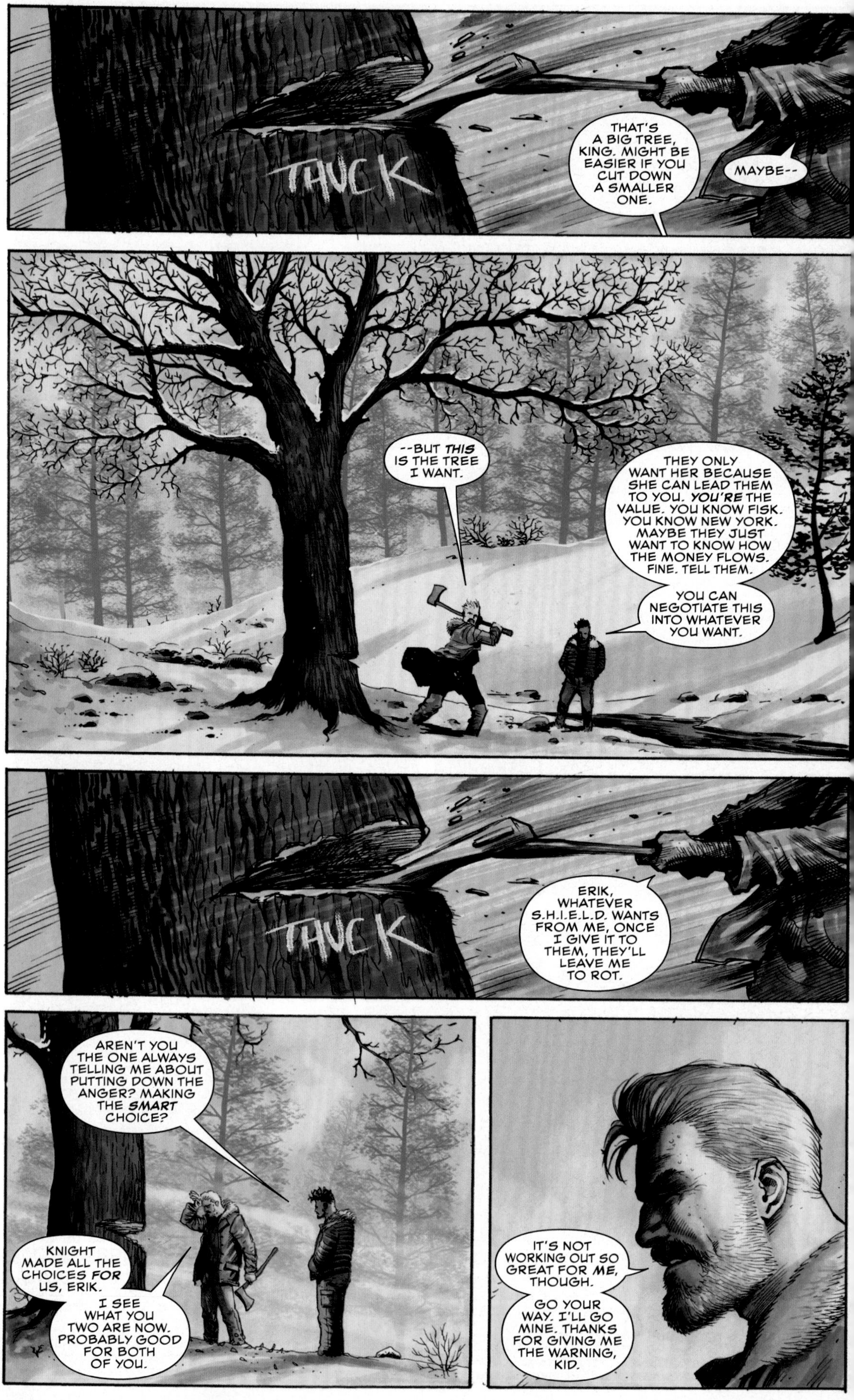
THUCK
THAT'S A BIG TREE, KING. MIGHT BE EASIER IF YOU CUT DOWN A SMALLER ONE.
MAYBE--
--BUT THIS IS THE TREE I WANT.
THEY ONLY WANT HER BECAUSE SHE CAN LEAD THEM TO YOU. YOU'RE THE VALUE. YOU KNOW FISK. YOU KNOW NEW YORK. MAYBE THEY JUST WANT TO KNOW HOW THE MONEY FLOWS. FINE. TELL THEM.
YOU CAN NEGOTIATE THIS INTO WHATEVER YOU WANT.
THUCK
ERIK, WHATEVER S.H.I.E.L.D. WANTS FROM ME, ONCE I GIVE IT TO THEM, THEY'LL LEAVE ME TO ROT.
AREN'T YOU THE ONE ALWAYS TELLING ME ABOUT PUTTING DOWN THE ANGER? MAKING THE SMART CHOICE?
KNIGHT MADE ALL THE CHOICES FOR US, ERIK.
I SEE WHAT YOU TWO ARE NOW. PROBABLY GOOD FOR BOTH OF YOU.
IT'S NOT WORKING OUT SO GREAT FOR ME, THOUGH.
GO YOUR WAY. I'LL GO MINE. THANKS FOR GIVING ME THE WARNING, KID.

YOU ARE HIS FRIEND?

HE MIGHT NOT SEE IT THAT WAY NOW.

LOOK, I'M NOT TRYING TO DESTROY YOUR LITTLE PARADISE. I'M TRYING TO HELP HIM.

YOU CAME HERE WITH A GUN. MY PARADISE IS ALREADY GONE.

WHY WARN US? WHY NOT JUST DO WHAT YOU WANT?

BECAUSE HE DESERVES MORE THAN THAT.

BUT NOT MUCH MORE, YES?

YOU WANT HIS PERMISSION TO TAKE AWAY HIS FREEDOM. HE WILL NEVER GIVE YOU THAT.

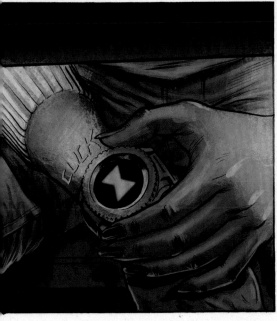

HE LIED TO YOU, CELIA.

PEOPLE LIKE US DON'T GET TO BE FREE.

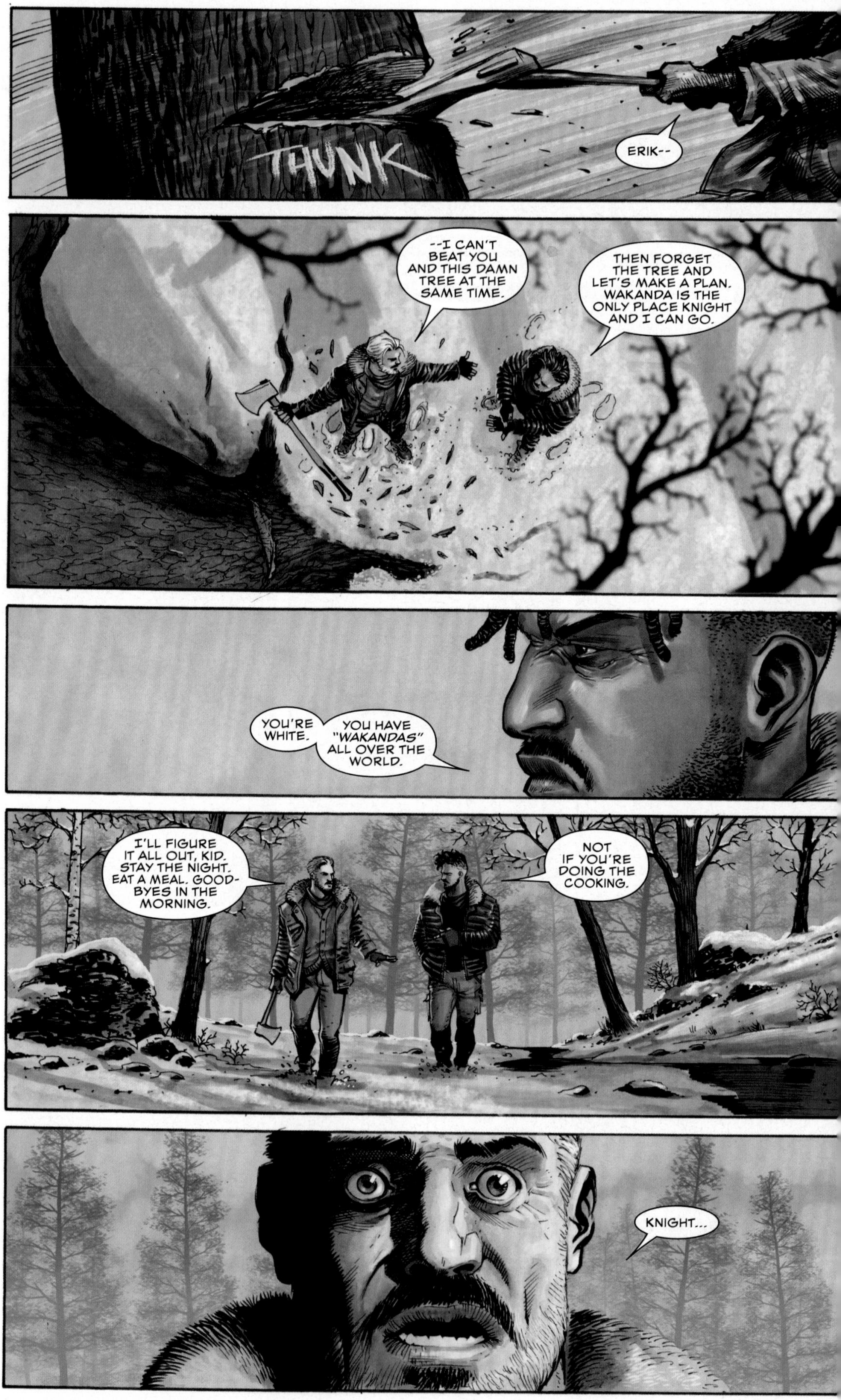
THUNK
ERIK--
--I CAN'T BEAT YOU AND THIS DAMN TREE AT THE SAME TIME.
THEN FORGET THE TREE AND LET'S MAKE A PLAN. WAKANDA IS THE ONLY PLACE KNIGHT AND I CAN GO.
YOU'RE WHITE.
YOU HAVE "WAKANDAS" ALL OVER THE WORLD.
I'LL FIGURE IT ALL OUT, KID. STAY THE NIGHT. EAT A MEAL. GOOD-BYES IN THE MORNING.
NOT IF YOU'RE DOING THE COOKING.
KNIGHT...

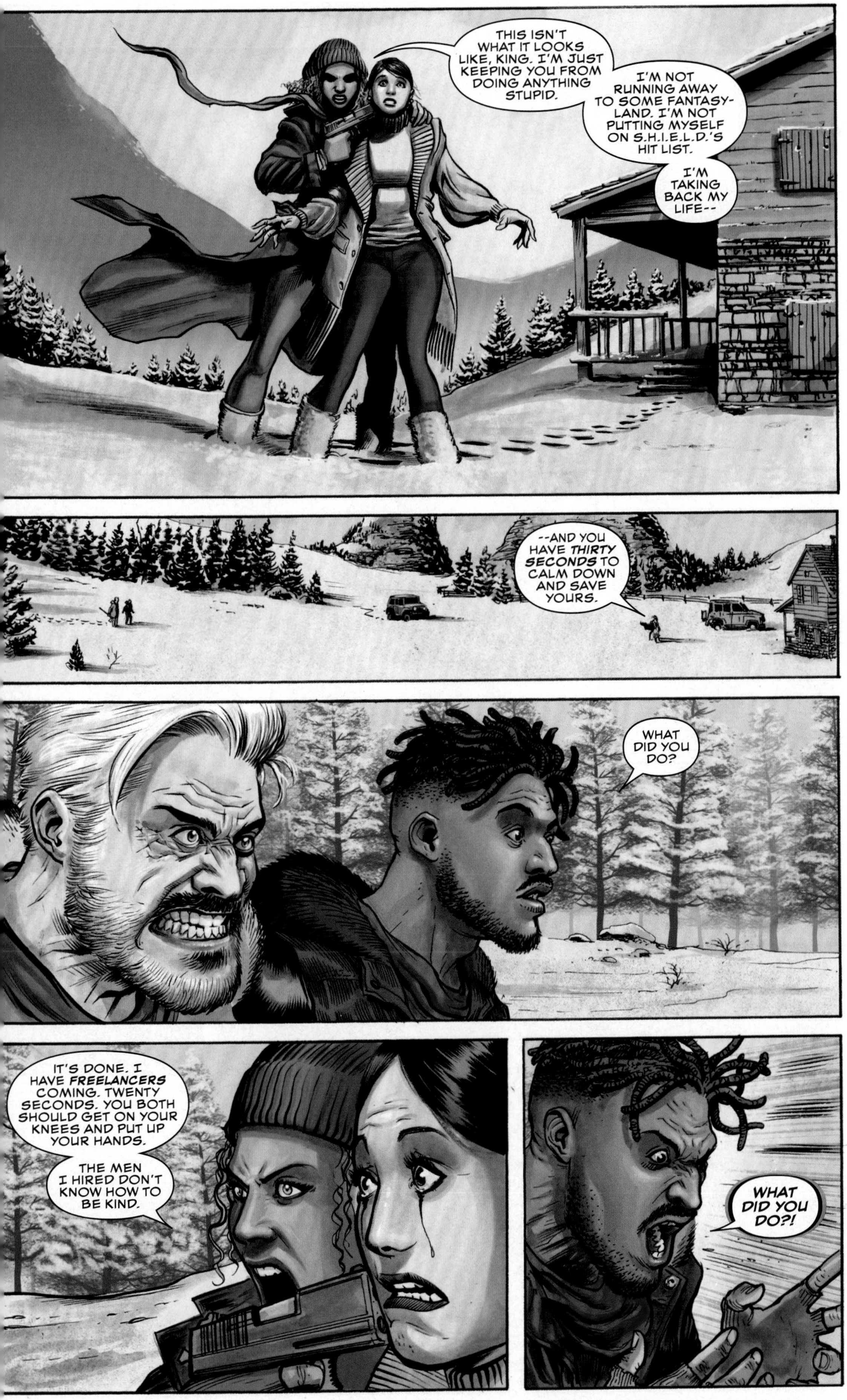
THIS ISN'T WHAT IT LOOKS LIKE, KING. I'M JUST KEEPING YOU FROM DOING ANYTHING STUPID.
I'M NOT RUNNING AWAY TO SOME FANTASY-LAND. I'M NOT PUTTING MYSELF ON S.H.I.E.L.D.'S HIT LIST.
I'M TAKING BACK MY LIFE--
--AND YOU HAVE THIRTY SECONDS TO CALM DOWN AND SAVE YOURS.
WHAT DID YOU DO?
IT'S DONE. I HAVE FREELANCERS COMING. TWENTY SECONDS. YOU BOTH SHOULD GET ON YOUR KNEES AND PUT UP YOUR HANDS.
THE MEN I HIRED DON'T KNOW HOW TO BE KIND.
WHAT DID YOU DO?!

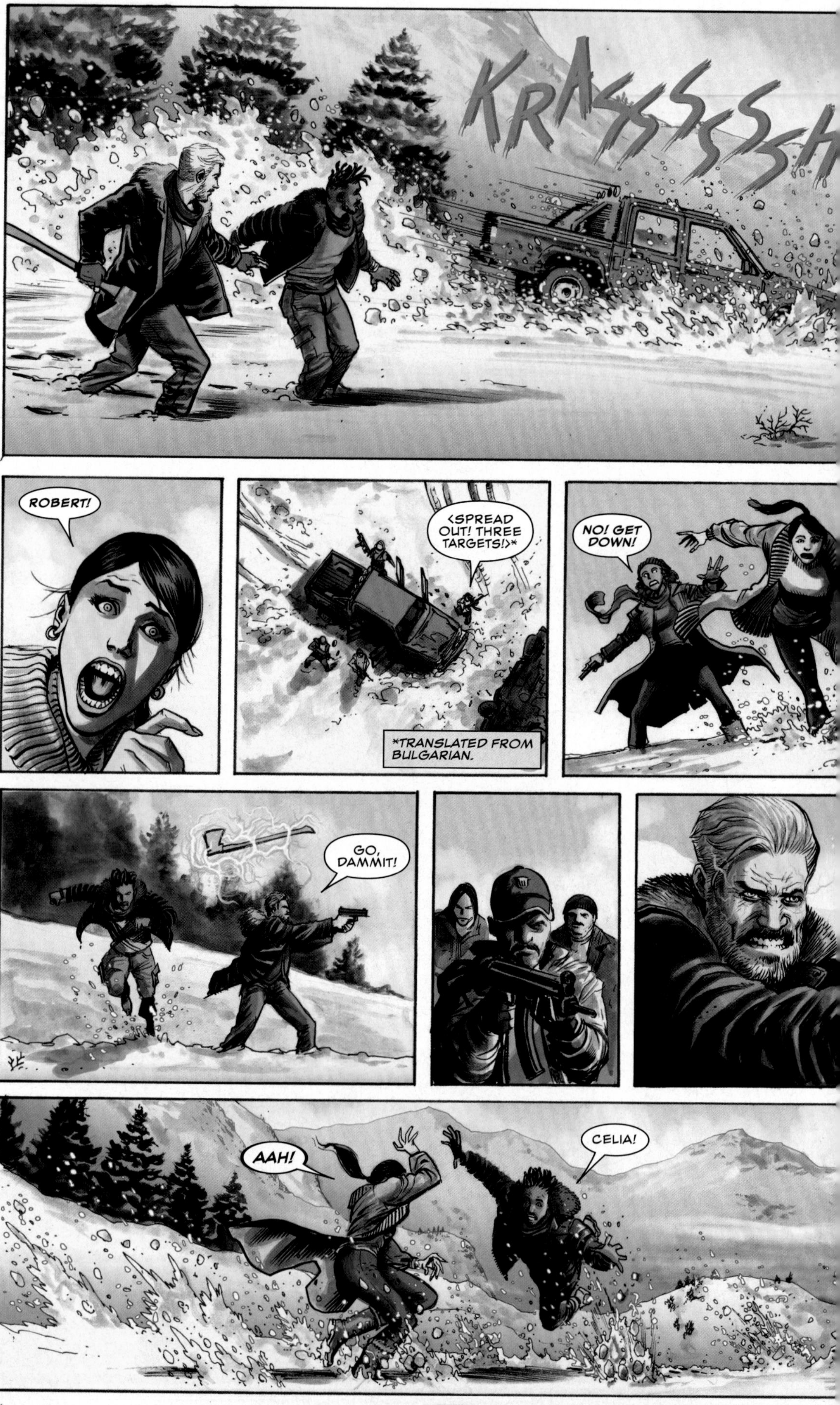
KRASSSSSSH
ROBERT!
<SPREAD OUT! THREE TARGETS!>*
*TRANSLATED FROM BULGARIAN.
NO! GET DOWN!
GO, DAMMIT!
AAH!
CELIA!

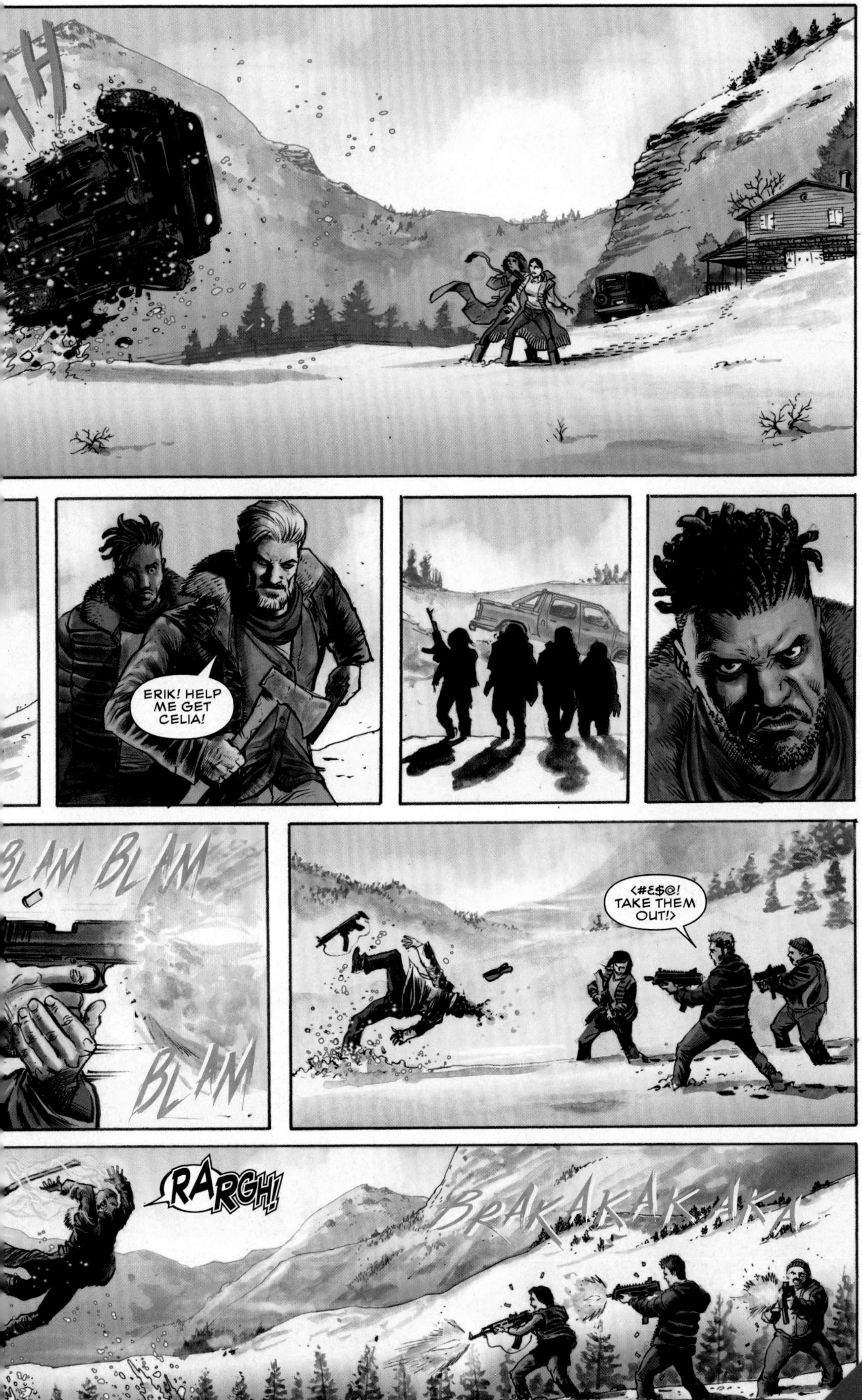

AH
ERIK! HELP ME GET CELIA!
BLAM BLAM
BLAM
<#£$@! TAKE THEM OUT!>
RARGH!
BRAKAKAKAKAKA

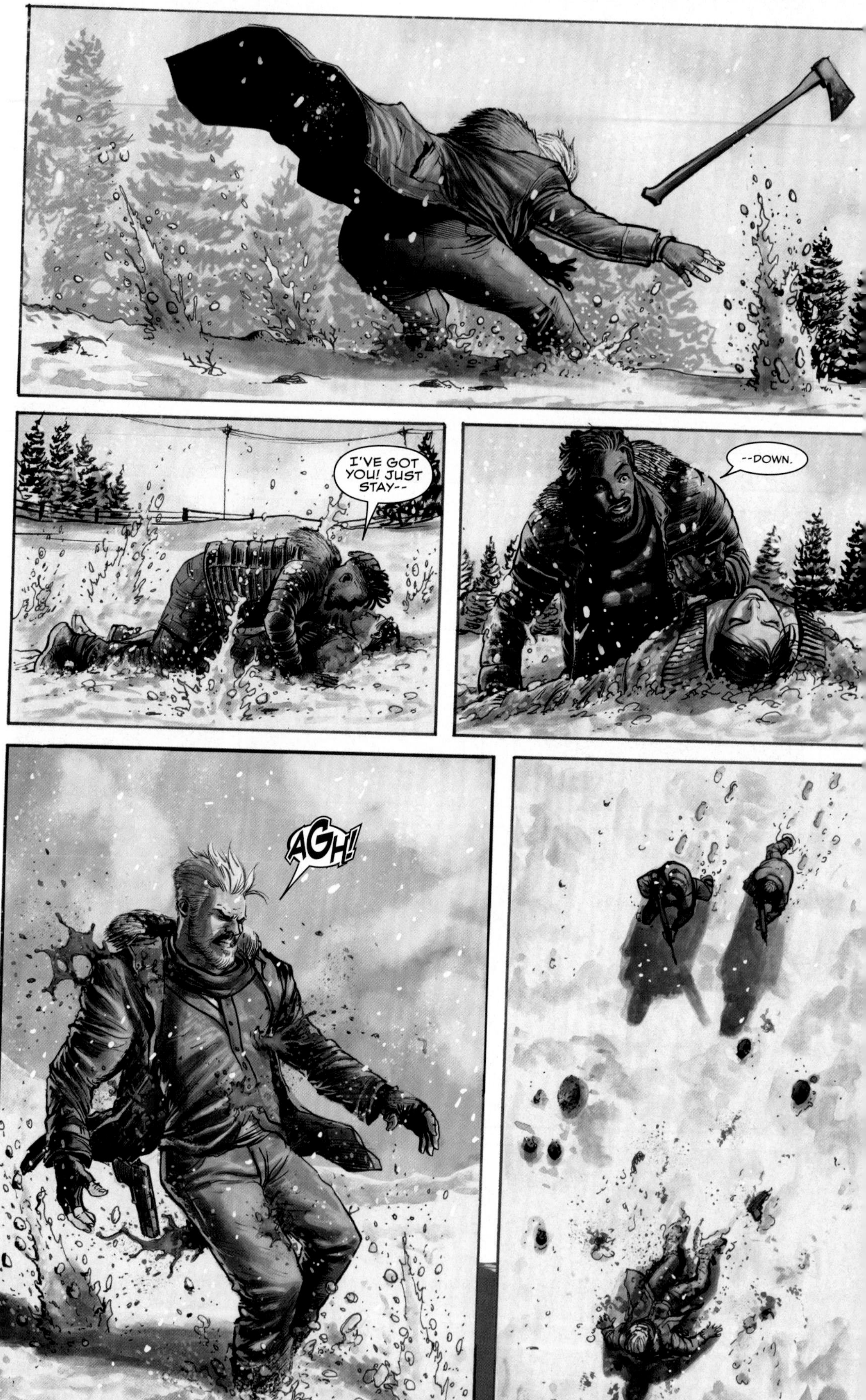
I'VE GOT YOU! JUST STAY--
--DOWN.
AGH!

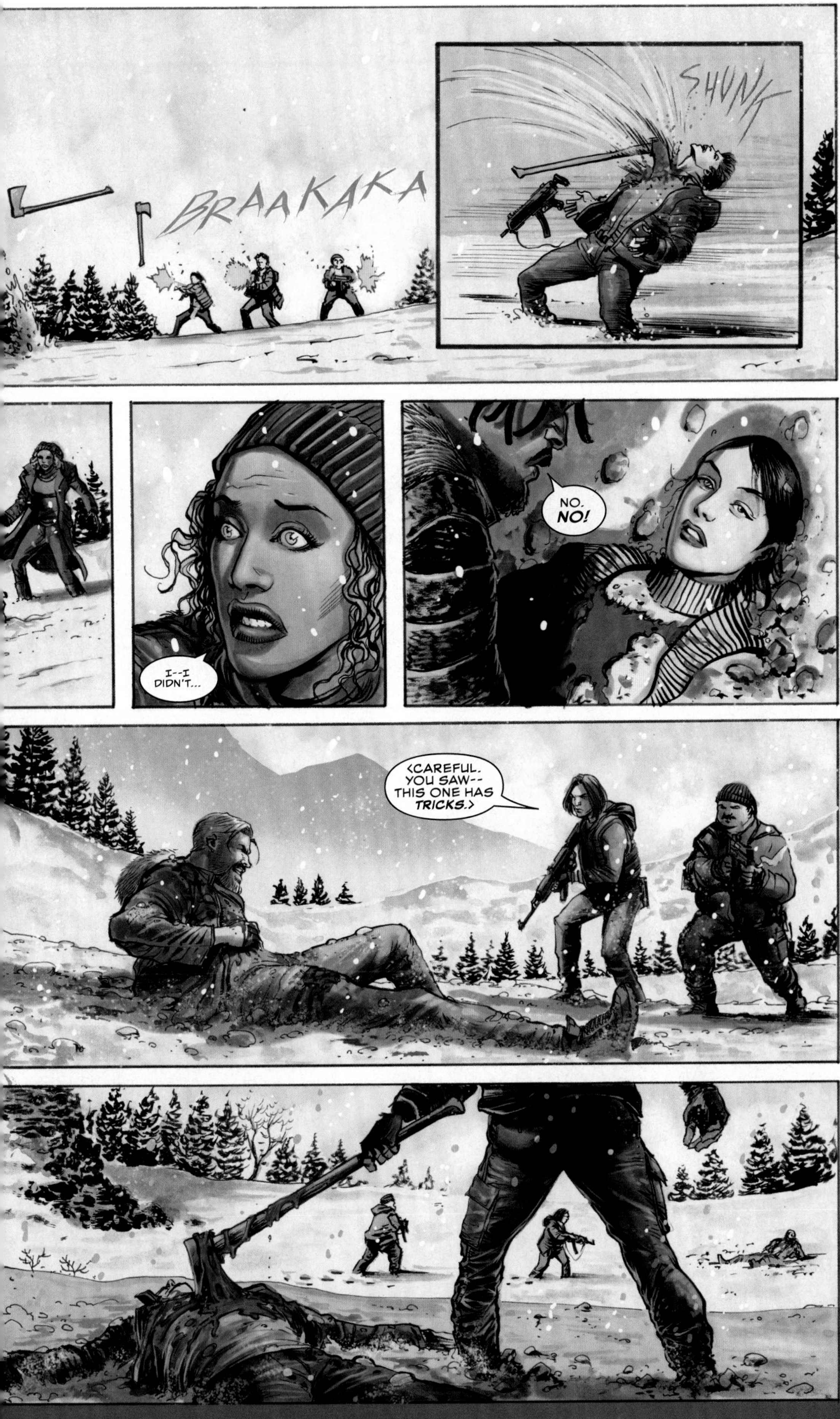
BRAAKAKA
SHUNK
I--I DIDN'T...
NO. NO!
<CAREFUL. YOU SAW-- THIS ONE HAS TRICKS.>

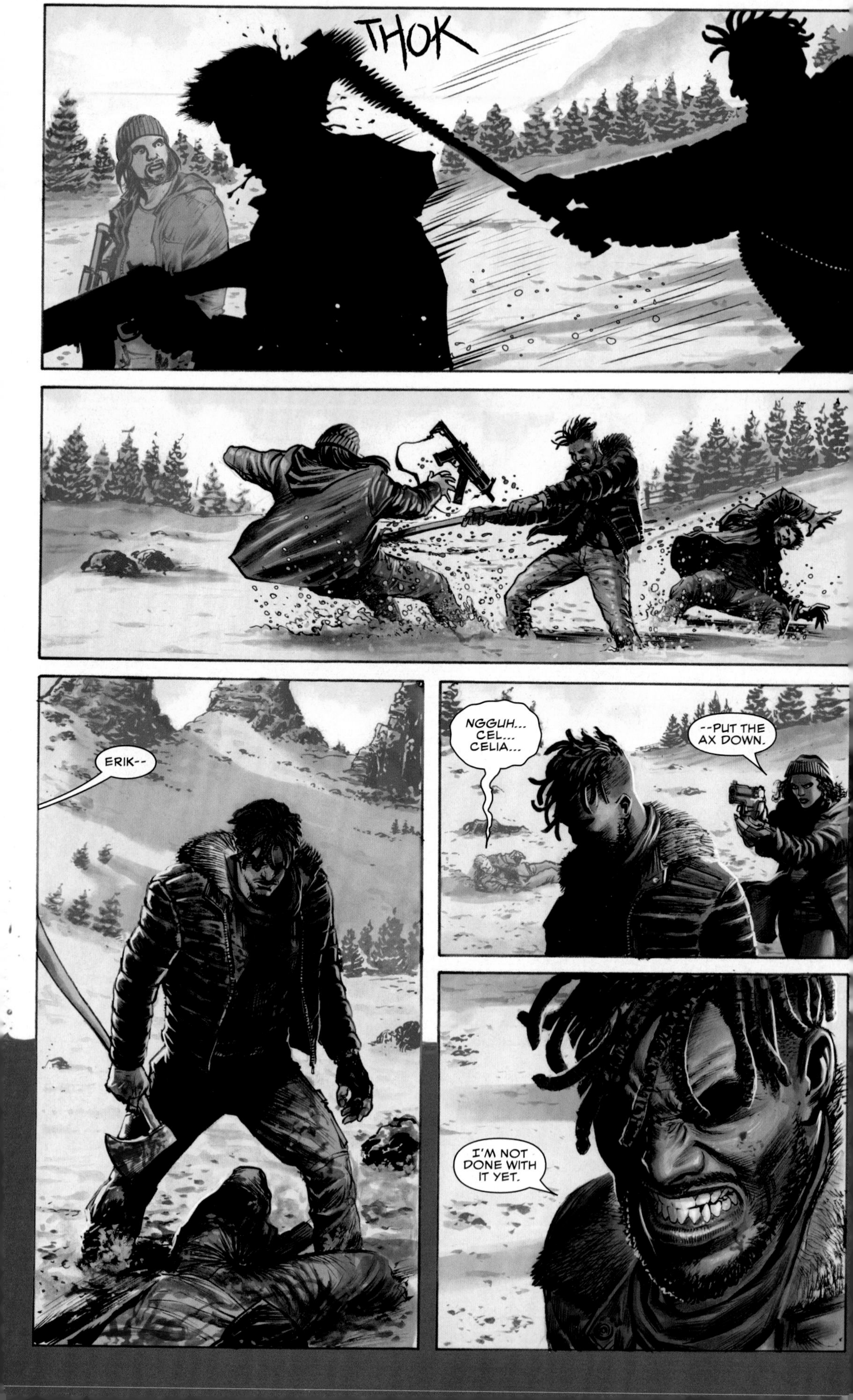
THOK
ERIK--
NGGUH... CEL... CELIA...
--PUT THE AX DOWN.
I'M NOT DONE WITH IT YET.

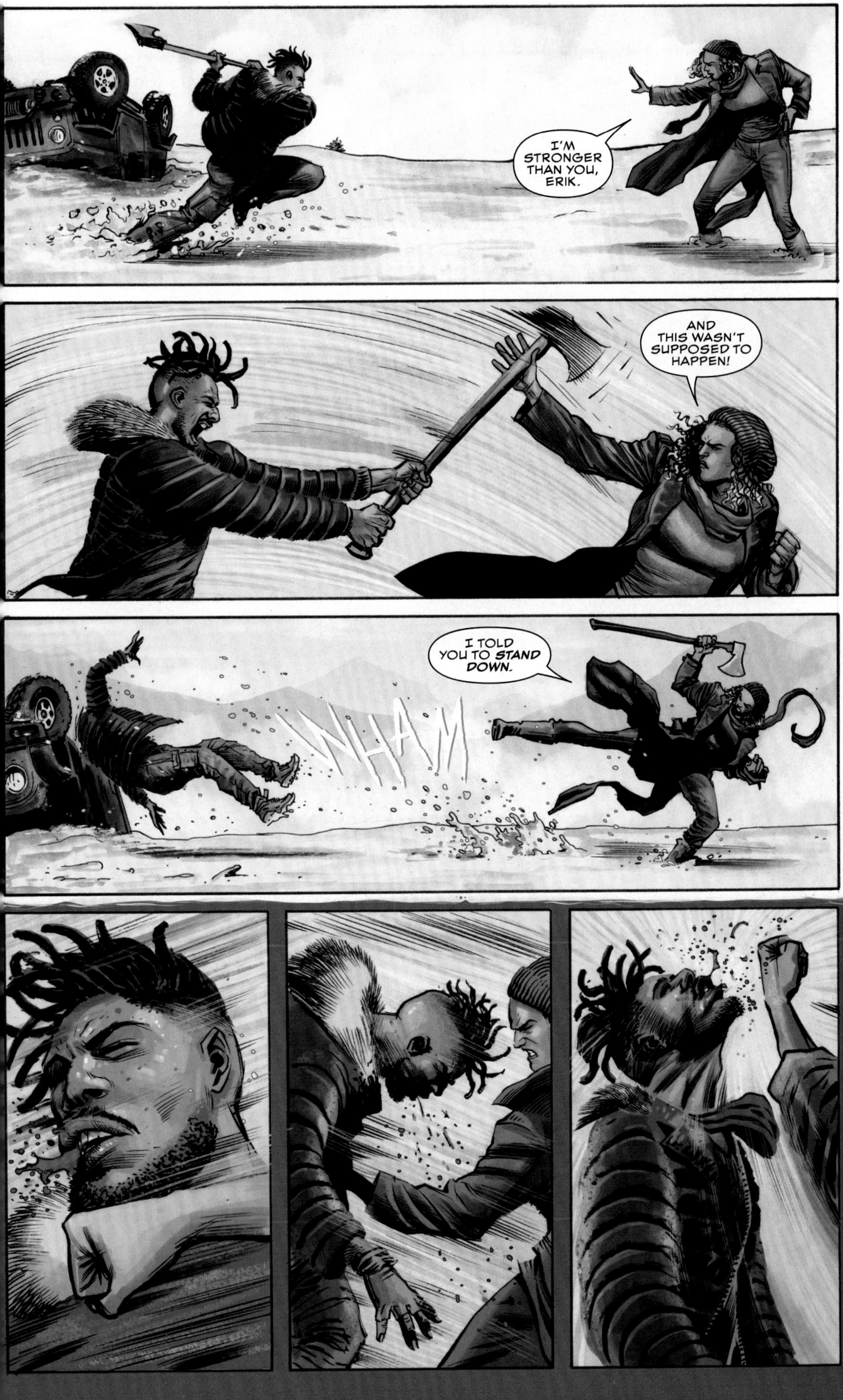
I'M STRONGER THAN YOU, ERIK.
AND THIS WASN'T SUPPOSED TO HAPPEN!
I TOLD YOU TO STAND DOWN.
WHAM

IF I WAS WHAT YOU THINK I AM, I'D KILL YOU.

I HAD TO MAKE A CHOICE, ERIK.

FORGET *ALL* OF THIS. I'LL TELL S.H.I.E.L.D. YOU'RE *DEAD*. GO FIND YOUR FAIRY TALE.

REMEMBER YOUR QUEEN HAD MERCY.

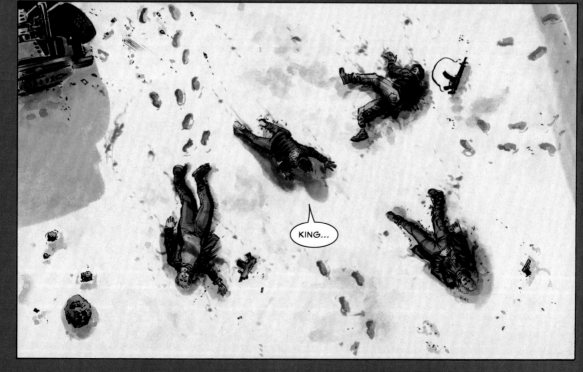

KING...

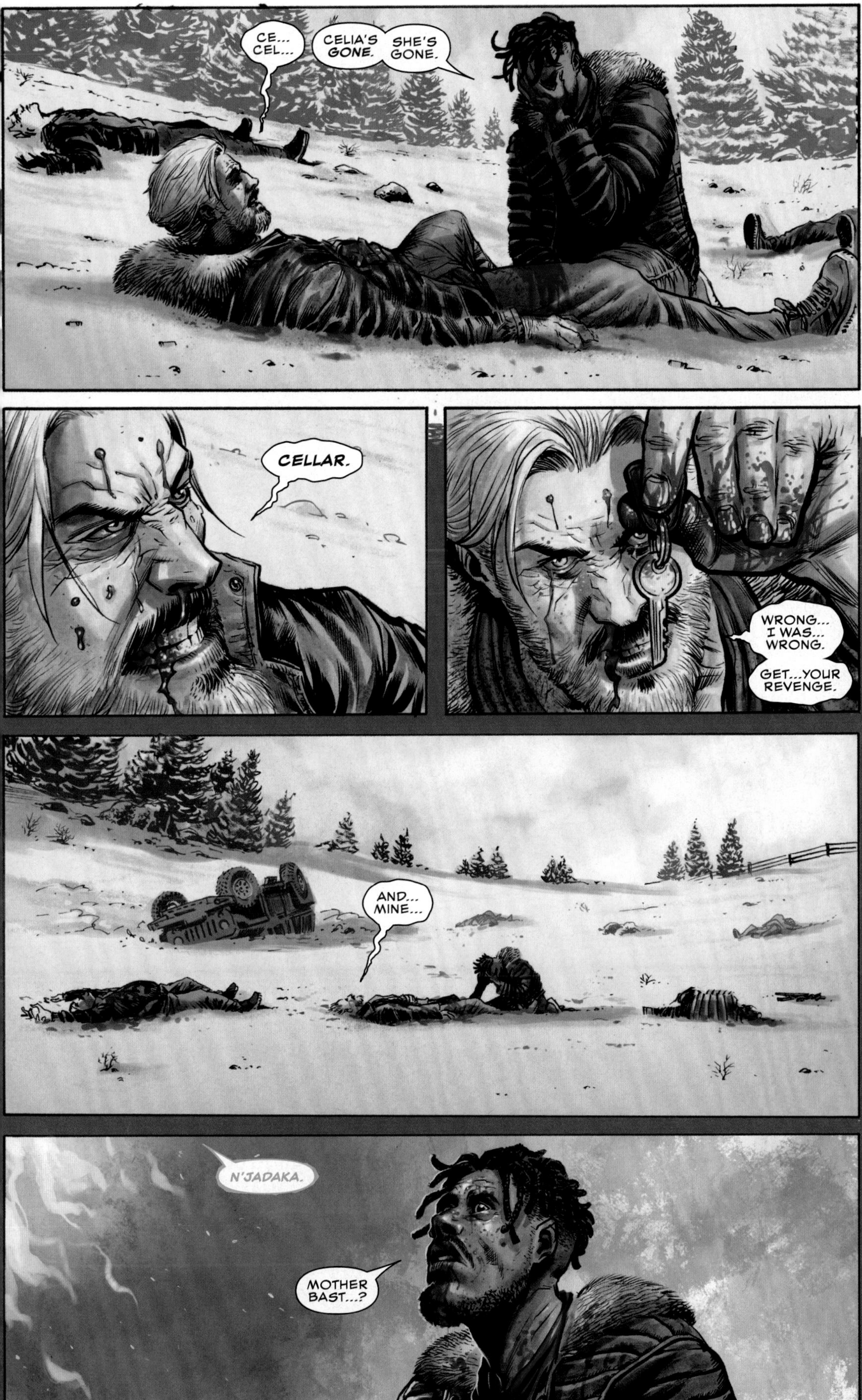
CE... CEL...
CELIA'S GONE.
SHE'S GONE.
CELLAR.
WRONG... I WAS... WRONG.
GET...YOUR REVENGE.
AND... MINE...
N'JADAKA.
MOTHER BAST...?

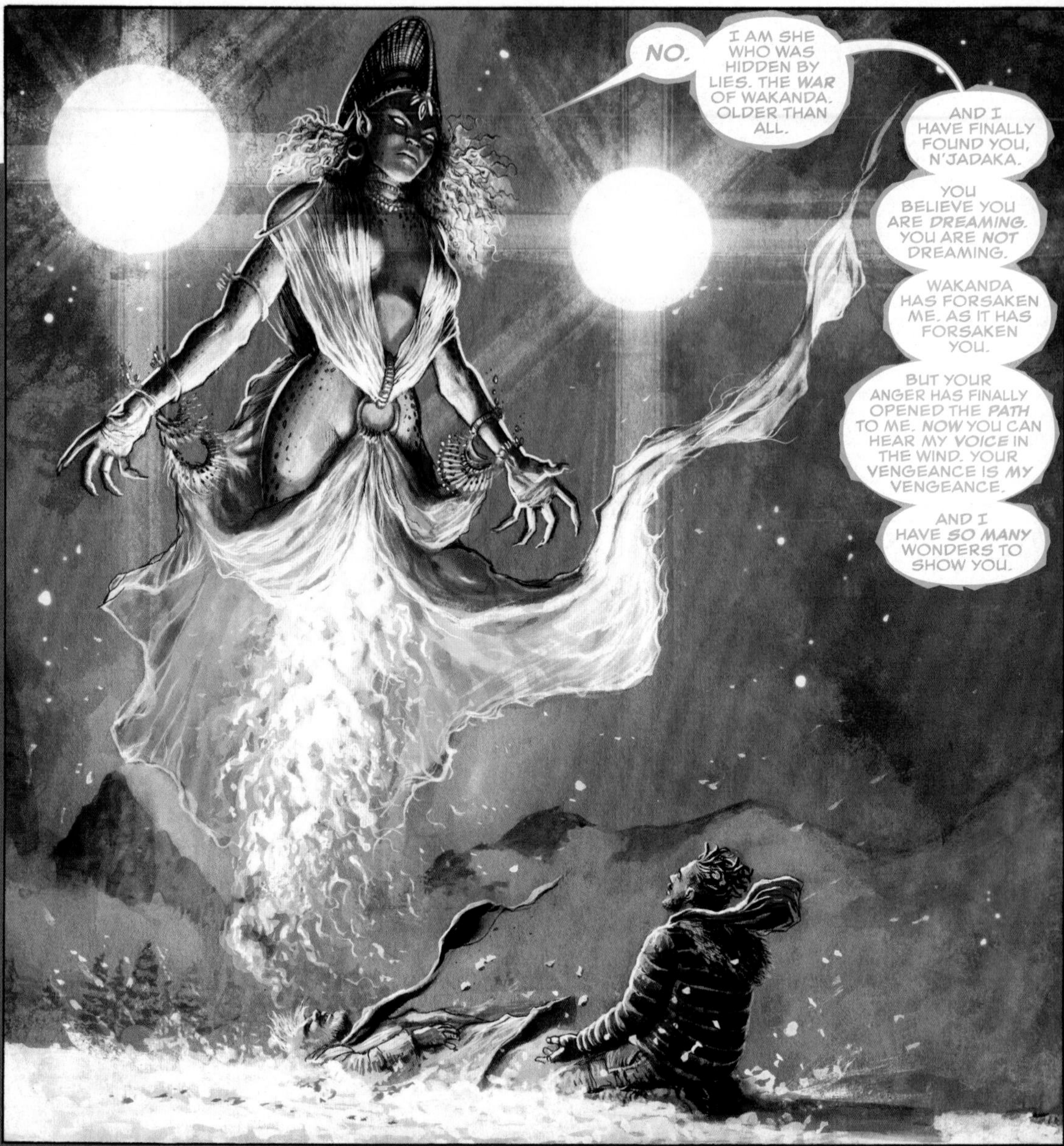
NO.
I AM SHE WHO WAS HIDDEN BY LIES. THE *WAR* OF WAKANDA. OLDER THAN ALL.
AND I HAVE FINALLY FOUND YOU, N'JADAKA.
YOU BELIEVE YOU ARE *DREAMING.* YOU ARE *NOT* DREAMING.
WAKANDA HAS FORSAKEN ME. AS IT HAS FORSAKEN YOU.
BUT YOUR ANGER HAS FINALLY OPENED THE *PATH* TO ME. *NOW* YOU CAN HEAR MY *VOICE* IN THE WIND. YOUR *VENGEANCE* IS *MY* VENGEANCE.
AND I HAVE *SO MANY* WONDERS TO SHOW YOU.

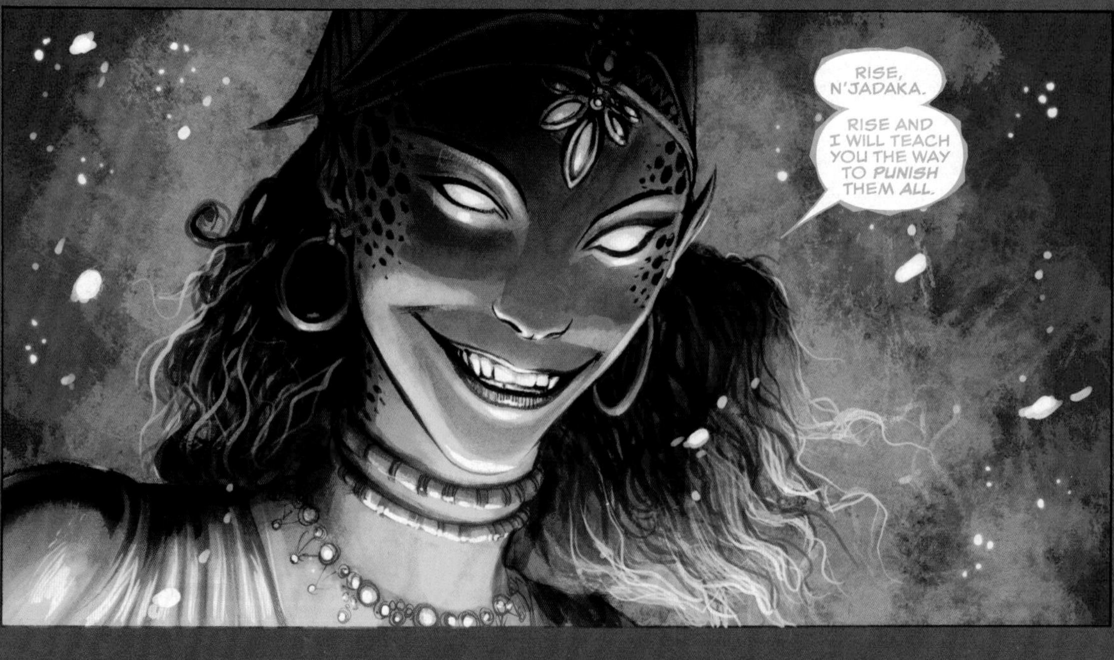
RISE, N'JADAKA.
RISE AND I WILL TEACH YOU THE WAY TO *PUNISH* THEM *ALL.*

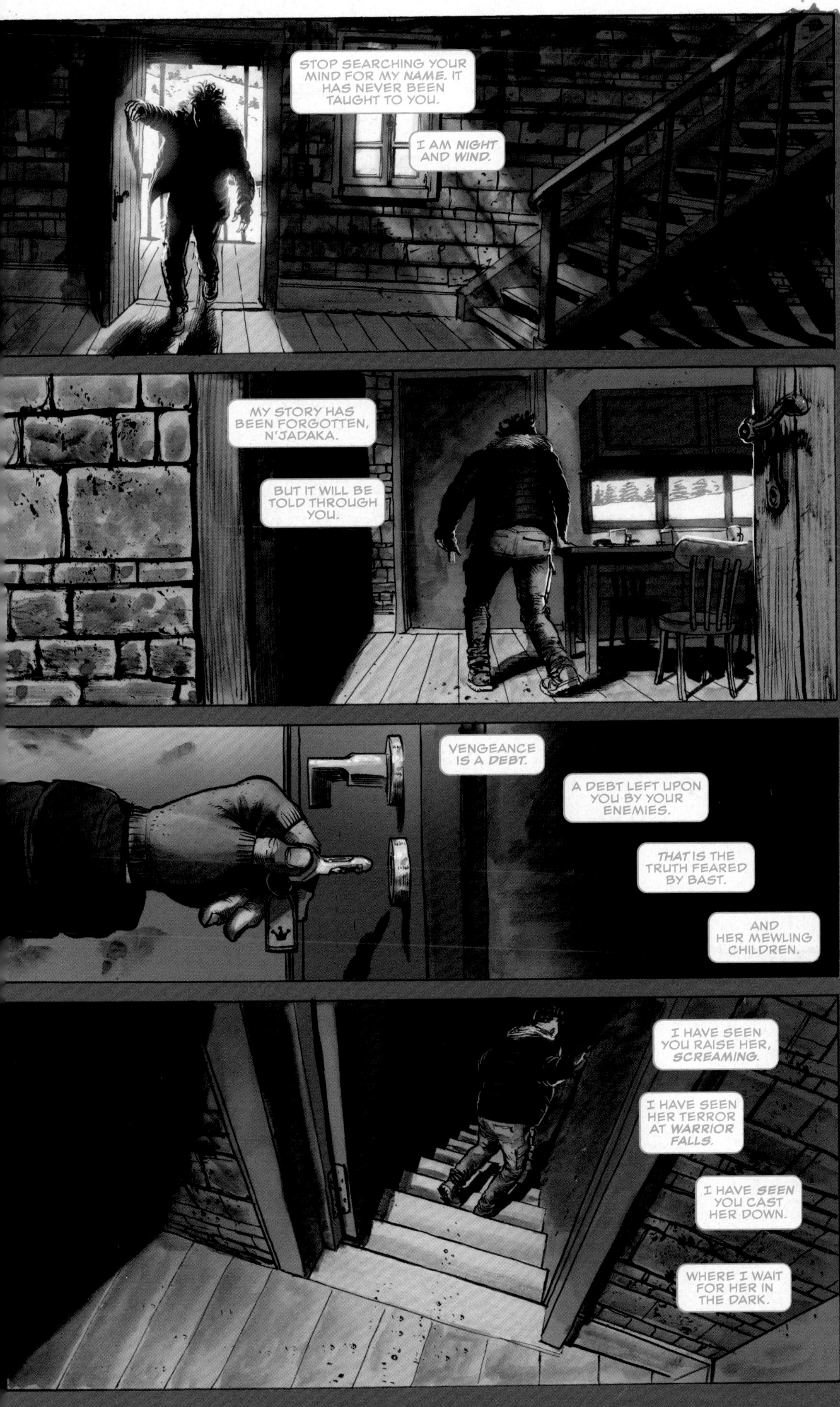

STOP SEARCHING YOUR MIND FOR MY NAME. IT HAS NEVER BEEN TAUGHT TO YOU.
I AM NIGHT AND WIND.
MY STORY HAS BEEN FORGOTTEN, N'JADAKA.
BUT IT WILL BE TOLD THROUGH YOU.
VENGEANCE IS A DEBT.
A DEBT LEFT UPON YOU BY YOUR ENEMIES.
THAT IS THE TRUTH FEARED BY BAST.
AND HER MEWLING CHILDREN.
I HAVE SEEN YOU RAISE HER, SCREAMING.
I HAVE SEEN HER TERROR AT WARRIOR FALLS.
I HAVE SEEN YOU CAST HER DOWN.
WHERE I WAIT FOR HER IN THE DARK.

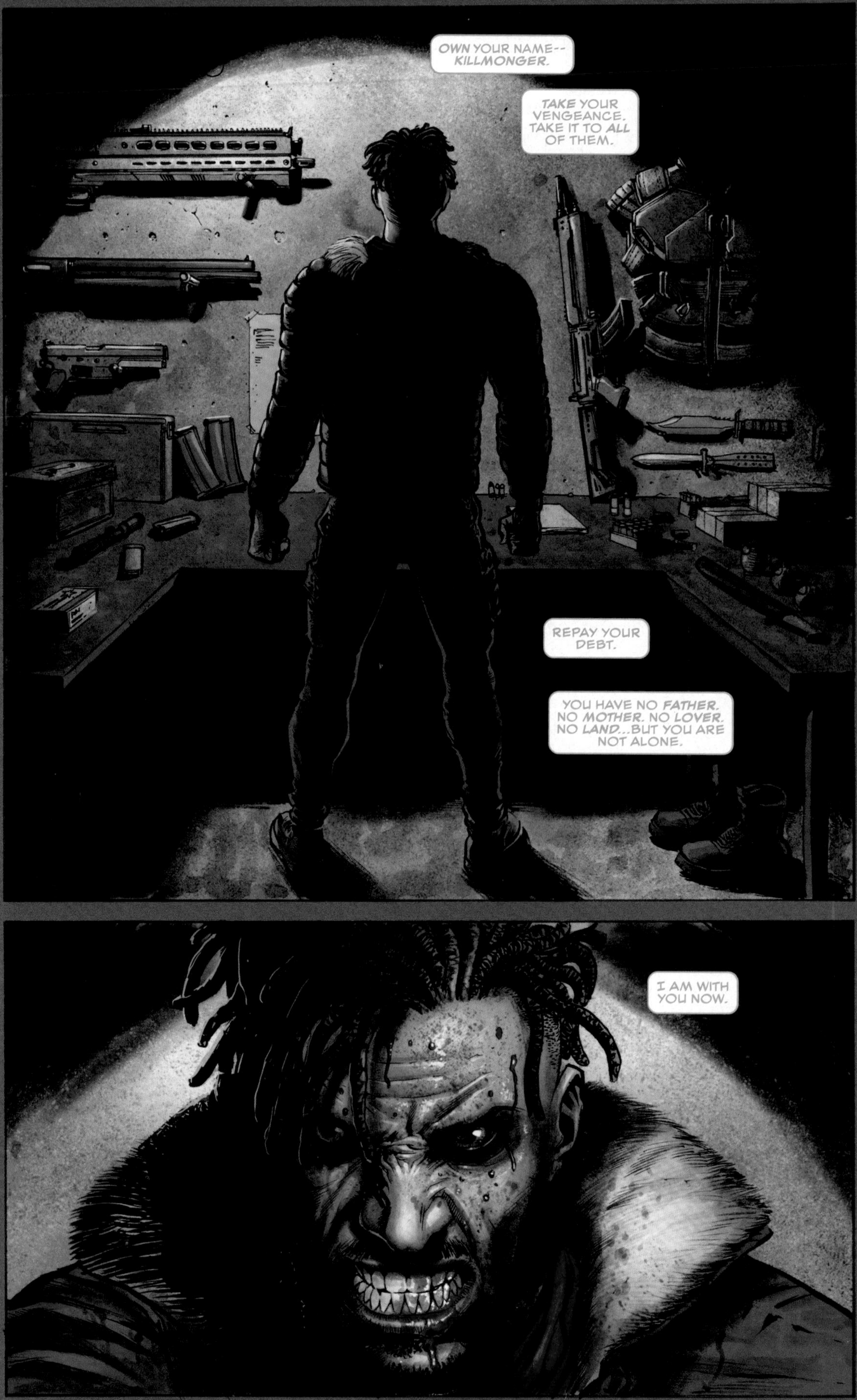
OWN YOUR NAME--KILLMONGER.
TAKE YOUR VENGEANCE. TAKE IT TO ALL OF THEM.
REPAY YOUR DEBT.
YOU HAVE NO FATHER. NO MOTHER. NO LOVER. NO LAND...BUT YOU ARE NOT ALONE.
I AM WITH YOU NOW.

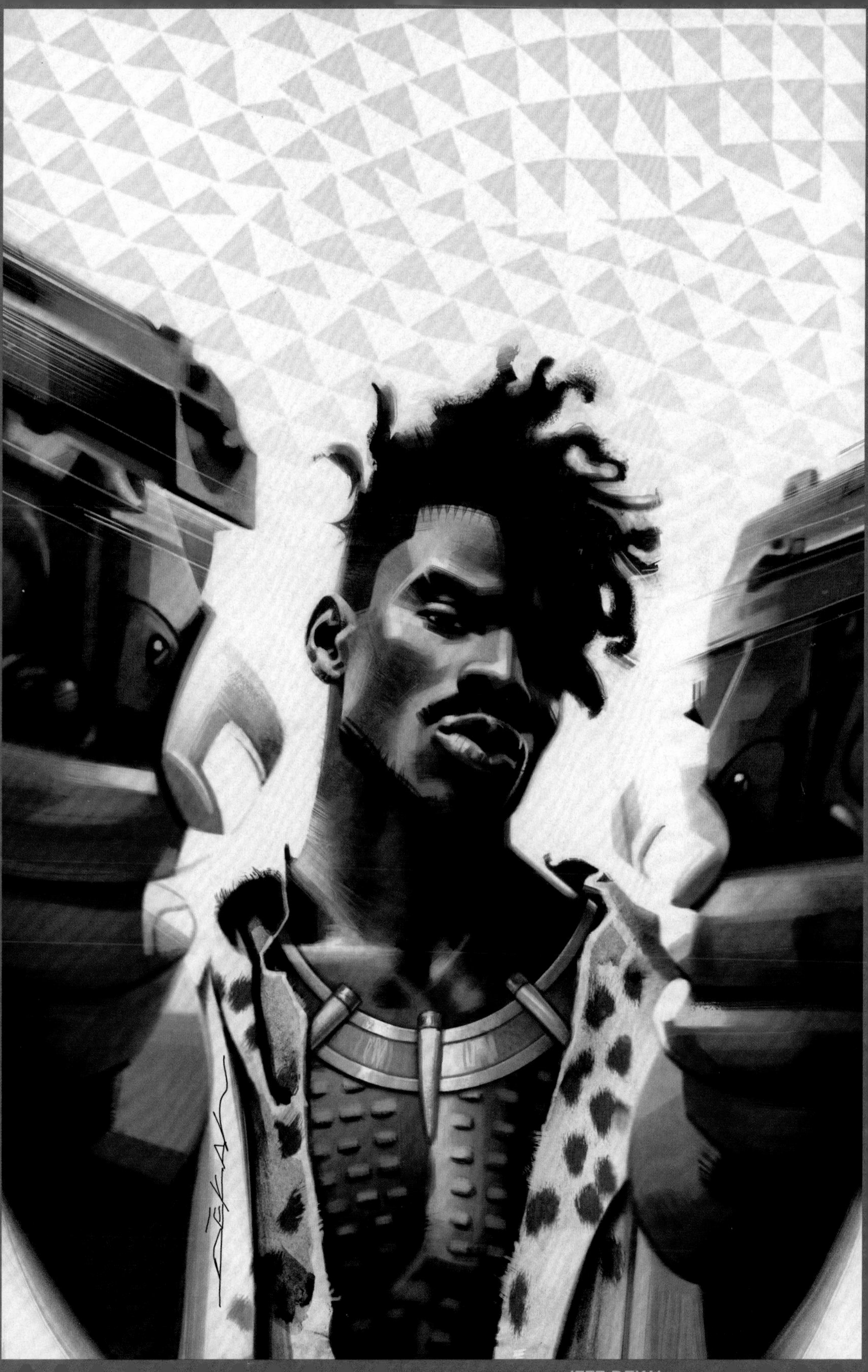

#2 VARIANT BY JEFF DEKAL

5

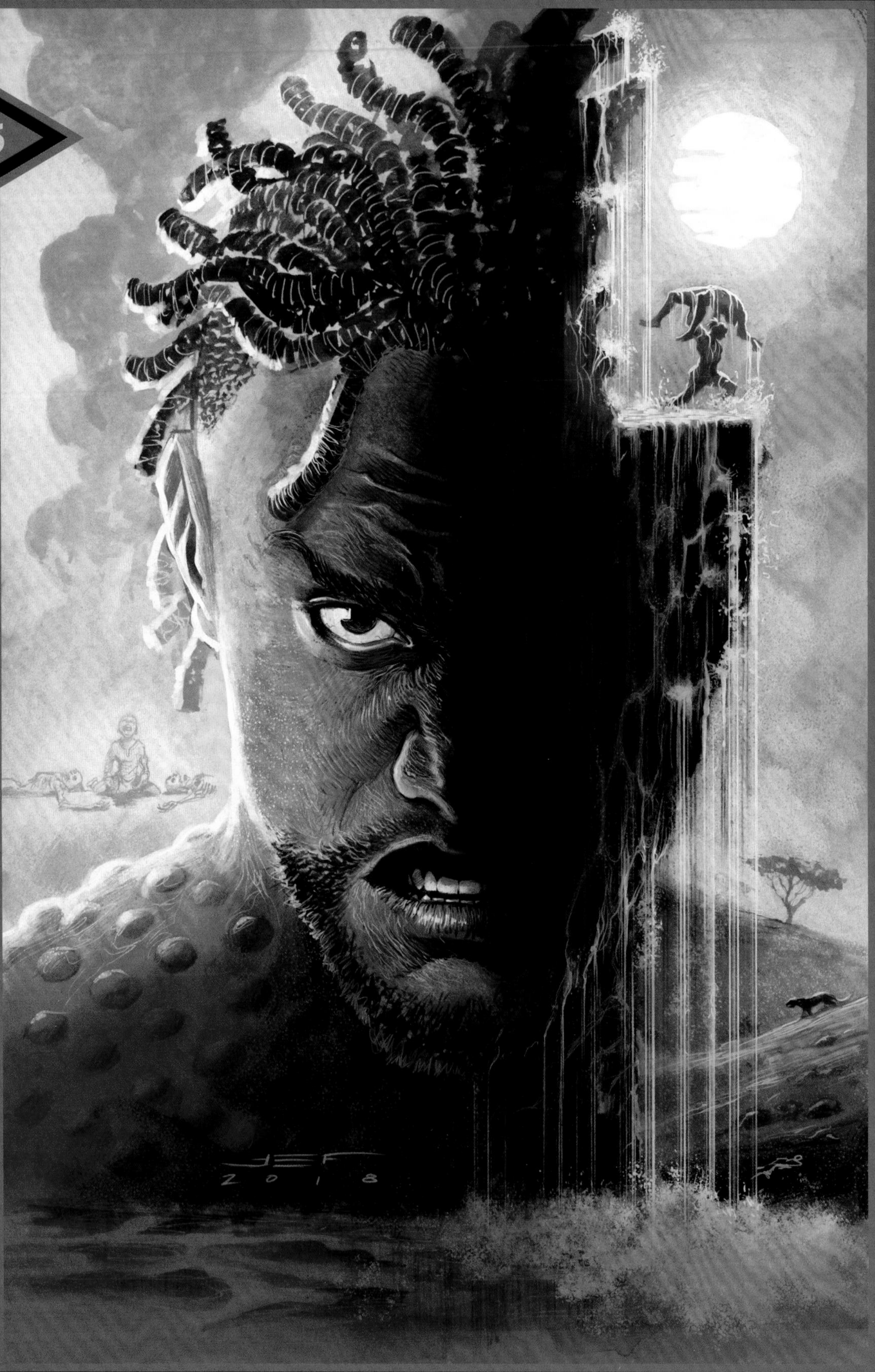

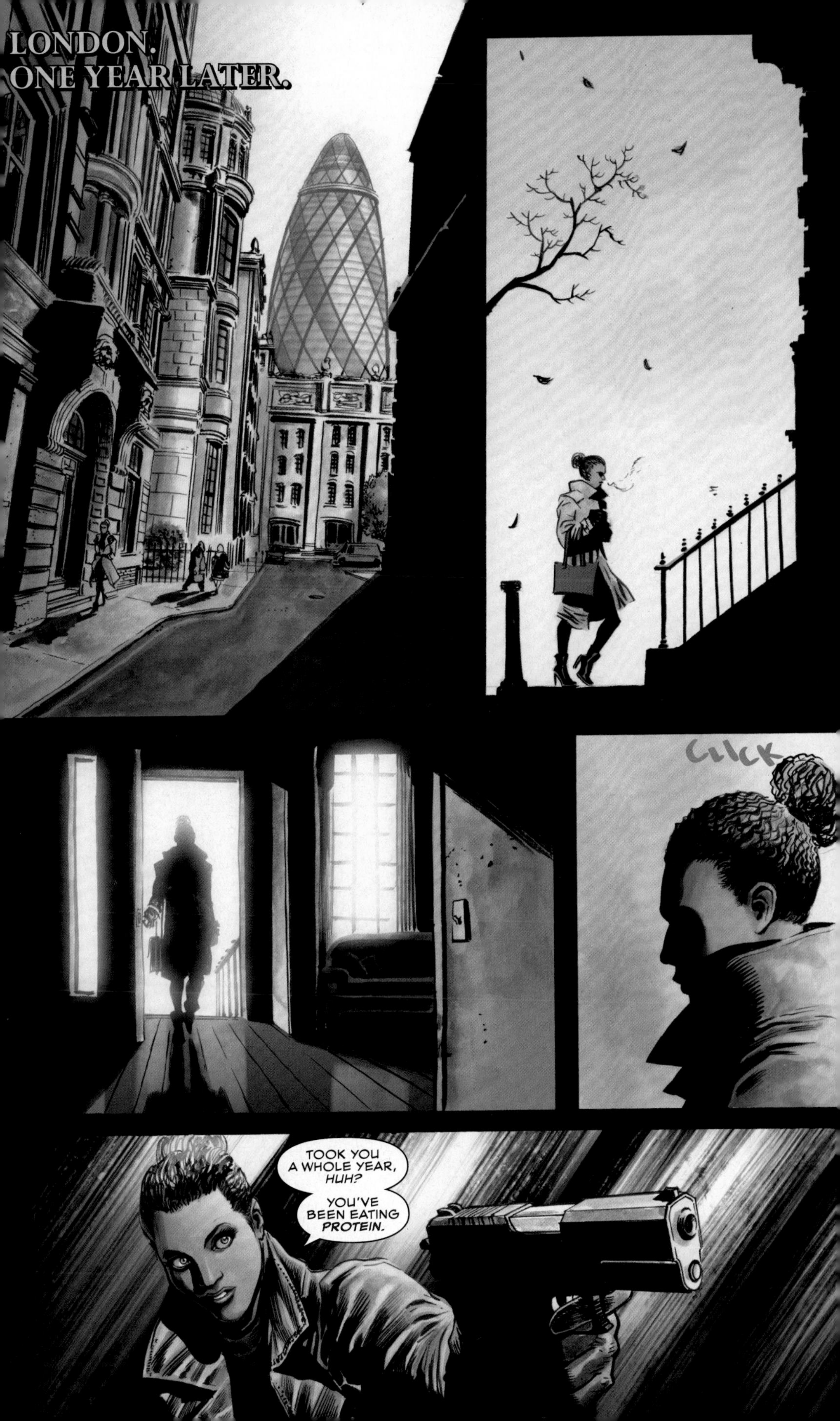
LONDON.
ONE YEAR LATER.
CLICK
TOOK YOU A WHOLE YEAR, HUH?
YOU'VE BEEN EATING PROTEIN.

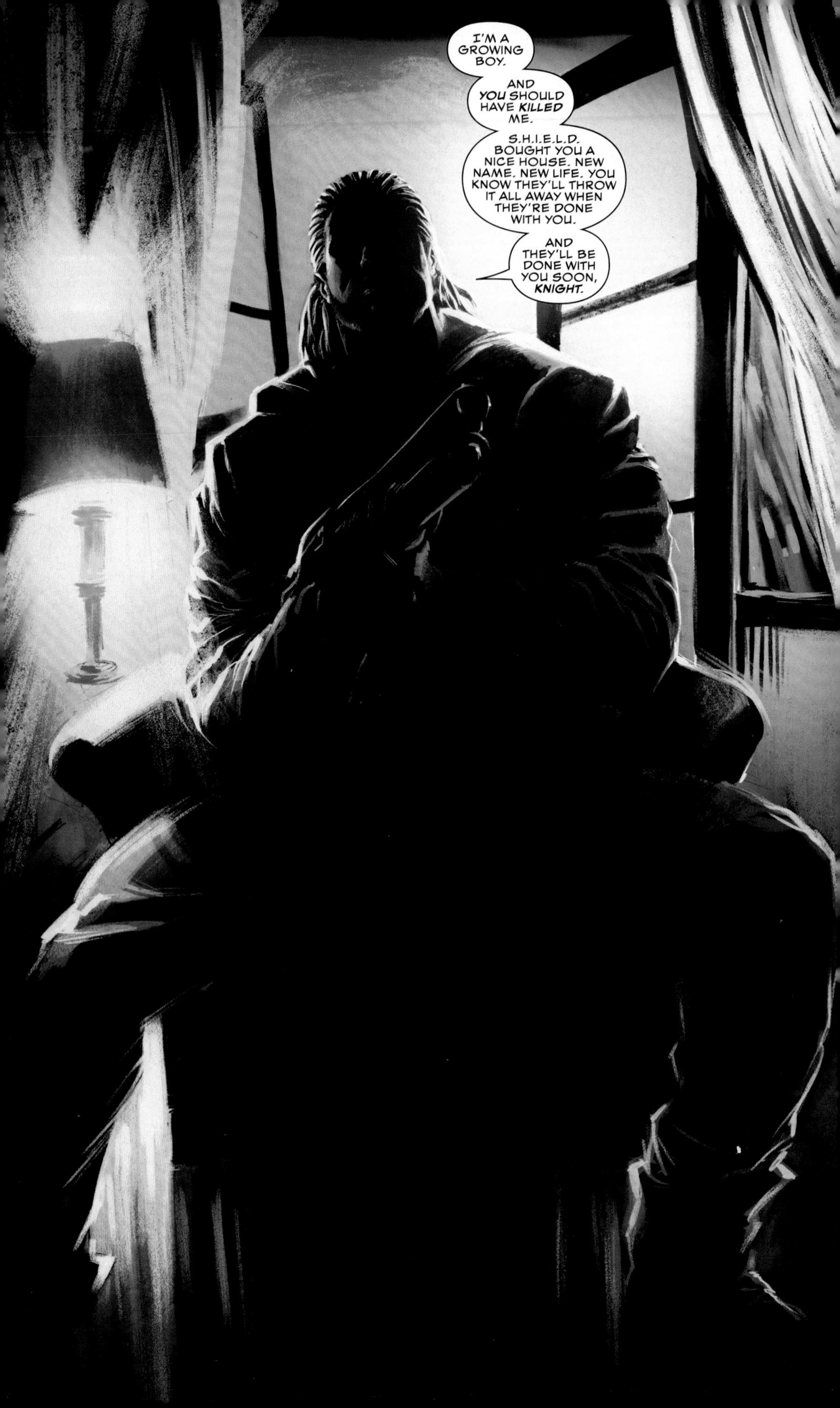

I'M A GROWING BOY.
AND YOU SHOULD HAVE KILLED ME.
S.H.I.E.L.D. BOUGHT YOU A NICE HOUSE. NEW NAME. NEW LIFE. YOU KNOW THEY'LL THROW IT ALL AWAY WHEN THEY'RE DONE WITH YOU.
AND THEY'LL BE DONE WITH YOU SOON, KNIGHT.

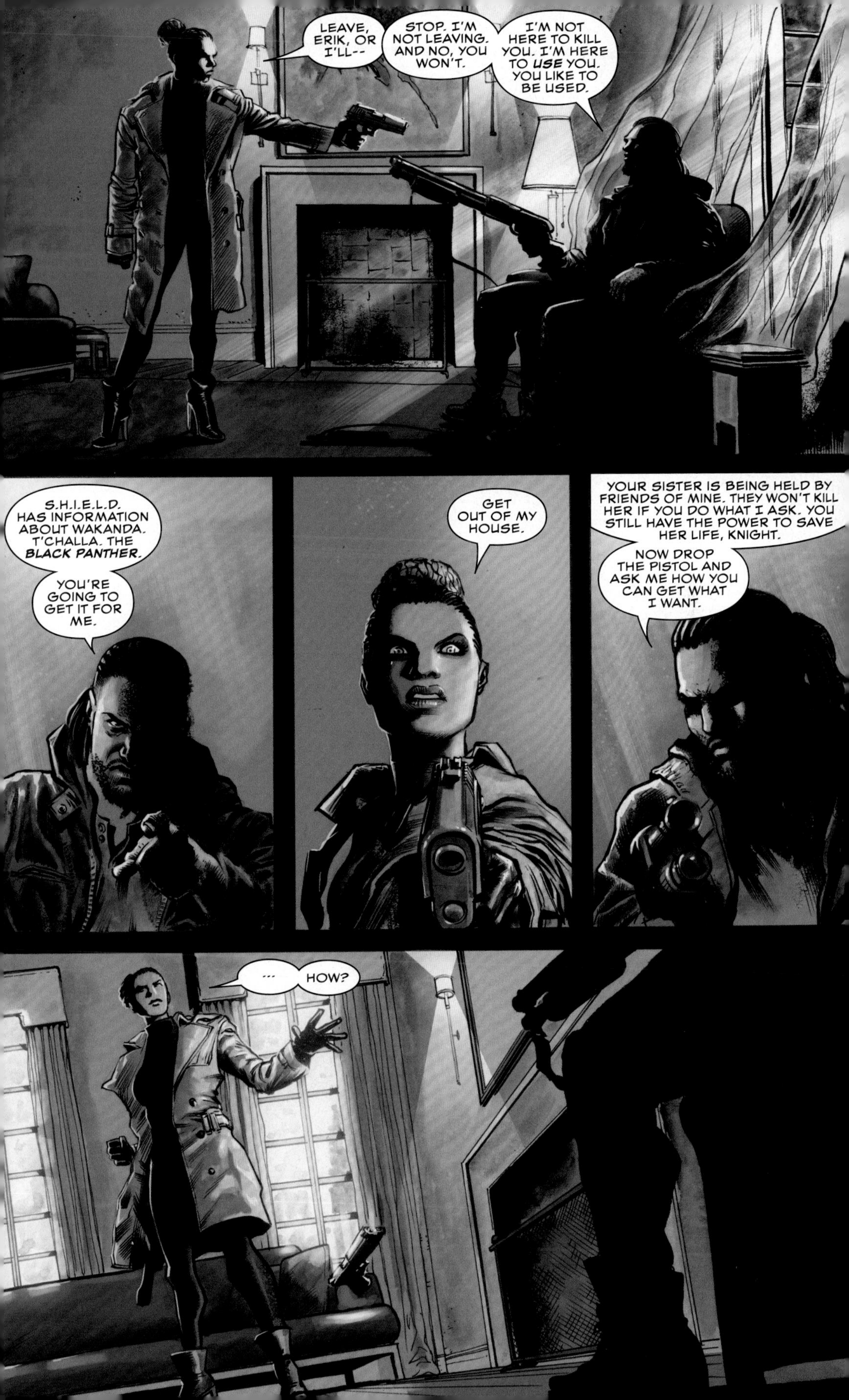
LEAVE, ERIK, OR I'LL--
STOP. I'M NOT LEAVING. AND NO, YOU WON'T.
I'M NOT HERE TO KILL YOU. I'M HERE TO USE YOU. YOU LIKE TO BE USED.
S.H.I.E.L.D. HAS INFORMATION ABOUT WAKANDA. T'CHALLA. THE BLACK PANTHER.
YOU'RE GOING TO GET IT FOR ME.
GET OUT OF MY HOUSE.
YOUR SISTER IS BEING HELD BY FRIENDS OF MINE. THEY WON'T KILL HER IF YOU DO WHAT I ASK. YOU STILL HAVE THE POWER TO SAVE HER LIFE, KNIGHT.
NOW DROP THE PISTOL AND ASK ME HOW YOU CAN GET WHAT I WANT.
...
HOW?

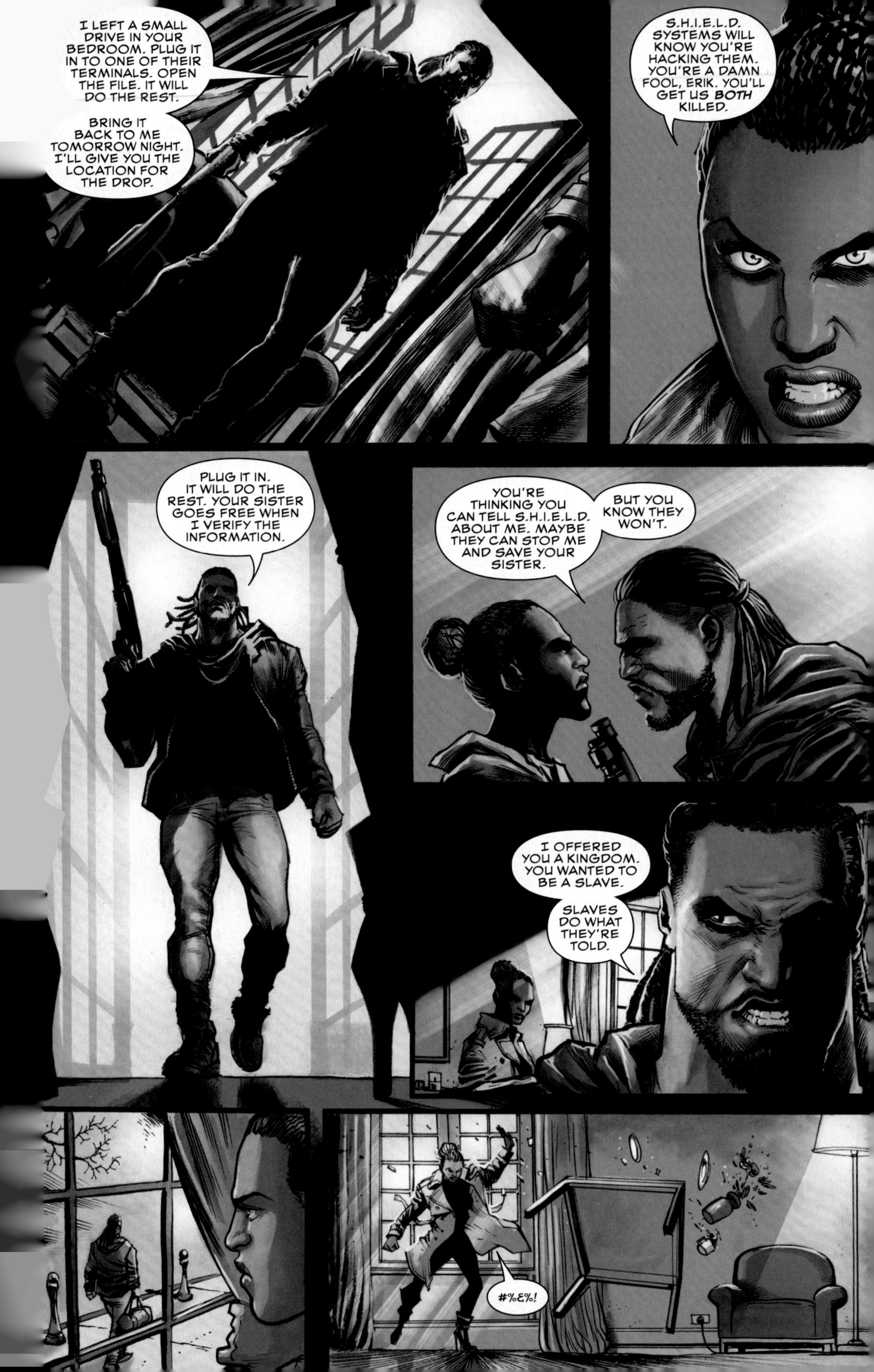
I LEFT A SMALL DRIVE IN YOUR BEDROOM. PLUG IT IN TO ONE OF THEIR TERMINALS. OPEN THE FILE. IT WILL DO THE REST.
BRING IT BACK TO ME TOMORROW NIGHT. I'LL GIVE YOU THE LOCATION FOR THE DROP.
S.H.I.E.L.D. SYSTEMS WILL KNOW YOU'RE HACKING THEM. YOU'RE A DAMN FOOL, ERIK. YOU'LL GET US BOTH KILLED.
PLUG IT IN. IT WILL DO THE REST. YOUR SISTER GOES FREE WHEN I VERIFY THE INFORMATION.
YOU'RE THINKING YOU CAN TELL S.H.I.E.L.D. ABOUT ME. MAYBE THEY CAN STOP ME AND SAVE YOUR SISTER.
BUT YOU KNOW THEY WON'T.
I OFFERED YOU A KINGDOM. YOU WANTED TO BE A SLAVE.
SLAVES DO WHAT THEY'RE TOLD.
#%&%!

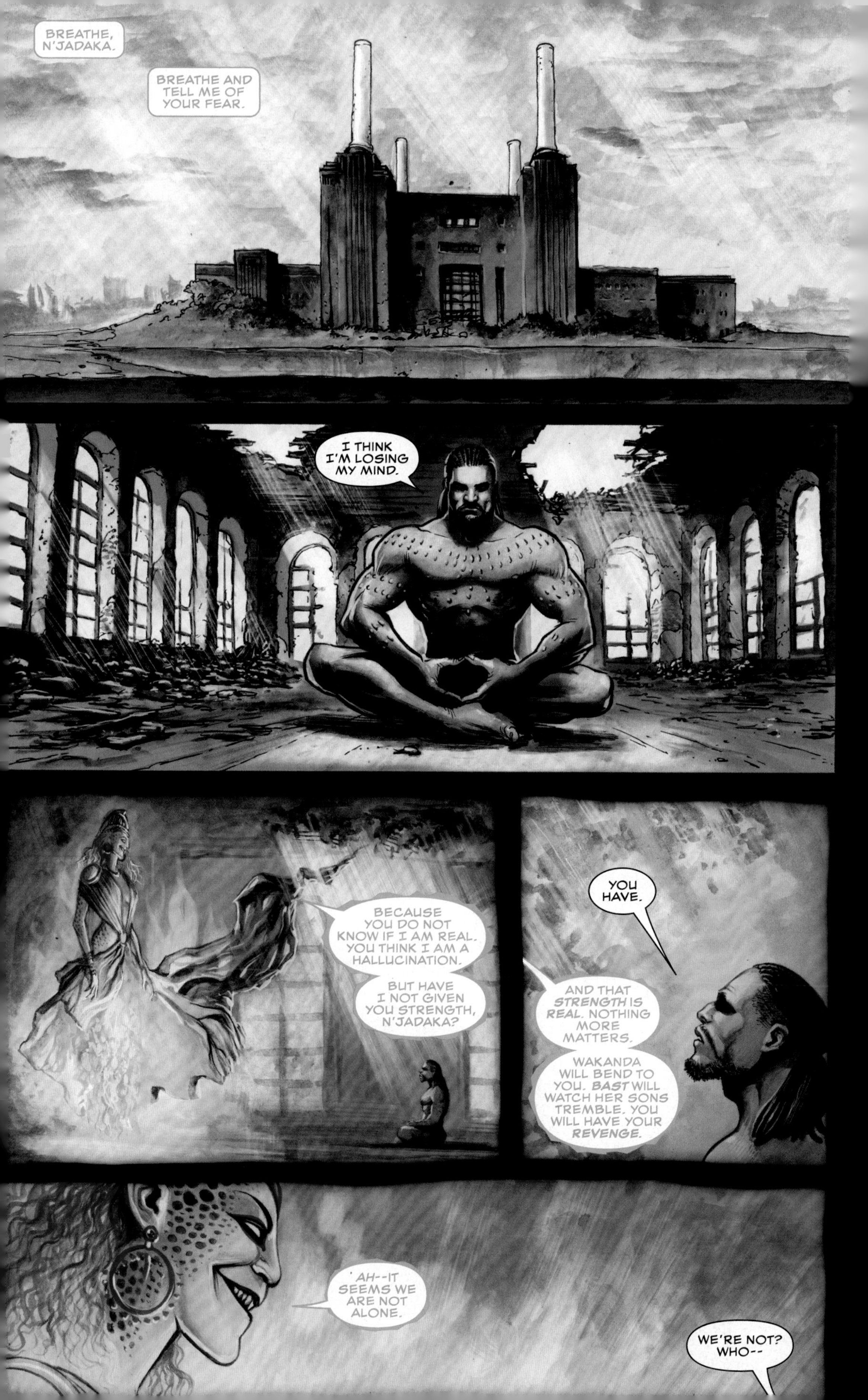
BREATHE, N'JADAKA.
BREATHE AND TELL ME OF YOUR FEAR.
I THINK I'M LOSING MY MIND.
BECAUSE YOU DO NOT KNOW IF I AM REAL. YOU THINK I AM A HALLUCINATION.
BUT HAVE I NOT GIVEN YOU STRENGTH, N'JADAKA?
YOU HAVE.
AND THAT STRENGTH IS REAL. NOTHING MORE MATTERS.
WAKANDA WILL BEND TO YOU. BAST WILL WATCH HER SONS TREMBLE. YOU WILL HAVE YOUR REVENGE.
'AH--IT SEEMS WE ARE NOT ALONE.
WE'RE NOT? WHO--

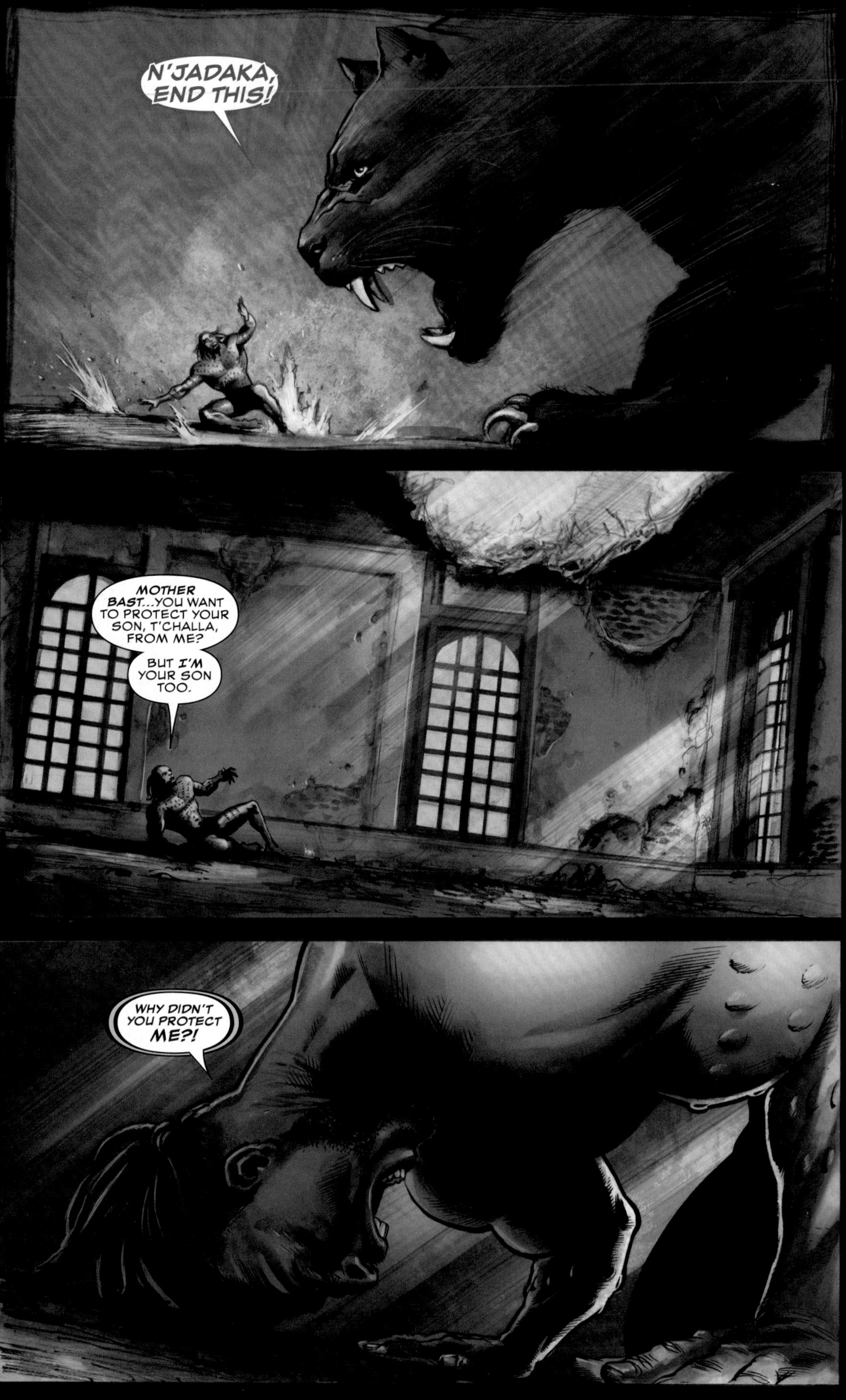
N'JADAKA, END THIS!
MOTHER BAST...YOU WANT TO PROTECT YOUR SON, T'CHALLA, FROM ME?
BUT I'M YOUR SON TOO.
WHY DIDN'T YOU PROTECT ME?!

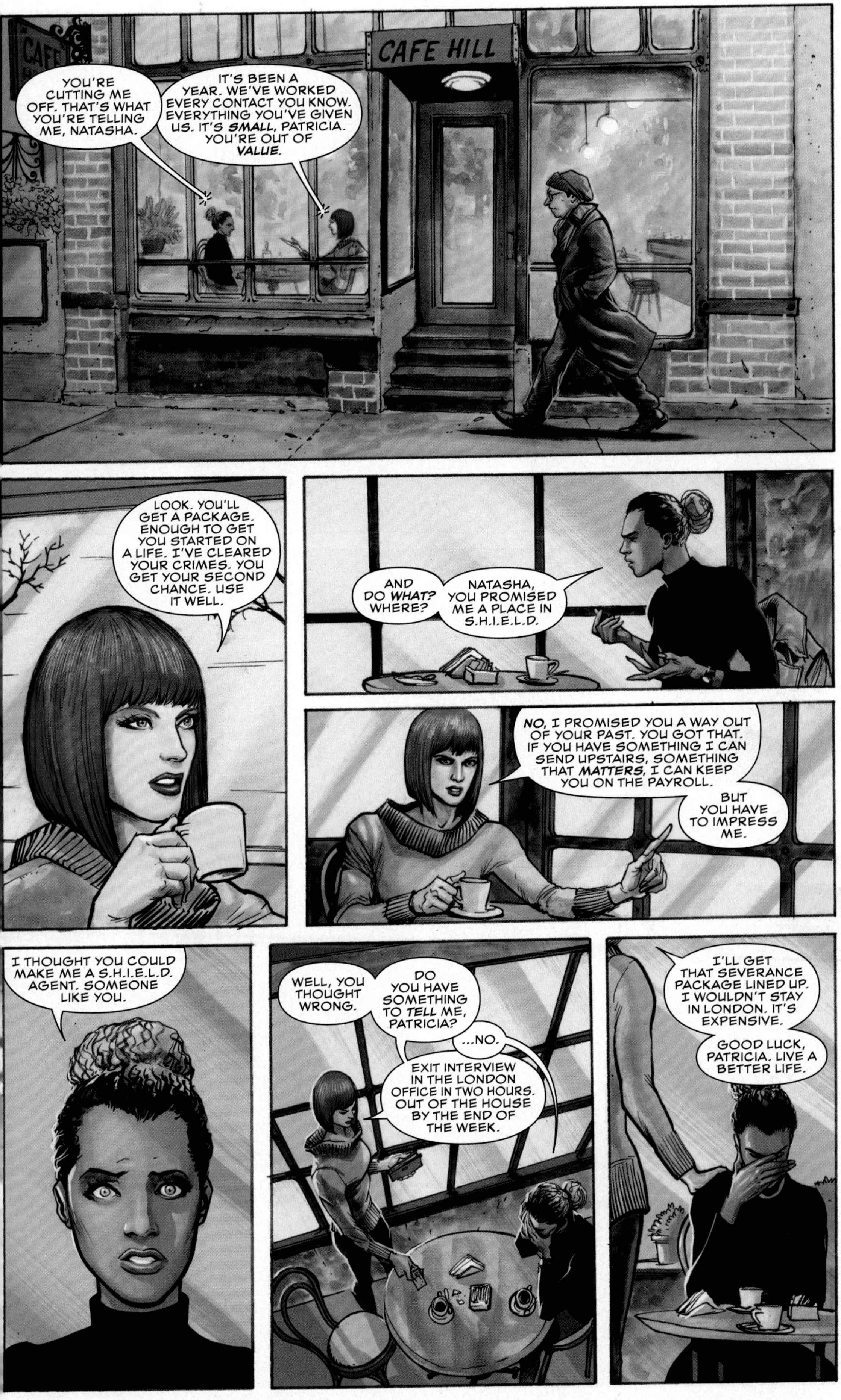
CAFE
CAFE HILL
YOU'RE CUTTING ME OFF. THAT'S WHAT YOU'RE TELLING ME, NATASHA.
IT'S BEEN A YEAR. WE'VE WORKED EVERY CONTACT YOU KNOW. EVERYTHING YOU'VE GIVEN US. IT'S SMALL, PATRICIA. YOU'RE OUT OF VALUE.
LOOK. YOU'LL GET A PACKAGE. ENOUGH TO GET YOU STARTED ON A LIFE. I'VE CLEARED YOUR CRIMES. YOU GET YOUR SECOND CHANCE. USE IT WELL.
NATASHA, YOU PROMISED ME A PLACE IN S.H.I.E.L.D.
AND DO WHAT? WHERE?
NO, I PROMISED YOU A WAY OUT OF YOUR PAST. YOU GOT THAT. IF YOU HAVE SOMETHING I CAN SEND UPSTAIRS, SOMETHING THAT MATTERS, I CAN KEEP YOU ON THE PAYROLL.
BUT YOU HAVE TO IMPRESS ME.
I THOUGHT YOU COULD MAKE ME A S.H.I.E.L.D. AGENT. SOMEONE LIKE YOU.
WELL, YOU THOUGHT WRONG.
DO YOU HAVE SOMETHING TO TELL ME, PATRICIA?
...NO.
EXIT INTERVIEW IN THE LONDON OFFICE IN TWO HOURS. OUT OF THE HOUSE BY THE END OF THE WEEK.
I'LL GET THAT SEVERANCE PACKAGE LINED UP. I WOULDN'T STAY IN LONDON. IT'S EXPENSIVE.
GOOD LUCK, PATRICIA. LIVE A BETTER LIFE.

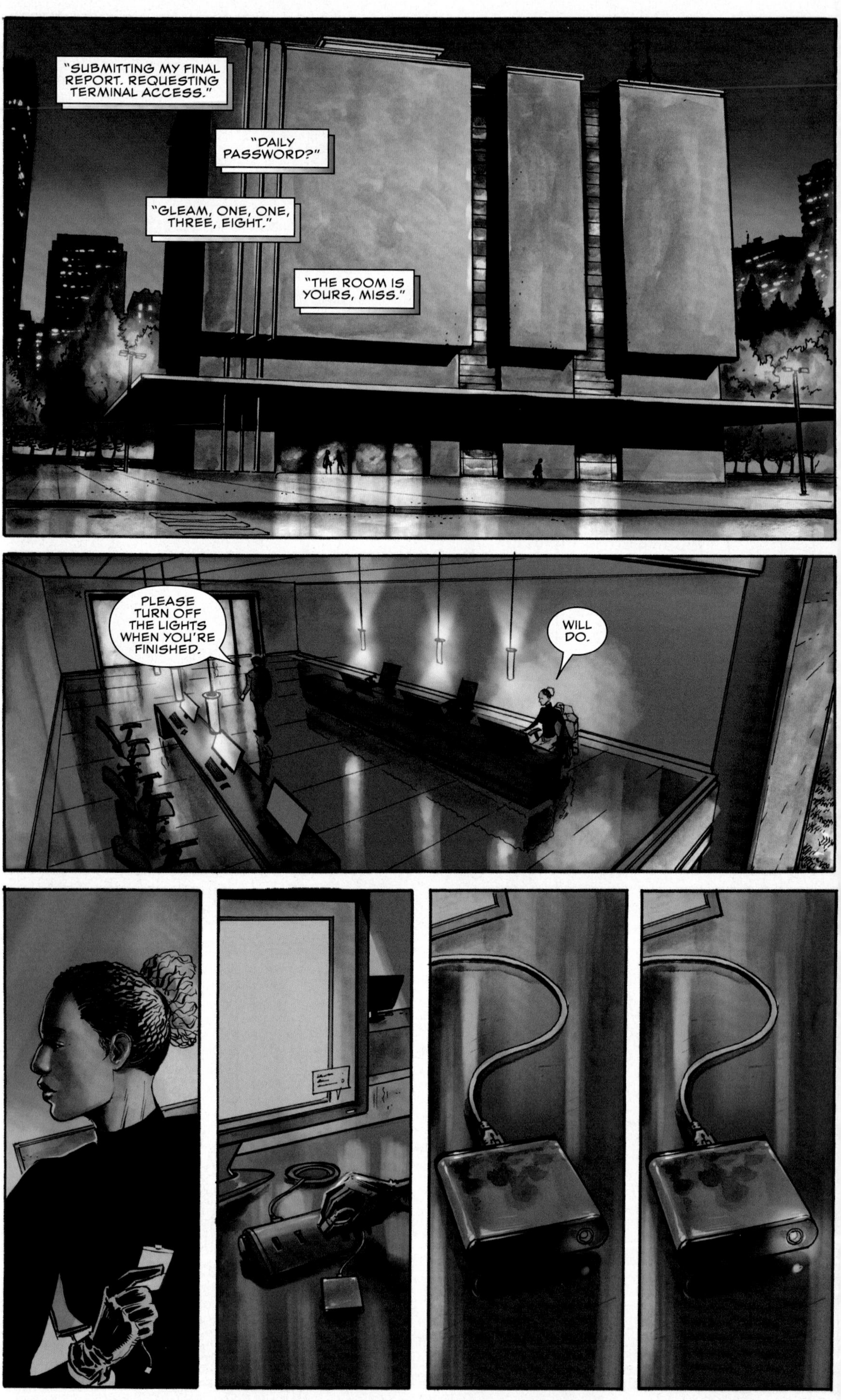
"SUBMITTING MY FINAL REPORT. REQUESTING TERMINAL ACCESS."
"DAILY PASSWORD?"
"GLEAM, ONE, ONE, THREE, EIGHT."
"THE ROOM IS YOURS, MISS."
PLEASE TURN OFF THE LIGHTS WHEN YOU'RE FINISHED.
WILL DO.

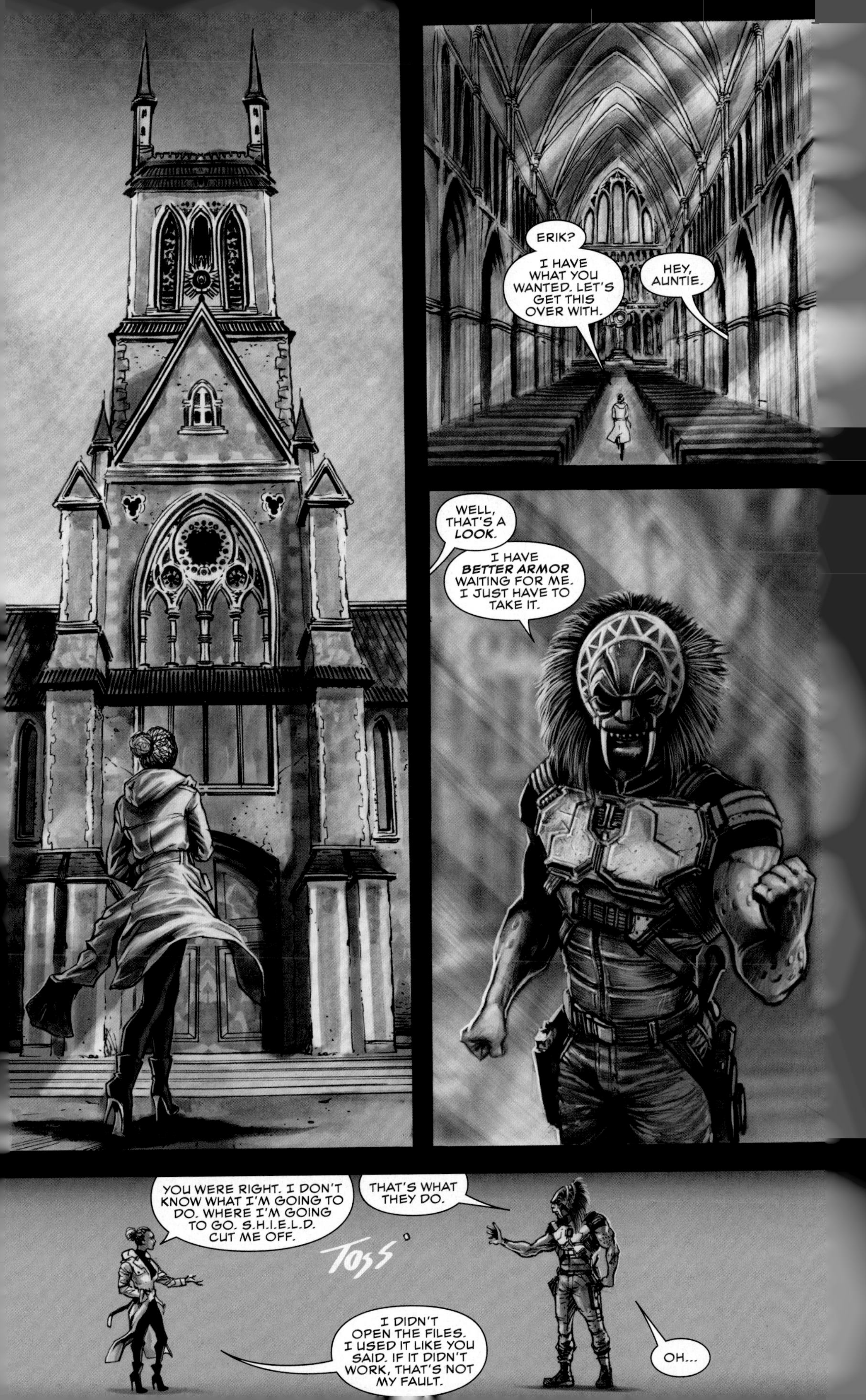
ERIK?
I HAVE WHAT YOU WANTED. LET'S GET THIS OVER WITH.
HEY, AUNTIE.
WELL, THAT'S A LOOK.
I HAVE BETTER ARMOR WAITING FOR ME. I JUST HAVE TO TAKE IT.
YOU WERE RIGHT. I DON'T KNOW WHAT I'M GOING TO DO. WHERE I'M GOING TO GO. S.H.I.E.L.D. CUT ME OFF.
THAT'S WHAT THEY DO.
TOSS
I DIDN'T OPEN THE FILES. I USED IT LIKE YOU SAID. IF IT DIDN'T WORK, THAT'S NOT MY FAULT.
OH...

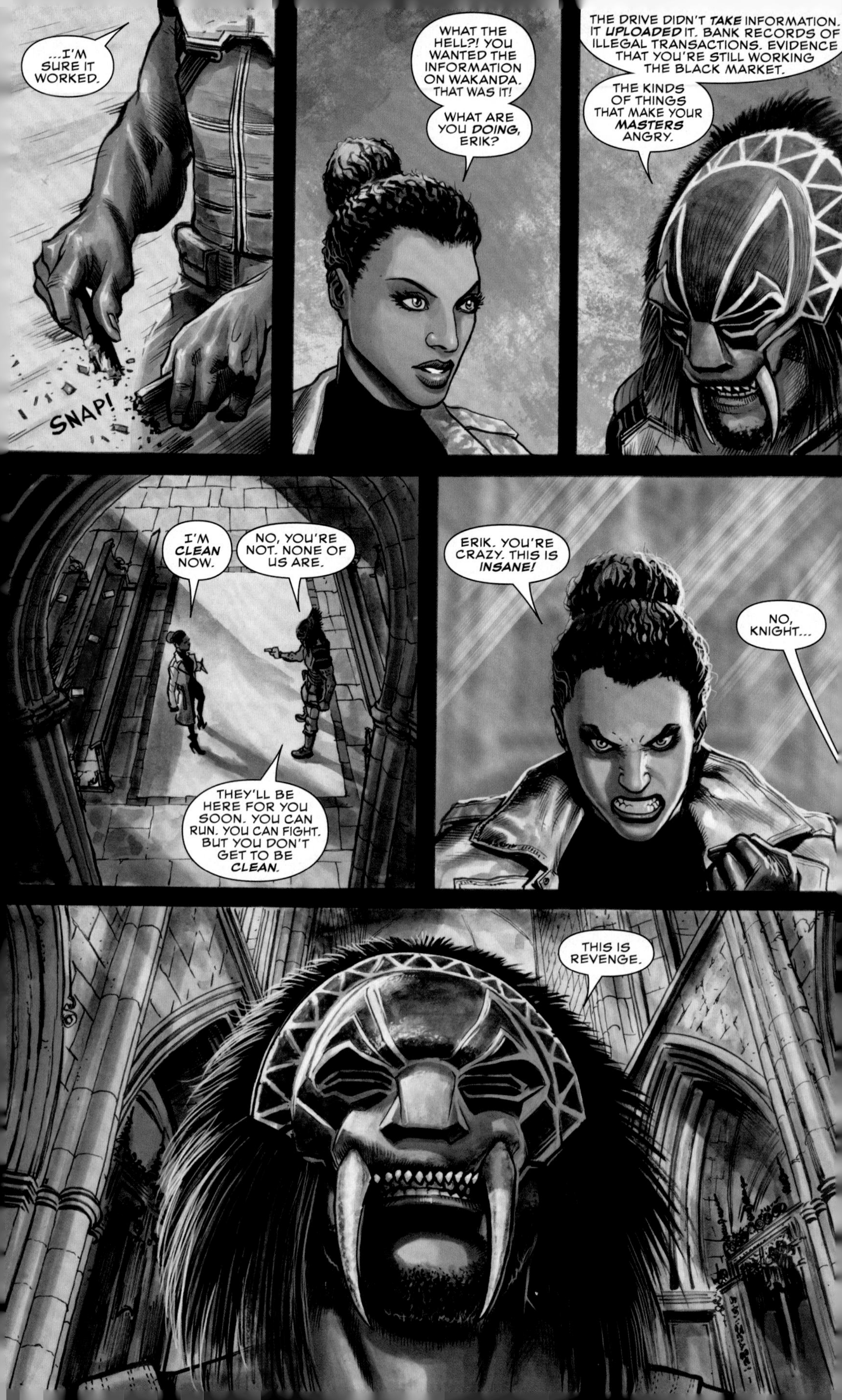
...I'M SURE IT WORKED.
SNAP!
WHAT THE HELL?! YOU WANTED THE INFORMATION ON WAKANDA. THAT WAS IT!
WHAT ARE YOU DOING, ERIK?
THE DRIVE DIDN'T TAKE INFORMATION. IT UPLOADED IT. BANK RECORDS OF ILLEGAL TRANSACTIONS. EVIDENCE THAT YOU'RE STILL WORKING THE BLACK MARKET.
THE KINDS OF THINGS THAT MAKE YOUR MASTERS ANGRY.
I'M CLEAN NOW.
NO, YOU'RE NOT. NONE OF US ARE.
THEY'LL BE HERE FOR YOU SOON. YOU CAN RUN. YOU CAN FIGHT. BUT YOU DON'T GET TO BE CLEAN.
ERIK. YOU'RE CRAZY. THIS IS INSANE!
NO, KNIGHT...
THIS IS REVENGE.

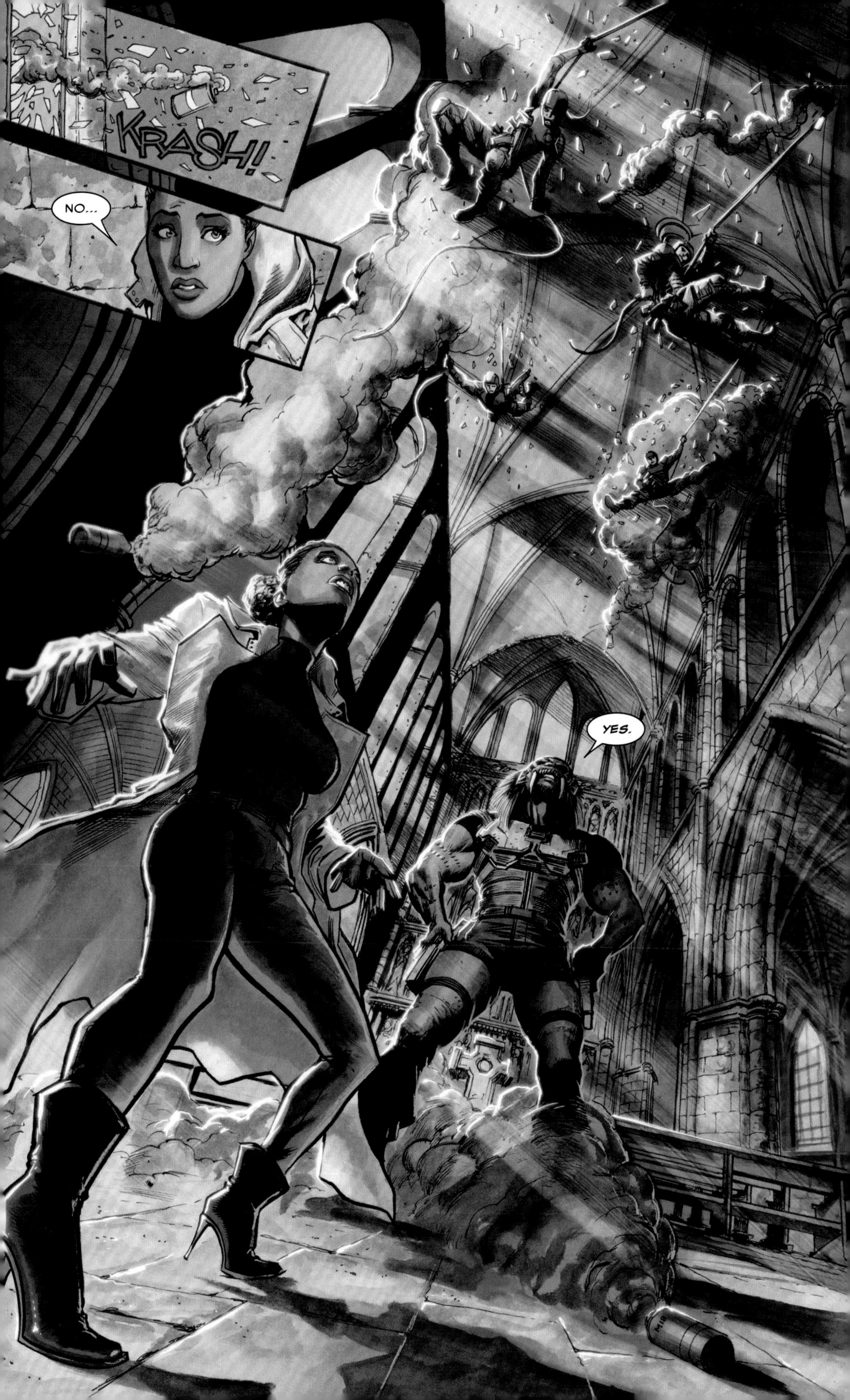
KRASH!
NO...
YES.

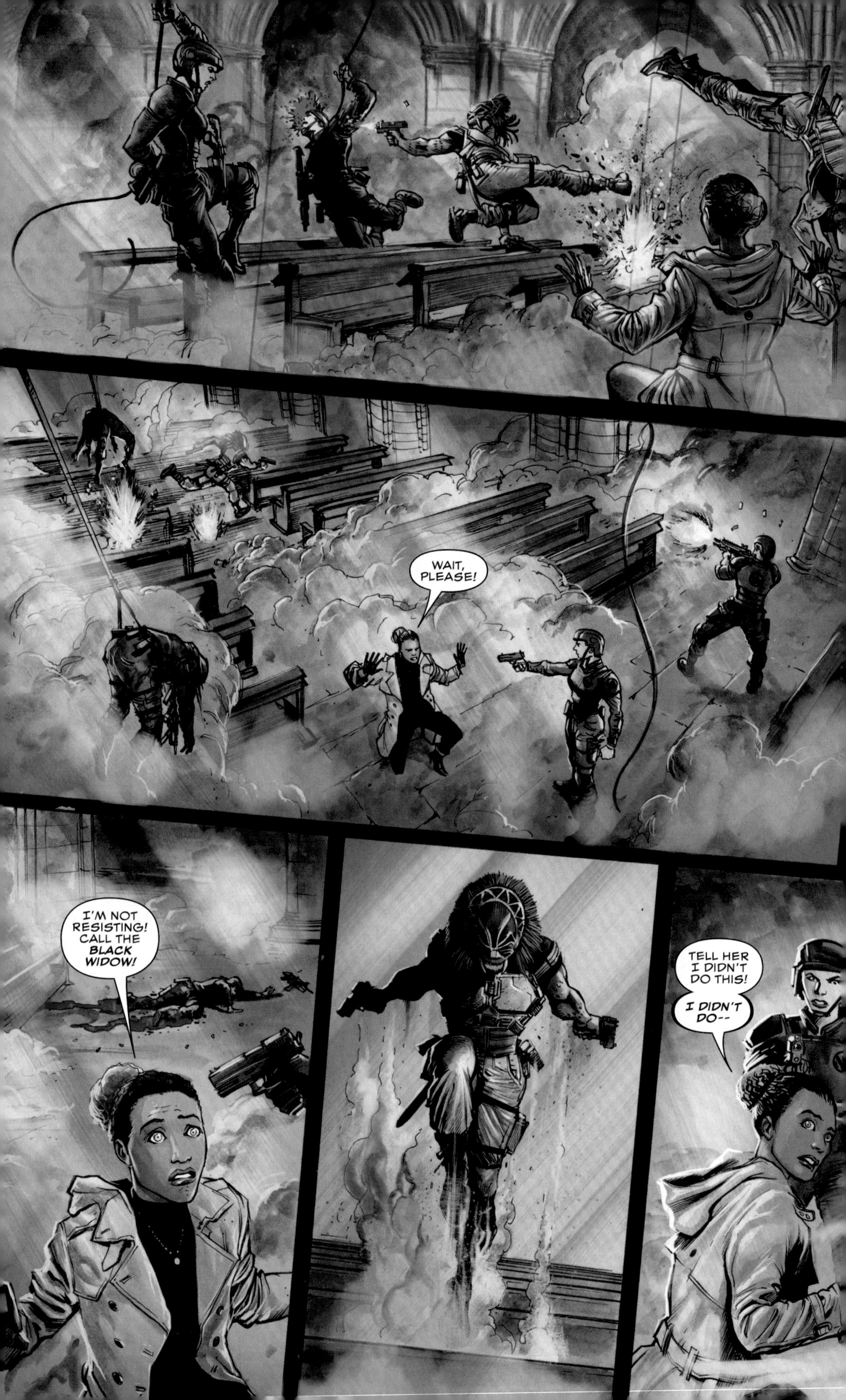
WAIT, PLEASE!
I'M NOT RESISTING! CALL THE BLACK WIDOW!
TELL HER I DIDN'T DO THIS!
I DIDN'T DO--

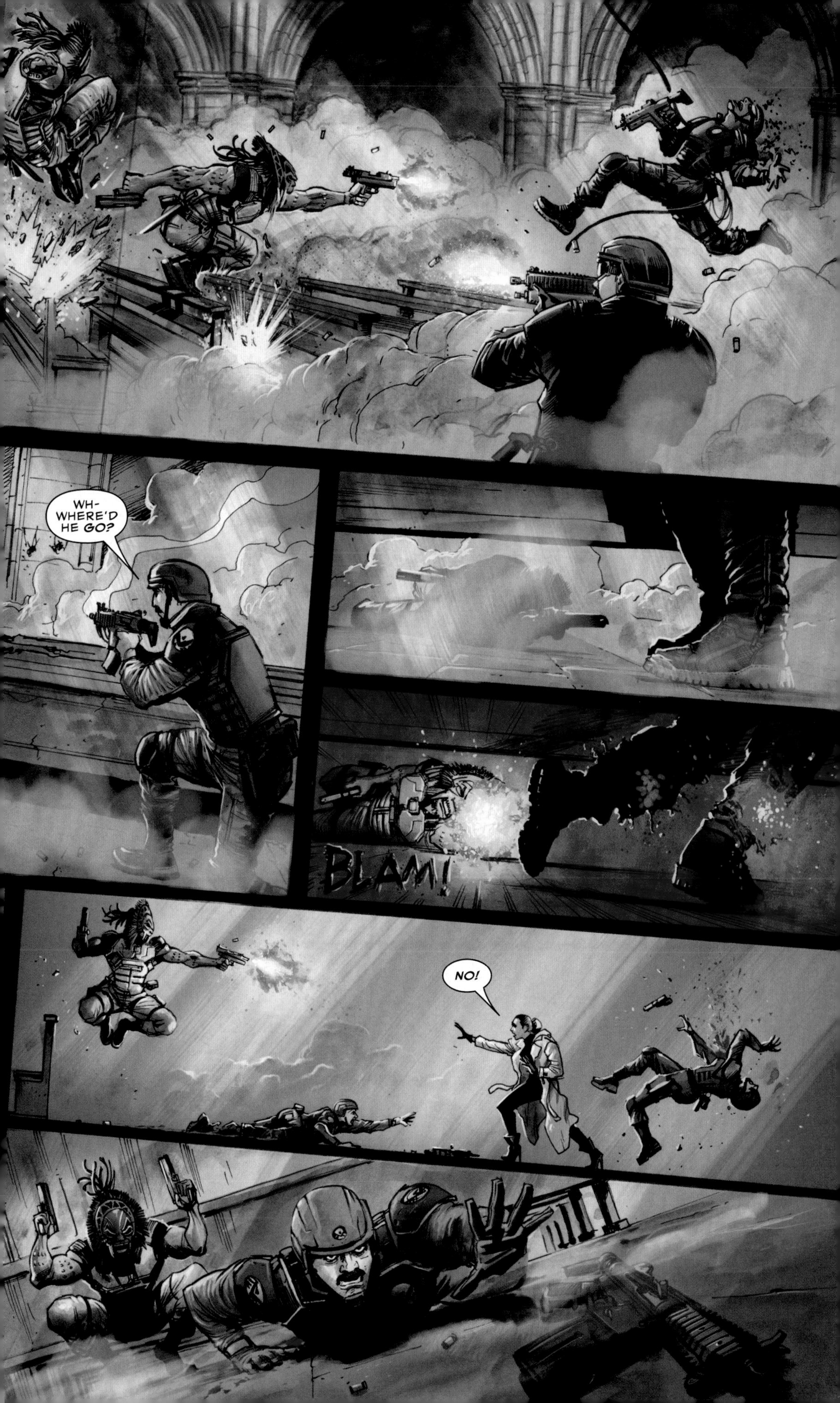
WH- WHERE'D HE GO?
BLAM!
NO!

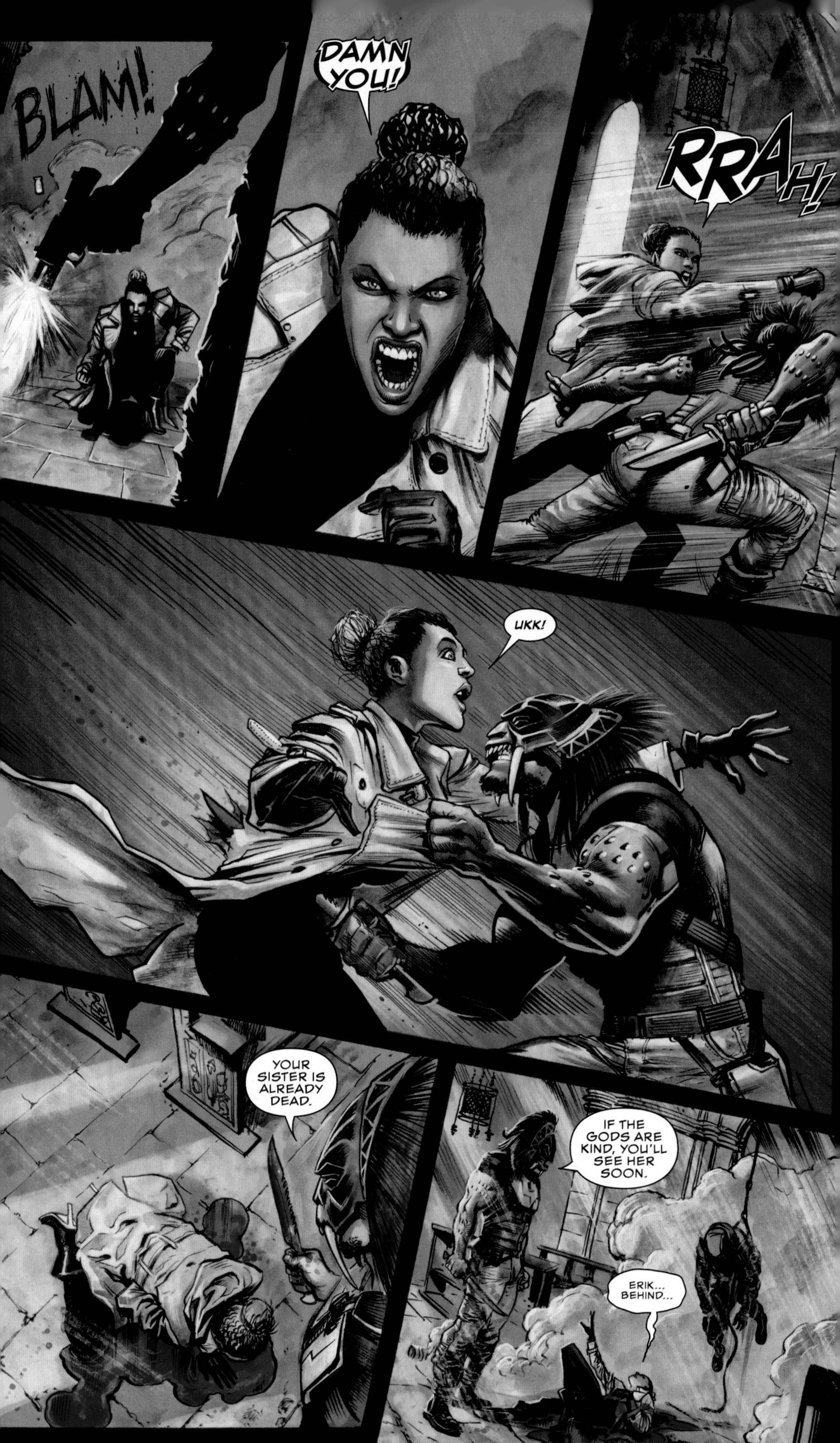
BLAM!
DAMN YOU!
RRAH!
UKK!
YOUR SISTER IS ALREADY DEAD.
IF THE GODS ARE KIND, YOU'LL SEE HER SOON.
ERIK... BEHIND...

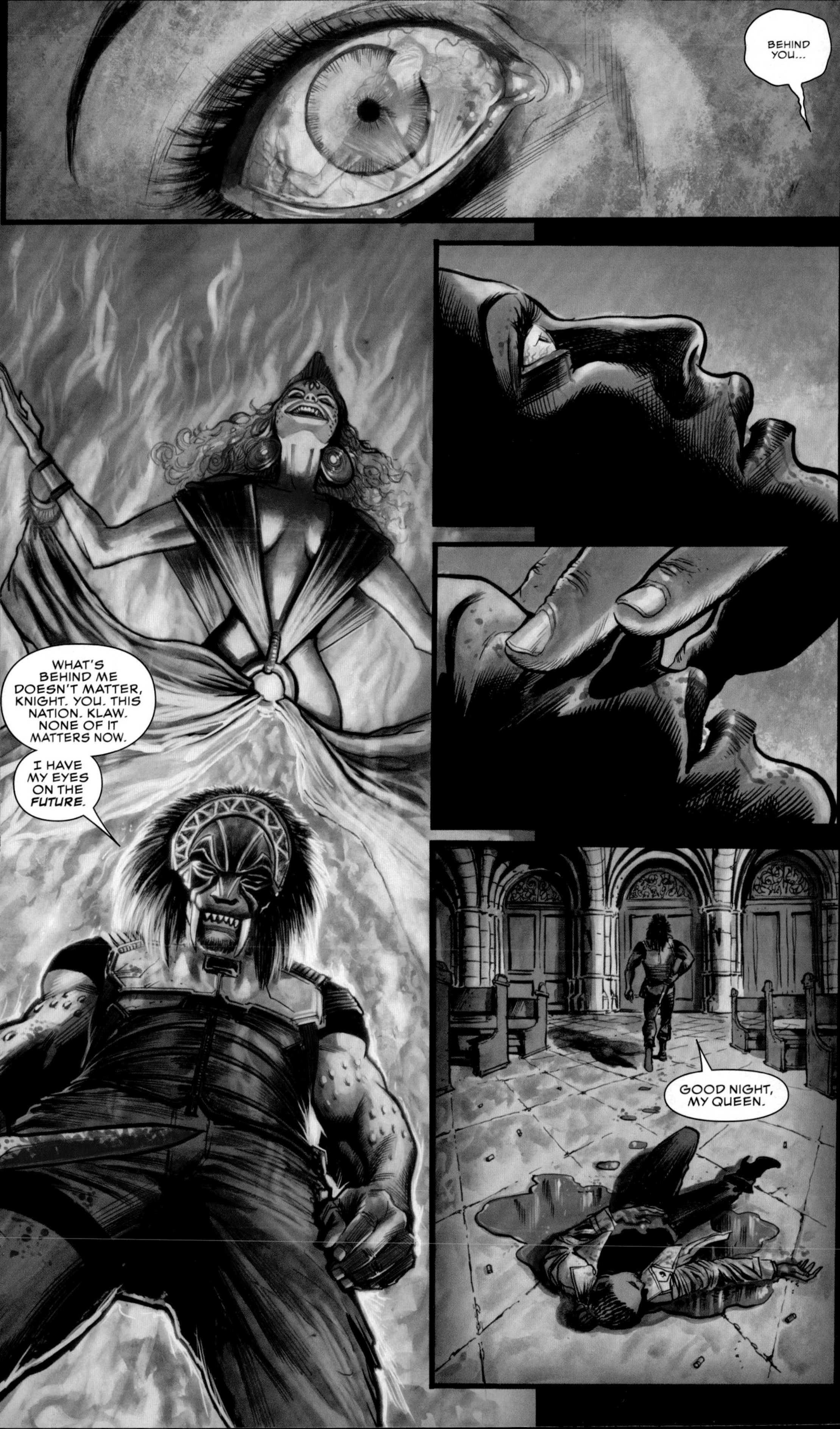
BEHIND YOU...
WHAT'S BEHIND ME DOESN'T MATTER, KNIGHT. YOU. THIS NATION. KLAW. NONE OF IT MATTERS NOW.
I HAVE MY EYES ON THE *FUTURE*.
GOOD NIGHT, MY QUEEN.

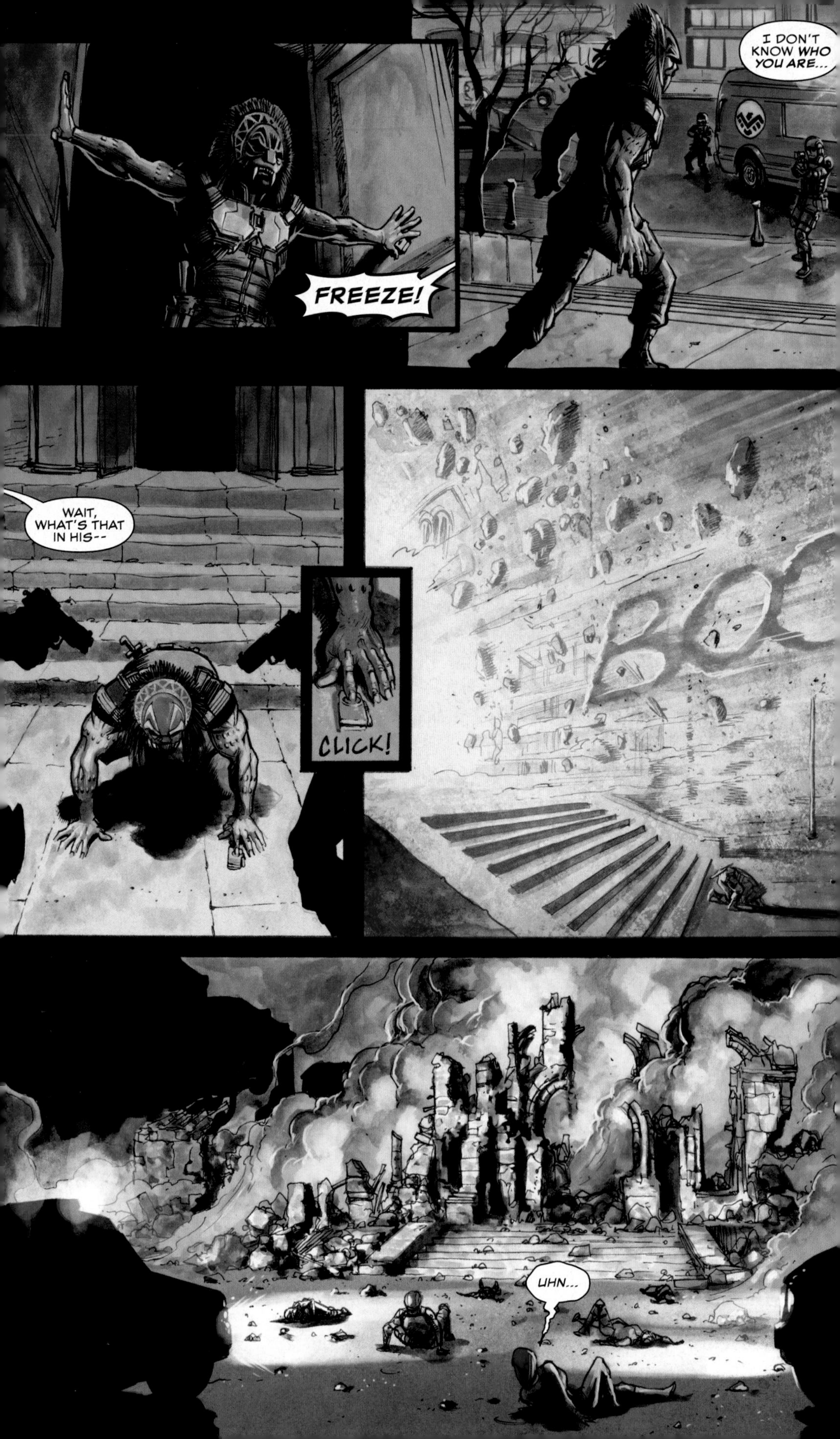
I DON'T KNOW WHO YOU ARE...
FREEZE!
WAIT, WHAT'S THAT IN HIS--
CLICK!
UHN...

...BUT YOU HAVE *THREE SECONDS* TO GET ON YOUR KNEES.

ONE.

TWO.

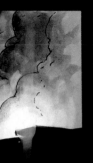

I NEED MEDEVAC ON MY LOCATION *NOW!*

PATRICIA, GOD...

WHOEVER THAT WAS IS GONE, MA'AM.

I ASSUMED. WHEREVER THAT SON OF A BITCH IS RUNNING--

--HE'D BETTER GO *FAR.*

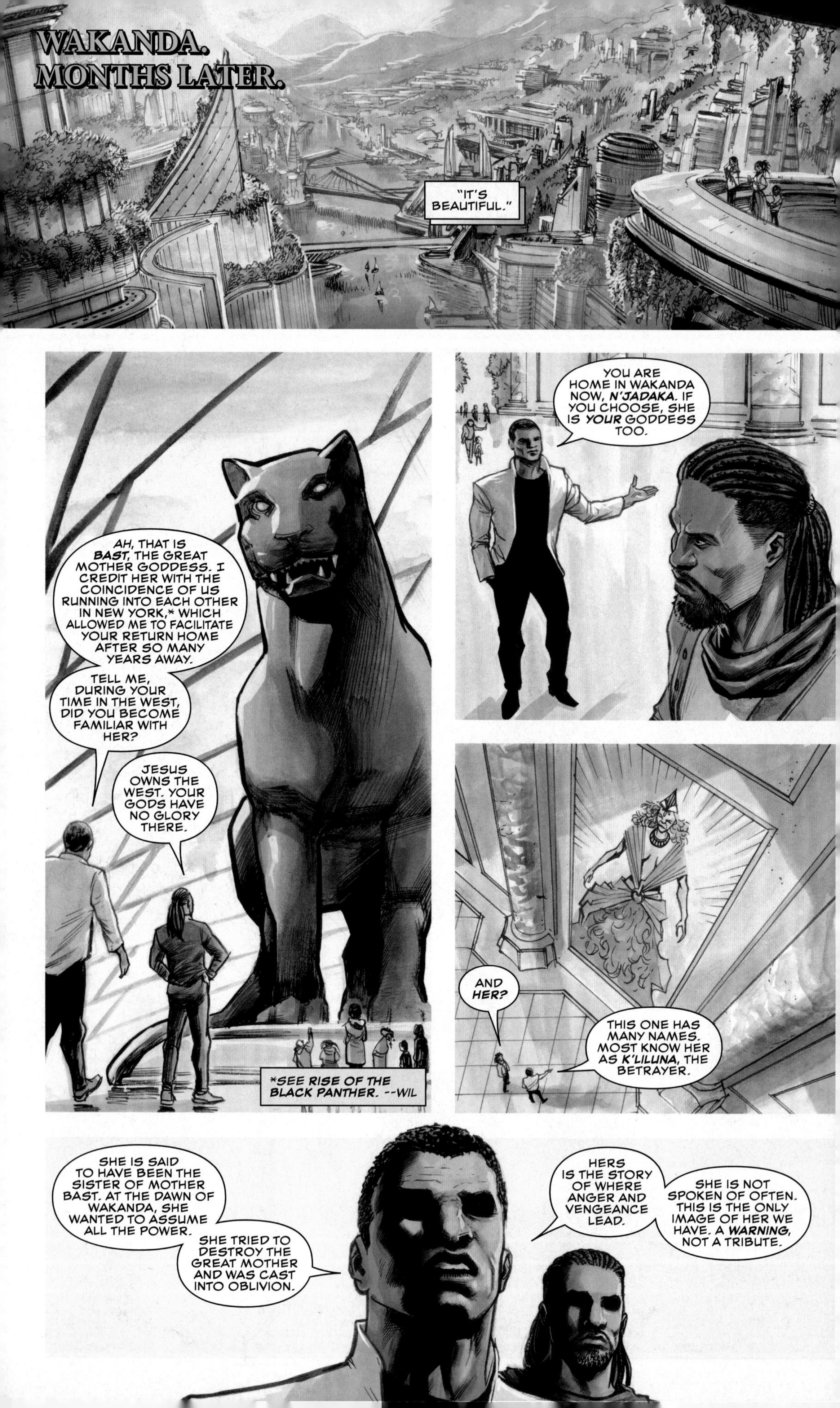
WAKANDA. MONTHS LATER.
"IT'S BEAUTIFUL."
AH, THAT IS BAST, THE GREAT MOTHER GODDESS. I CREDIT HER WITH THE COINCIDENCE OF US RUNNING INTO EACH OTHER IN NEW YORK,* WHICH ALLOWED ME TO FACILITATE YOUR RETURN HOME AFTER SO MANY YEARS AWAY.
TELL ME, DURING YOUR TIME IN THE WEST, DID YOU BECOME FAMILIAR WITH HER?
JESUS OWNS THE WEST. YOUR GODS HAVE NO GLORY THERE.
*SEE RISE OF THE BLACK PANTHER. --WIL
YOU ARE HOME IN WAKANDA NOW, N'JADAKA. IF YOU CHOOSE, SHE IS YOUR GODDESS TOO.
AND HER?
THIS ONE HAS MANY NAMES. MOST KNOW HER AS K'LILUNA, THE BETRAYER.
SHE IS SAID TO HAVE BEEN THE SISTER OF MOTHER BAST. AT THE DAWN OF WAKANDA, SHE WANTED TO ASSUME ALL THE POWER.
SHE TRIED TO DESTROY THE GREAT MOTHER AND WAS CAST INTO OBLIVION.
HERS IS THE STORY OF WHERE ANGER AND VENGEANCE LEAD.
SHE IS NOT SPOKEN OF OFTEN. THIS IS THE ONLY IMAGE OF HER WE HAVE. A WARNING, NOT A TRIBUTE.

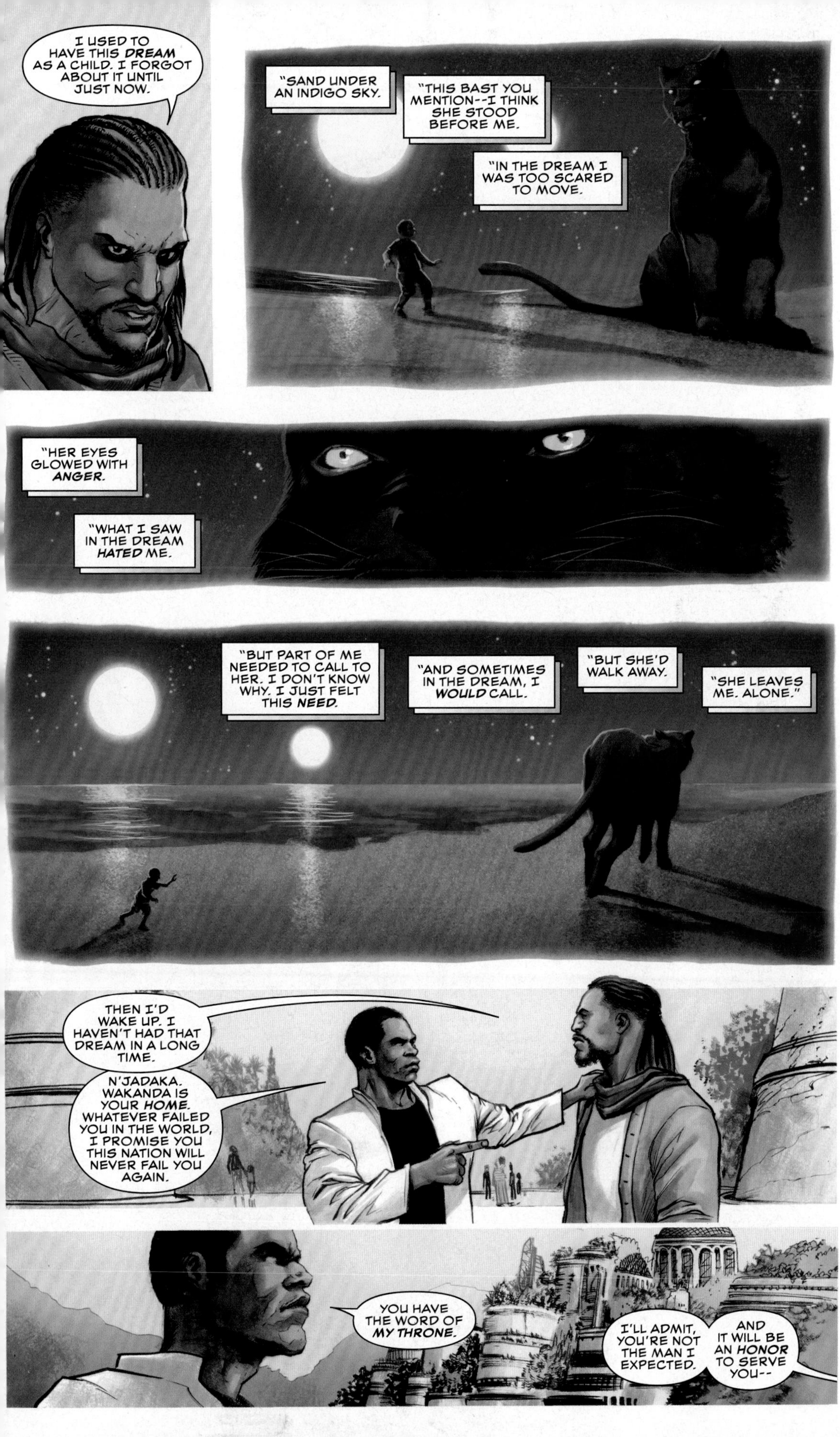
I USED TO HAVE THIS DREAM AS A CHILD. I FORGOT ABOUT IT UNTIL JUST NOW.
"SAND UNDER AN INDIGO SKY.
"THIS BAST YOU MENTION--I THINK SHE STOOD BEFORE ME.
"IN THE DREAM I WAS TOO SCARED TO MOVE.
"HER EYES GLOWED WITH ANGER.
"WHAT I SAW IN THE DREAM HATED ME.
"BUT PART OF ME NEEDED TO CALL TO HER. I DON'T KNOW WHY. I JUST FELT THIS NEED.
"AND SOMETIMES IN THE DREAM, I WOULD CALL.
"BUT SHE'D WALK AWAY.
"SHE LEAVES ME. ALONE."
THEN I'D WAKE UP. I HAVEN'T HAD THAT DREAM IN A LONG TIME.
N'JADAKA. WAKANDA IS YOUR HOME. WHATEVER FAILED YOU IN THE WORLD, I PROMISE YOU THIS NATION WILL NEVER FAIL YOU AGAIN.
YOU HAVE THE WORD OF MY THRONE.
I'LL ADMIT, YOU'RE NOT THE MAN I EXPECTED.
AND IT WILL BE AN HONOR TO SERVE YOU--

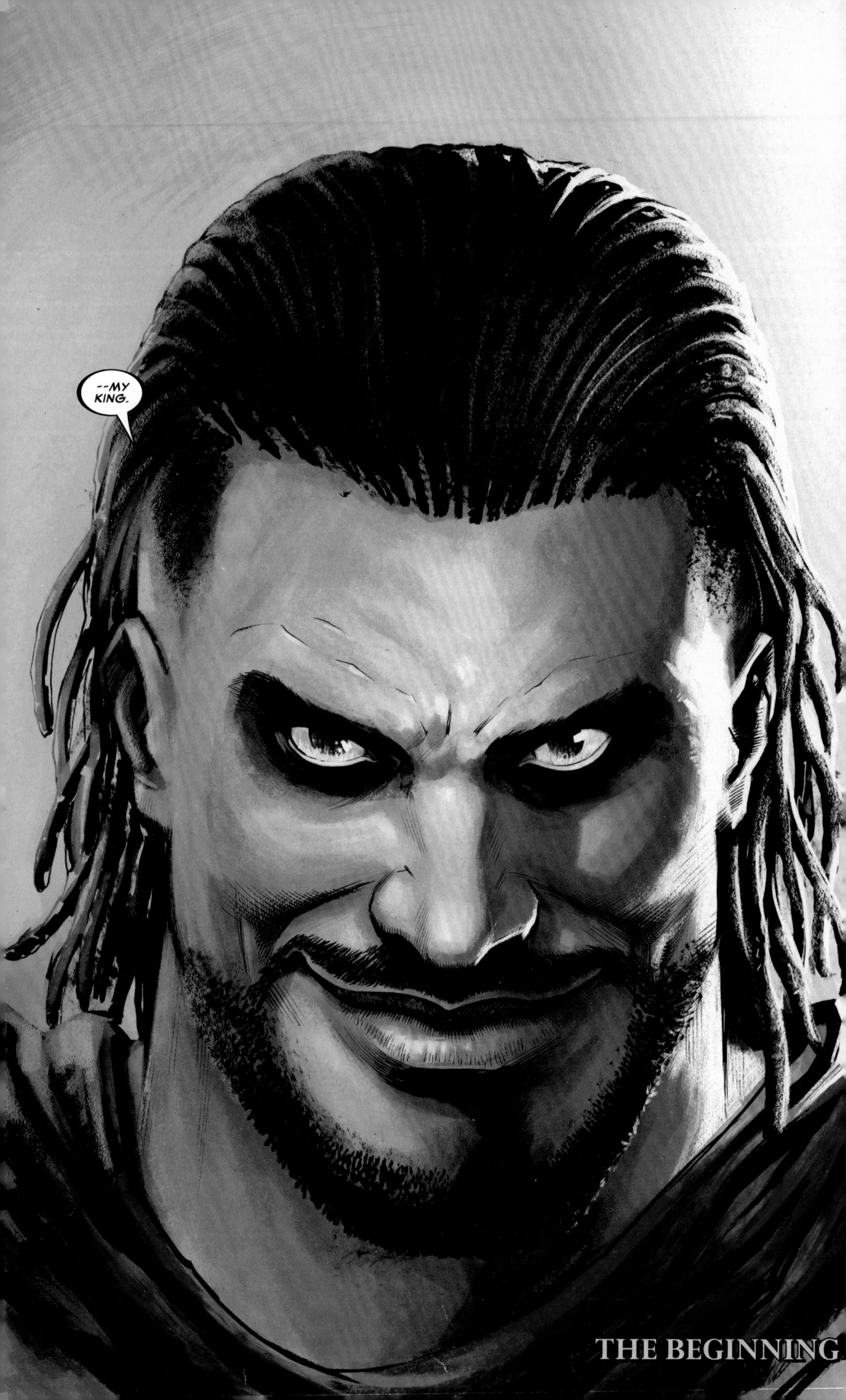
--MY KING.
THE BEGINNING